THE COMPLETE
15-MINUTE
GOURMET

Creative Cuisine Made Fast and Fresh

PAULETTE MITCHELL

Photographs by NANCY BUNDT

THOMAS NELSON
Since 1798

NASHVILLE   DALLAS   MEXICO CITY   RIO DE JANEIRO   BEIJING

Published in Nashville, Tennessee, by Thomas Nelson. Thomas Nelson is a
trademark of Thomas Nelson, Inc.

Photographs by Nancy Bundt.
Cover design by Kristen Vasgaard.
Page design by Mandi Cofer.

Thomas Nelson, Inc. titles may be purchased in bulk for educational, business,
fund-raising, or sales promotional use. For information, please e-mail
SpecialMarkets@ThomasNelson.com.

Library of Congress Cataloging-in-Publication Data

Mitchell, Paulette.
    The complete 15-minute gourmet : creative cuisine made fast and fresh
/ Paulette Mitchell ; Nancy Bundt, photographer.
        p. cm.
    Includes index.
    ISBN 978-1-4016-0355-7
    1. Quick and easy cookery. 2. Entrées (Cookery) 3. Cookery, International.
I. Title. II. Title: Complete fifteen-minute gourmet.
  TX833.5.M577 2008
  641.5′55—dc22
                                    2008002237

Printed in Singapore
08 09 10 11 12 TWP 5 4 3 2 1

TO MY FRIENDS around the world,

who have shared

thoughts and **adventures,**

as well as many

memorable meals

Contents

Acknowledgments

I offer a special thank you to my friends and culinary assistants Cindy Jurgensen and Judy Tills, for their diligence and meticulous attention to detail as they tested recipes; much appreciation also goes to Judy for skillfully styling the photographed recipes. To my dear friend and photographer Nancy Bundt, thank you for sharing your joyful sense of being and artistic talents in the photos that showcase my creations on the pages of this book.

Gratitude also goes to the staff at Lund's, who happily filled specific grocery requests, and the staffs of Cooks of Crocus Hill and Sur La Table, who provided props for the photos.

Many thanks to my son, Brett Mitchell, who enthusiastically consumes my culinary creations, offers his valued opinions, solves my computer woes, and adds infinite joy to my life. My extraordinary, cherished friends and colleagues contributed favorite recipes, tested and tasted mine, and patiently kept in touch during this project; heartfelt thanks go to Arthur Cores, Bret Bannon, Mary Brindley, Stephanie Browner, Shelli Chase, Barbara Cook, Lori English, Conrad and Uni Farinola, Nathan Fong, Carol Frieberg, Mary Hunter, Kristine Igo, Raghavan Iyer, June Jones, Dr. Mumtaz Kazim, Barb Kennedy, Donna Kuehn, Fran Lebahn, Dorothy Long, Leah Mann, Loretta McCarthy, Elisa Lobo Neese, Mary Margaret Ness, An Nguyen, Tom Nugent, Linda Platt, Karen Schmit, Gale and Sue Smieja, Darryl Trones, Ann Ulrich, Claudia Wagner, Carla Waldemar, Judy Witts Francini, and John Yee.

I am grateful to Crescent Dragonwagon, Emeril Lagasse, and Anne Willan, who offered endorsements for this book.

Finally, I offer my sincere appreciation to those responsible for making this book come to be: my agent Jane Dystel, her business partner Miriam Goodrich, and the staff at Thomas Nelson, including publishers Pamela Clements and Joel Miller, editor Jennifer Greenstein, Kristen Parrish, Kristen Vasgaard, Mandi Cofer, Scott Harris, Beth Hood, and Jason Jones.

Introduction

Welcome to *The Complete 15-Minute Gourmet.* The first book in this series was published in 1987. How things have changed! We thought we were busy then, but the pace of life has only quickened.

Just as important, in these 20 years, the world has become smaller. Holidays to faraway places have increased our awareness of different foods; restaurants on every street corner now offer cuisines from lands that, not so long ago, we'd hardly heard of. We also have access to ingredients that were obscure just two decades ago. In fact, some of these recipes are old favorites that appeared in previous versions of my 15-Minute cookbooks. They've been updated because most of us have become more adventuresome eaters.

Many who cooked from my books in the 1980s have sent their sons and daughters off to their own kitchens with several of the volumes in the 15-Minute Gourmet series. This is gratifying because my goal is to offer speedy dishes sophisticated enough to inspire experienced, savvy gourmets, but at the same time, I want to tempt and teach novices with simple, basic 15-Minute dishes that are also incredibly delicious. After all, it's important even for new cooks to be able to make a few great meals that please and amaze friends.

My culinary students often ask me for advice in dealing with the challenges of preparing family fare on busy weeknights. Most of us agree that prepackaged and frozen meals aren't satisfying, but the challenges of busy schedules deter us from cooking from scratch. This book addresses that concern—I developed many of these dishes specifically to help balance the demands on my time. Whether cooking for family or for a dinner party, anyone can use fresh, flavorful ingredients and the 15-Minute game plan to achieve remarkable and beautiful results with minimum effort—guaranteed!

Fast meals are simplified meals. In this book, I've made a point to feature dishes that are substantial enough to anchor a menu with little or no accompaniment. These incredibly delicious and satisfying one-dish meals can stand alone or be served with salad, bread, wine, and dessert for easy elegance when company's coming.

The 15-Minute recipes are organized by protein source. Within the chapters, you'll find soups, salads, sandwiches, pasta recipes, dishes to be served with rice, stovetop preparation, and oven preparation that will provide variety for your quick meals. The Basics chapter includes sauces, salsas, dressings, and other meal components that are called for in other recipes in this book and can also be used to inspire your own creations. In the Desserts chapter are some of my easy-to-prepare favorites for perfect finales to your 15-Minute meals.

Plan ahead to have the right ingredients on hand. Then preparation itself is a breeze—and so is cleanup.

You'll be astonished at what's possible in just 15 minutes. Be organized. Be creative. And be known as a great cook who can get a superb meal on the table with little fuss. This is my style of cooking and the kind of food I love. Join me on this culinary adventure.

Since my first book was published, my work has taken me around the globe. My primary inspiration comes from those travels, which have offered opportunities to experience many of the world's renowned dishes. I embrace and share their diversity.

Wander with me through noisy markets in Vietnam. Observe noodles being meticulously prepared by soba masters in Japan. Watch fishermen unload the catch of the day at dawn at a picturesque fish market in Valparaiso, and ride in a long-tail boat alongside vendors at the floating market in Bangkok.

Enjoy recipes inspired as I devoured pasta in some of the world's great Italian cities, nibbled on noodles at tiny shops in Shanghai, and learned to love tapas in Barcelona. Fruit recipes came to mind as I sipped on freshly squeezed pomegranate juice at a street stand in Turkey and ate juicy, sweet tree-ripened tropical fruits in the South Pacific. Seafood became a passion as I sampled fresh fish and coconut served on banana leaves on an unspoiled beach in Ile de Pins. In Marseille, I savored the ritual of serving and eating bouillabaisse. Many times I have cleaned my plate of tuna salade niçoise at its home in Nice.

Along the way, I've made acquaintances and celebrated friendships over memorable meals. These experiences are reflected in the wide range of recipes in this book. In private homes I've learned to cook with local ingredients, taking part in time-tested family culinary traditions. And I've found that every cuisine in the world has quick-to-prepare specialties.

Fast and easy does not make a dish less desirable, nor does it mean sacrificing complex flavors and beautiful appearance. Here, you'll find some recipes that represent "home cooking" at its best. Other dishes are decidedly "gourmet." These 15-Minute recipes can free you from long hours in the kitchen while adding an international flair and style to the meals you prepare.

INGREDIENTS

Great food starts with great ingredients. But keep it simple. Pairing fresh foods with some pantry staples, these recipes don't require a long list of components. And quick cooking retains their bright, fresh flavors. For this reason, I insist on using top-quality ingredients because each makes a vital contribution to flavor and texture—and that combination makes these dishes work. The best items, especially fresh, beautiful produce, may cost more, but a superior dish is well worth it.

As you shop for fresh ingredients for the individual recipes, you'll also be stocking your pantry with ethnic sauces, condiments, and other jarred staples. Thai curry paste, hoisin sauce, fish sauce, plum sauce, and dark sesame oil are just some of the Asian flavorings that quickly and easily add flavor to your dishes.

I rely on some canned goods, such as tomatoes. They are now available in so many useful varieties—some chopped, others already flavored with herbs and spices. Legumes require hours of soaking and cooking, but canned ones are a delicious, ready-to-serve alternative.

Chicken broth is essential to have on hand. I prefer reduced-sodium broth so that I can control the amount of salt in my recipe; for the same reason, my recipes nearly always call for unsalted butter. And you can always use the low-sodium variety of soy sauce, if you like.

In these recipes, use the type of dairy product that suits you best. If you have a preference for fat-free sour cream over regular sour cream, that's fine. When it comes to milk, skim yields a lighter texture than whole milk in a recipe, but the choice is yours.

A few frozen food staples, too, make sense, such as peas and corn kernels, which are tasty when cooked and save considerable time. I don't favor storing leftovers in the freezer, so I dedicate much of my freezer space to storing ingredients, such as nuts and seeds.

Pasta is another staple that's perfect for simple meals. In the summer it provides a canvas for the robust flavors of garden-fresh produce, and in the cooler seasons, pasta warms us as a sublime comfort food. It pairs well with everything from vegetables to chicken, seafood, and meat. The toppings can be easily prepared in the 15 minutes (or less) it takes to cook the noodles.

We all know that the Italians have a love affair with pasta. In Asian countries, too, noodles are a staple in everyday life. Making noodles there is an art form, and noodles symbolize long life. While Italian pastas are made almost exclusively from wheat flour, Asian noodles are more diverse. They can be made from wheat, rice, or beans, and they cook especially quickly. Both dried Italian pastas and Asian noodles keep well in your pantry, so it's a good idea to have an assortment of varieties on hand. If you choose to use fresh noodles or pasta, cooking takes only a few minutes.

Couscous is one of my favorite meal accompaniments, and it's easy to use in place of rice. It's actually a pasta in a shape so small that it needs only soaking rather than cooking, and this can be done as you prepare your recipe, so that it's ready to put on the table when your dish is completed.

Rice is the staple food for more than 1.5 billion people in the world; in many countries, people consider a meal without rice as not to have eaten at all. I do not recommend quick-cooking rice because it lacks flavor and texture, as well as nutritional value. Basmati rice is perfect for the 15-Minute gourmet because it cooks in just 15 minutes, which is quicker than standard long-grain rice. It's helpful to own an electric rice cooker, which allows you to make a big pot of any rice without fuss. Cooked rice keeps for about a week in the refrigerator; I like to have some on hand for use in recipes and as an accompaniment to others.

Fresh herbs are used throughout this book, and when dried herbs are acceptable, you'll find them mentioned, too, in the ingredient list. Some herbs, such as cilantro and parsley, are completely unacceptable in their dried forms. For times when I want to make a dish on the spur of the moment, I keep on hand frozen chopped basil and cilantro, which are available in some supermarkets. These products come in handy when only a small amount is needed. And, of course, my homemade Basil Pesto (page 274) is always in my freezer, ready to add its heady flavor and aroma to a variety of dishes.

Our sense of smell determines how we perceive flavors, so I love the aroma of freshly ground pepper as a final touch just before serving many dishes. For convenience, though, preground pepper is acceptable when cooking. Regarding salt, I use sea salt rather than iodized salt because I prefer the flavor.

Remember, it's fine to take a few shortcuts to speed preparation. When my time is especially limited, I select some prechopped vegetables from the supermarket's salad bar, where I can buy exactly the amount needed so nothing goes to waste. Also, most produce departments stock shredded carrots, sliced mushrooms, stemmed pea pods, broccoli in florets, washed salad spinach, coleslaw, trimmed green beans, and peeled and cored pineapple. I also specify garlic by the teaspoon measurement because it's handy to use preminced garlic in a jar. Some stores also sell frozen crushed garlic in convenient cubes. In addition, I buy jars of oil-packed sun-dried tomatoes that are already chopped to cut down on preparation and clean-up time.

Although I nearly always prefer fresh fruit, I've found that mango spears in a jar (with light syrup) always provide the perfect ripeness and just-right texture. When I know that I'll need grated or shredded cheese, that's how I buy it. Packaged polenta is just fine; it's delicious when freshly cooked just before serving. I also buy sesame seeds already toasted for a ready-to-use garnish. The quality of your cooking is not diminished because someone else has done some of the preparations for you. And the savings in time and effort are worth the additional cost.

But some prepackaged ingredients are unacceptable. Good-quality Parmesan cheese, for example, is an important flavor element in many recipes. The pregrated, non-refrigerated variety found on the supermarket shelf cannot offer the right element to your recipe. Instead, you will want to freshly shred or grate Parmesan cheese or buy the preshredded or pregrated cheese available in the refrigerated section of many supermarkets, cheese shops, and delis.

In my favorite supermarkets, I've made it a point to become acquainted with the butchers, who are available to offer advice on the best meat to buy. They are also helpful when it comes to thinly slicing meat for stir-fry, removing the skin from fish for certain recipes, and filling special orders when I am planning for company. Don't hesitate to ask for help. Also, look for shrimp that have already been peeled and deveined, another timesaver.

You'll need cooking oils in your pantry. Canola oil is my choice for a flavorless cooking medium when I want other flavors in the recipe to shine. It is high in mono-unsaturated fatty acids that have been shown to reduce blood cholesterol levels and has the lowest amount of saturated fat of all commonly used vegetable oils. Olive oil,

another monounsaturated oil, is important for the wonderful aroma and flavor it provides. And in some recipes, especially salads, I use flavoring oils such as hazelnut and walnut oil to contribute the essence of those nuts.

Some recipes simply require nonstick cooking spray, which is good to have on hand. You will find empty oil spray cans in many gourmet shops, which allow you to apply a spray of your favorite oil.

It's important to be organized. Make a grocery list before you shop. Then, once you've made certain you have all the ingredients for your recipe, set them out on the counter, along with all the necessary equipment, before you begin to prepare your meal.

EQUIPMENT

Elaborate equipment is not necessary to prepare speedy meals. When it comes to pans, all you really need is a Dutch oven (which doubles as a soup pot and a pasta cooker), a stovetop grill pan, a medium saucepan, a large skillet, and a large sauté pan—the most-used pan in my kitchen. In fact, the sauté pan has replaced my wok for stir-frying. The straight sides, which make the pan deeper than a skillet, are better for recipes that call for a liquid to be stirred into the pan.

Most of my recipes require just one pan, and many of mine are nonstick, which allows for quick cleanup. I don't like to spend more time cleaning up after a meal than I spent preparing it. Select high-quality nonstick pans because the surface is permanent, will not peel off, and is less likely to scratch.

It's also important to have heavy, good-quality pans because they will last longer and conduct heat more evenly. Be sure all have covers, which are needed for some recipes. I also often use a splash shield for recipes cooked in uncovered pans; that cuts down on stove cleanup, too.

Some recipe steps, such as steaming vegetables, are efficiently accomplished in the microwave. It's a good idea to have several sizes of glass microwave-proof dishes with lids. Microwaving in plastic containers or with plastic covers is believed by many to be hazardous.

I learned to love panini sandwiches at wine bars in Italy, and I enjoy them at home, too, for their crusty, toasted exteriors and savory fillings. For the 15-Minute gourmet, a panini grill is very efficient because the appliance toasts both sides of sandwiches at the same time, while creating attractive grill marks on the bread.

A set of good-quality, sharp knives is indispensable. I also use kitchen shears for snipping herbs and cutting chicken. My food processor is invaluable. It's used daily for rough chopping and for shredding ingredients like carrots. For smaller quantities, I use my mini-chop. This tiny version of a food processor has a blade that spins faster than the larger appliance and is good for cutting small amounts of nuts, for example, that would get lost in a conventional food processor.

Several important gadgets serve as time-savers, too. Whisks often blend ingredients together more efficiently than a spoon. Microplanes in various sizes also come in handy for quick shredding or grating of ingredients, such as blocks of Parmesan cheese. A wide and long fish spatula guarantees that tender and fragile cooked fish won't break when being transferred from the cooking pan to the serving plate. Tongs and ladles are important for serving your creations. And, of course, it's a good idea to have several sets of measuring spoons and cups so you can proceed through a recipe without taking time to wash them.

Some of the soups and sauces in my recipes require blending; I recommend an immersion blender, which eliminates the need to transfer hot liquids to a blender container. Instead, the shaft of this handheld appliance goes directly into a soup or sauce to purée the cooked ingredients and achieve a smooth, creamy texture right in the cooking pan. There's nothing to wash except the blade and the shaft, which rinse clean when held under the kitchen faucet.

Keep on hand a supply of kitchen parchment and aluminum foil (the instant-release type is best) so that you can line baking sheets, eliminating the need to oil pans and cutting down on clean-up time.

TECHNIQUES

By using fresh ingredients paired with some staples in an organized way, you'll find you do not need a great deal of time to create colorful, tasty meals. These recipes rely more on the imaginative use of ingredients than on elaborate techniques.

Most of these recipes are cooked on the stovetop. I usually begin with high or medium-high heat to get things going. I like to cook (sauté and stir-fry) with a high temperature when possible, which is how restaurant chefs can turn out meals in a hurry. For simmering, reduce the temperature. Some recipes require broiling or baking in the oven, which does require preheating time. And the microwave will come in handy for steaming vegetables. Of course, I usually reheat leftovers in the microwave, too.

PRESENTATION

Quick and efficient need not be slapdash, so I've suggested garnishes and presentation tips for most of the dishes. Your meals will look as though they were prepared by a trained gourmet chef rather than a hurried cook. And garnishes are also a quick and easy way to add a dash of extra flavor and an unexpected texture to your dishes. It takes only seconds to add a sprig of fresh herbs or a sprinkling of sesame seeds to top a dish. If you plan in advance, you can have crunchy croutons on hand to top a creamy soup.

MORE TIPS FOR 15-MINUTE COOKING

● Prep some ingredients to have on hand for future meals. If you're chopping onions for today's soup, chop extra for tomorrow's pasta dish. They will keep in a tightly covered container in the refrigerator.

● For entertaining, prep most of the ingredients in advance. Also, organize all the cooking equipment and serving plates. When possible, mix sauces and dressings ahead of time. This eliminates last-minute mess and reduces time in the kitchen.

● Advance preparation of some recipes from the Basics chapter will save you time in the long run. Keep several homemade salad dressings on hand in the refrigerator and Basil Pesto (page 274) in the freezer. Of course, you can purchase these items ready-made at the supermarket, if you prefer.

● Always read the recipe before you begin and think through the steps that may be handled simultaneously. Some procedures can't be hurried. So get things going— start water boiling (with a lid to shorten the time) and preheat the broiler or oven. Do these things first if needed for the recipe, and then set out all the ingredients. Clean and start chopping foods before you begin to cook.

● Follow the sequence of steps as described. Efficient cooking does not follow a linear progression, so you won't be completing one step before going on to another. It's easy to do two things at once, as directed in many of the recipes with the terms "meanwhile" or "while the meat cooks." Chop the vegetables as the water comes to a boil. Make the sauce as the pasta cooks. For example, when making the Rotini with Creamy Three-Herb Pesto and Chicken (page 58), begin by bringing a large pot of water to a boil. During that time, assemble all the recipe ingredients on the kitchen counter. Add the pasta to the boiling water. Cut the chicken and begin to cook it in the skillet. Meanwhile, process all the pesto ingredients while the pasta and chicken cook. As directed by the recipe, you will drain the pasta, add the cooked chicken and pesto, and toss the dish together. By doing three simple procedures at the same time in an organized manner, you will complete the recipe in less than 15 minutes.

● Read the tips that accompany the recipes. They offer useful information about some of the ingredients.

● Cooking times are always approximate and may vary according to your pan type, gas or electric heat, type of microwave, and differences among ingredients. Judge doneness by appearance, aroma, and taste. The recipe procedures provide you with cues. When cooking with high and medium-high heat, stir the ingredients as they cook to prevent burning. Garlic and shallots, for example, become bitter if they brown.

● Use salt and pepper, as well as spicy ingredients such as red pepper flakes or Tabasco sauce, according to your personal taste. Sample the completed dish and adjust the seasonings before serving. Ingredients that require personal adjustment are noted.

● Let your creativity flow. Once you have become proficient at 15-Minute techniques, feel free to make substitutions, such as using your favorite vegetables or odds and ends you may have on hand. Good cooking is all about personal expression.

● Most of the recipes make main courses to serve four. Some, especially those in the vegetarian chapter, could serve as starters or side dishes. Most of the recipes multiply easily, though you may not need to increase herbs and seasonings in the same proportion as other ingredients. For example, if doubling a recipe, first add 1½ times the amount of herbs, then taste and adjust. Be aware that multiplying a recipe may increase the preparation and cooking time.

● Most of the recipes in this book taste best when served immediately (exceptions are some of the desserts and basics). Many leftovers can be refrigerated for a day or two and then reheated. But I don't recommend freezing these dishes. Fresh flavors and crisp-tender textures deteriorate after being frozen and thawed.

The steps are so quick, it's easier to create new than to revive old.

These 15-Minute recipes have all been thoroughly tested, so I guarantee your success—even if you are a novice. Yet these dishes are sophisticated enough to satisfy experienced cooks and demanding diners.

It's true that we have less time to cook—at least the laborious, old-fashioned, day-in, day-out cooking Grandma is remembered for. The good news is that in just 15 minutes, a variety of delicious meals, inspired by cuisines from around the world, can be on the table. And I promise you that these dishes will be some of the best you've eaten because they are made at home, from scratch, by you.

That's it in a nutshell: a world of quick, easy, and intriguing dishes packed with flair and flavor.

Here's wishing you, your family, and your guests many a memorable meal. Enjoy!

Paulette's Tips

For more fast and fresh cooking tips,
visit paulettemitchell.com.

Poultry

THROUGHOUT CENTURIES, chicken has played a starring role in many of the world's cuisines. In the late 1990s, I accepted my editor's challenge to develop 100 quick-to-prepare chicken recipes. Creating them meant eating lots of chicken, but I discovered that the possibilities are unlimited. Chicken is used in many cuisines, and its mild flavor is compatible with an almost endless variety of herbs and spices, fruits and vegetables. It can be enjoyed hot, at room temperature, or chilled. You can serve chicken with pasta, chicken with rice, chicken with fruit or vegetables, chicken with wine, chicken salads, chicken sandwiches in many forms, and the ultimate comfort food, chicken soup.

The process of disjointing and deboning whole chickens is time-consuming. But boneless, skinless chicken breasts (which are, more accurately, breast halves) are perfect for 15-Minute recipes. If the meat is cut into chunks or strips, it cooks in just five minutes. Whole chicken breasts take five minutes per side when cooked in a skillet, broiler, or stovetop grill pan. "Chicken tenders" or "tenderloins," which are small chicken fillets cut from the most delicate part of the breast, are also used in some recipes. These smaller pieces require less chopping. I do take a minute to snip away the tendon; some chicken producers remove it before packaging. The size of the tenders varies among brands and may alter cooking time. And, of course, many supermarkets offer "chicken for stir-fry," which comes completely chopped and ready to use.

One word of warning: Fresh chicken is highly perishable and must be handled and cooked properly. Bring chicken directly home from the market and store it in the coldest part of your refrigerator. If the chicken can-

not be used within two days, freeze it. Thaw the frozen chicken in the refrigerator, not on the kitchen counter. Rinse chicken quickly under cool running water and pat it dry before cooking. Be sure to carefully wash all work surfaces that held the raw chicken, as well as your knives and hands. (Clean the cutting board with a sanitizing spray or with a solution of 2 tablespoons chlorine bleach to 1 quart hot water.) I often use poultry shears to cut both raw and cooked chicken. This speedy method eliminates some of the chicken safety concerns because it's not necessary for the chicken to touch a cutting board.

Also important is thorough cooking. Properly cooked chicken breasts will be white throughout, with no traces of pink, and the juices will run clear rather than red.

Most of the chicken recipes in this chapter are cooked on the stovetop. In addition to sautéing, several recipes are "braised." In braising, the chicken is lightly coated with a seasoned flour mixture (for efficiency and less mess, I use a large zip-top plastic bag for chicken in strips). It is then lightly browned, a sauce is stirred in, and the entire mixture simmers until the chicken is thoroughly cooked and tender.

Some recipes call for cooked rotisserie chicken, which is a godsend for days when you are especially pressed for time. Right away when I get home from the supermarket, I remove the skin and pull the chicken from the bone because it's most efficient to do this while the meat is warm. Keep in mind that the seasoning added before the chicken is cooked is of little importance; most remains in the skin and does not alter the flavor of the meat. A rotisserie chicken yields about 2½ cups white meat and about 1½ cups dark meat. I include both in many of my recipes calling for rotisserie chicken. In fact, both light and dark meat are used in some cuisines, and the dark meat actually offers the most flavor. If you prefer, in these recipes you can substitute chicken that you have cooked for the rotisserie chicken. In other recipes, such as Spicy Chicken and Rice (page 73) and Red Sweet Potato Salad with Chicken (page 25), you can use chopped rotisserie chicken rather than cooking chicken yourself.

Here, you'll find chicken salads that go miles beyond the tired scenario of cubes of chicken tossed with bits of celery and smothered in mayonnaise. Some of the chicken salads are warm, such as Warm Chicken Salad with Peaches and Blueberries (page 17)—others chilled, like Chinese Chicken Salad with Hoisin Dressing (page 27). Some are artfully composed, such as Grilled Chicken Salad with Herbed Tomato Vinaigrette (page 20)—others tossed, as is Chopped Salad with Balsamic Vinaigrette (page 21). They are all beautiful and uniquely delicious.

Chicken soup has established quite a reputation as the quintessential cure-all comfort food. In this chapter, you'll find not only a quick-to-prepare version of chicken noodle soup but also others that showcase many cuisines, including intriguing Japanese, Italian, and Mexican meals in a bowl.

It's no longer necessary to stew a chicken to arrive at a tasty broth. I make homemade soups in no time, thanks to good-quality canned or aseptically packaged chicken broth. I prefer using the reduced-sodium type, which allows me to salt dishes as I choose. For recipes calling for less than a whole can or box, I usually use chicken broth cubes, concentrates, or granules, which I always keep on hand. Partially used aseptic boxes can also be refrigerated for use later. Some soup recipes that don't call for chicken are included in this chapter because they include chicken broth, which is itself an important flavor component.

In addition to chicken, in this chapter you will find recipes calling for turkey cutlets, another convenience poultry cut. One recipe also calls for ground turkey; if lean meat is important to you, look for the label "ground breast meat." Also, recipes calling for rotisserie chicken are delicious destinations for holiday turkey leftovers. For the rotisserie chicken, simply substitute an equal amount of cooked turkey.

Warm Chicken Salad
with Peaches
and Blueberries

Salads

WARM CHICKEN SALAD WITH PEACHES AND BLUEBERRIES
Makes **4** servings

Celebrate the fruits of summer, and serve this artfully composed salad on a warm summer evening. If you prefer, cook boneless, skinless chicken breasts on your outdoor grill rather than indoors in a skillet. Cut them into diagonal strips before adding to the salads.

For the vinaigrette:

¼	cup red wine vinegar
¼	cup canola oil
1	tablespoon honey mustard
1	teaspoon minced garlic
	Salt and pepper to taste

For the salad:

1	tablespoon canola oil
12	ounces chicken tenders, halved lengthwise and cut crosswise into strips
1	teaspoon lemon pepper
8	cups mesclun (mixed baby greens)
2	peaches, cut into ⅜-inch wedges
1	cup fresh blueberries

○ Whisk together the vinaigrette ingredients in a small bowl.

○ Heat the oil in a large skillet over medium-high heat. Add the chicken and sprinkle with lemon pepper. Cook, stirring occasionally, for 5 minutes or until lightly browned and thoroughly cooked.

○ Meanwhile, spread the greens on plates.

○ Arrange the warm chicken strips and peach slices over the greens. Drizzle with the vinaigrette and sprinkle with blueberries. Serve immediately.

CHICKEN SALAD WITH RED GRAPES, DRIED CHERRIES, AND TOASTED PECANS
Makes **4** servings

This salad is ideal for a casual fall lunch or light evening meal with guests. It offers a palette of sweet and tart flavors paired with the equally alluring contrast of both crunchy and soft textures. Serve the scrumptious mixture with warm rolls or soft breadsticks.

2	cups coarsely chopped rotisserie chicken, skin removed, cooled
1	cup halved seedless red grapes
½	cup finely chopped celery
½	cup coarsely chopped toasted pecans
⅓	cup dried cherries
⅔	cup Creamy Poppy Seed Dressing (page 270)
	Bibb lettuce leaves
	Small bunches of red seedless grapes for garnish

○ Combine the chicken, grapes, celery, pecans, and dried cherries in a large bowl. Add the dressing and stir until evenly combined.

○ Serve on lettuce leaves and garnish with grapes.

GRILLED CHICKEN AND SPINACH SALAD WITH POMEGRANATE-RASPBERRY VINAIGRETTE

Makes **4** servings

This warm chicken salad jeweled with raspberries is a gorgeous dish perfect for serving guests. And because it's so quick and easy to toss together, you can relax with your friends in the evening breezes instead of spending precious time in the kitchen.

4	boneless, skinless chicken breasts
	Olive oil for brushing
	Dash of salt and pepper
10	cups salad spinach
1	cup fresh raspberries
½	red onion, thinly sliced
¾	cup Pomegranate-Raspberry Vinaigrette (page 271), divided
½	cup coarsely chopped walnuts

▶ Heat a stovetop grill pan over high heat. Lightly brush both sides of the chicken breasts with oil and sprinkle with salt and pepper. Reduce the heat to medium-high; cook for 5 minutes per side or until lightly browned and thoroughly cooked. Transfer to a plate and set aside to cool slightly.

▶ Meanwhile, toss the spinach, raspberries, and onion in a large bowl. Add ½ cup vinaigrette and toss until evenly combined.

▶ Divide the salad among 4 salad plates. Cut the chicken into ¼-inch slices. Fan a chicken breast over each salad. Sprinkle with the walnuts and drizzle with the remaining ¼ cup vinaigrette.

GRILLED CHICKEN AND PEAR SALAD WITH HAZELNUT VINAIGRETTE

Makes **4** servings

The pronounced flavor of hazelnut oil is especially pleasing on bitter greens such as Belgian endive. (Other greens it complements include curly endive, dandelion greens, and escarole.) An artful arrangement of these leaves topped with chicken, pears, and hazelnuts creates a memorable salad indeed.

For the chicken:

16	ounces boneless, skinless chicken breasts
	Olive oil for brushing
	Dash of salt and pepper

For the vinaigrette:

¼	cup red wine vinegar
3	tablespoons hazelnut oil
1	tablespoon extra-virgin olive oil
1	teaspoon Dijon mustard
⅛	teaspoon pepper, or to taste
	Salt to taste

To complete the recipe:

2	large ripe pears, halved lengthwise, each half cut into ⅜-inch slices
	Olive oil for brushing
20	leaves Belgian endive (2 heads)
12	leaves leaf lettuce
	Freshly ground pepper, crumbled mild feta cheese, and toasted hazelnuts for garnish

▶ Heat a stovetop grill pan over high heat. Lightly brush both sides of the chicken breasts with oil. Reduce the heat to medium-high; cook for 5 minutes per side or until lightly browned and thoroughly cooked. Transfer to a plate and sprinkle with salt and pepper. Cover to keep warm.

◗ While the chicken is cooking, whisk together the vinaigrette ingredients in a small bowl.

◗ Lightly brush the pear slices with oil; cook on the preheated grill for 10 to 15 seconds per side or just until the grill markings become light brown. Transfer to a plate.

◗ To assemble the salads, arrange the endive and leaf lettuce on plates. Slice the chicken into thin strips; arrange atop the greens along with the pear slices. Drizzle with the vinaigrette, sprinkle with pepper, and garnish with feta cheese and hazelnuts.

WARM RASPBERRY-WALNUT CHICKEN SALAD

Makes **4** servings

Serve this dish as a special summer treat to dazzle both the eyes and the taste buds when fresh raspberries are at their best. In the winter, I compose the plates with additional orange slices. For advance preparation, assemble the salads, cover, and refrigerate; drizzle with room temperature raspberry-walnut vinaigrette just before serving.

For the chicken:

16	ounces boneless, skinless chicken breasts
	Olive oil for brushing
	Dash of salt and pepper

For the raspberry-walnut vinaigrette:

⅓	cup raspberry vinegar
⅓	cup walnut oil
2	teaspoons raspberry jam
1	teaspoon Dijon mustard
⅛	teaspoon salt, or to taste
⅛	teaspoon pepper, or to taste

To complete the recipe:

10	cups mesclun (mixed baby greens)
4	green onions, finely chopped
1	large orange, peeled and cut into 6 thin slices
1	cup fresh raspberries
½	cup (4 ounces) chèvre cheese
	Toasted coarsely chopped walnuts for garnish

◗ Heat a stovetop grill pan over high heat. Lightly brush both sides of the chicken breasts with oil. Reduce the heat to medium-high; cook for 5 minutes per side or until lightly browned and thoroughly cooked. Transfer to a plate and sprinkle with salt and pepper. Cover to keep warm.

◗ While the chicken is cooking, whisk together the vinaigrette ingredients in a measuring cup. Microwave on HIGH for 30 seconds or until the jam is melted.

◗ Toss together the mesclun and green onions in a large bowl. Stir the warm vinaigrette; add ⅓ cup to the bowl and toss again.

◗ To assemble the salads, spread the dressed greens on dinner plates. Diagonally slice the warm chicken into thin strips. Top the greens with a composed arrangement of chicken strips, orange slices, raspberries, and dollops of chèvre cheese. Stir the remaining warm vinaigrette and drizzle over the salads. Garnish with walnuts. Serve immediately while the chicken is warm.

GRILLED CHICKEN SALAD WITH HERBED TOMATO VINAIGRETTE

Makes **4** servings

Served on a bed of wilted greens and drizzled with herbed tomato vinaigrette, this chicken salad is a nice change from the usual fresh spinach salad. Plus, it's a complete meal.

For the chicken:

16 ounces boneless, skinless chicken breasts
Olive oil for brushing
Dash of salt and pepper

For the vinaigrette:

¼ cup extra-virgin olive oil
¼ cup red wine vinegar
¼ cup water
2 tablespoons tomato paste
2 tablespoons finely chopped fresh basil
1 tablespoon finely chopped fresh oregano
1 teaspoon minced garlic
1 teaspoon sugar
¼ teaspoon pepper, or to taste
Salt to taste

To complete the recipe:

10 cups spinach leaves, stems removed (this yields 4 cups after steaming)
½ cup frozen corn kernels, thawed
½ cup (4 ounces) chèvre cheese, coarsely crumbled

- Heat a stovetop grill pan over high heat. Lightly brush both sides of the chicken breasts with oil. Reduce the heat to medium-high; cook for 5 minutes per side or until lightly browned and thoroughly cooked. Transfer to a plate and sprinkle with salt and pepper. Cover to keep warm.

- While the chicken is cooking, whisk together the vinaigrette ingredients in a small bowl.

- Rinse the spinach in cool water. Transfer to a Dutch oven over medium-high heat. Cover and cook without additional water, except for the drops that cling to the leaves, for 2 minutes or until slightly wilted. Uncover and remove the pan from the heat.

- Slice the chicken into ½-inch diagonal strips.

- To assemble the salads, spread steamed spinach on each plate. Top with the chicken strips, corn, and chèvre cheese.

- Stir the vinaigrette and drizzle it over the salads.

TIP

Concentrated tomato paste is available in tubes, ideal for recipes calling for less than a 6-ounce can. Refrigerate the tube after opening.

WARM CHICKEN STIR-FRY SALAD WITH GINGERED PLUM DRESSING

Makes **4** servings

Chinese wheat-flour noodles, with their curly shape and tender texture, form a delectable foundation for the vegetables and chicken, all flavored with a hint of ginger and plum.

1 tablespoon canola oil
12 ounces chicken tenders, cut into 2-inch pieces

2	cups asparagus in 2-inch pieces
½	red bell pepper, cut into ¼-inch strips
3	green onions, coarsely chopped
1	teaspoon minced garlic
⅔	cup Gingered Plum Dressing (page 270), divided
4	ounces Chinese wheat-flour noodles
3	cups salad spinach

⊙ Bring a medium saucepan of water to a boil over high heat.

⊙ Heat the oil in a large sauté pan over medium-high heat. Add the chicken, asparagus, and bell pepper; cook, stirring occasionally, for 5 minutes. Add the green onions and garlic; continue to cook for 1 more minute. The chicken should be lightly browned and thoroughly cooked, the asparagus crisp-tender. Reduce the heat to low. Add ⅓ cup dressing and stir gently until warm, taking care that the vinaigrette does not evaporate.

⊙ Drop the noodles into the pan of boiling water; cook according to package instructions. Drain well; rinse with cool water, drain again, and pour into a medium bowl. Add the remaining ⅓ cup dressing and toss until evenly combined.

⊙ To serve, spread noodles on the plates and add a layer of spinach. Top with the warm stir-fried chicken and vegetables.

CHOPPED SALAD WITH BALSAMIC VINAIGRETTE

Makes **4** servings

Here's a colorful, complete, and satisfying meal in a bowl that's perfect for your family on a busy night.

You'll get lots of fresh, healthful vegetables and protein, and top-notch flavor, too. You can make the vinaigrette in advance, but toss it with the salad just before serving. If there's time to plan ahead, chill the salad bowls for that special added touch.

4	strips bacon
4	cups shredded romaine lettuce
2	plum tomatoes, cut into ½-inch cubes
1	avocado, cut into ½-inch cubes
½	cup coarsely crumbled yellow corn tortilla chips
2	green onions, finely chopped
¼	cup frozen corn kernels, thawed
½	cup Balsamic Vinaigrette (page 268) or bottled balsamic vinaigrette
2	cups coarsely chopped rotisserie chicken, skin removed, cooled
½	cup coarsely crumbled blue cheese

⊙ Cook the bacon in a small nonstick skillet over medium heat, turning occasionally, for 5 minutes or until crisp. (Or place the bacon on a triple layer of paper towels on a microwave-safe plate, and cover with a double layer of towels. Microwave on HIGH for 2 minutes. Continue to microwave for 1-minute intervals until done.) Transfer to a paper-towel lined plate. Crumble when cool.

⊙ Toss together the lettuce, tomatoes, avocado, tortilla chips, green onions, corn, and bacon in a large bowl.

⊙ Add the vinaigrette and toss again.

⊙ Divide the salad among 4 large salad bowls. Top with the chicken and blue cheese.

Pesto Chicken Salad
with Red Grapes

PESTO CHICKEN SALAD WITH RED GRAPES

Makes **4** servings

This is one of my favorites for do-ahead entertaining because it multiplies well and is a guaranteed crowd-pleaser. The splendid dish becomes the focal point when served on a large platter on a buffet. For advance preparation, add half the dressing before refrigerating the salad, and then toss with the rest just before serving. I like to make my own Basil Pesto using the recipe on page 274, but you can buy it in a ready-to-use tub in most supermarkets.

For the pasta:

6   ounces penne rigate

For the creamy pesto dressing:

¼   cup Basil Pesto (page 274)

¼   cup sour cream

¼   cup red wine vinegar

1   teaspoon sugar
     Salt and pepper to taste

To complete the recipe:

1½   cups rotisserie chicken in ¾-inch pieces,
     skin removed, cooled

1   cup coarsely shredded carrots

1   cup halved seedless red grapes
     (about 6 ounces)

2   green onions, coarsely chopped
     Salt and pepper to taste

8   leaves red leaf lettuce
     Freshly ground pepper, freshly shredded
     Parmesan cheese, and small bunches of
     red grapes for garnish

▶ Cook the penne according to package instructions.

▶ Meanwhile, whisk together the dressing ingredients in a large bowl.

▶ When the penne is done, drain well. Rinse in cold water, and then drain again.

▶ Add the penne, chicken, carrots, grapes, and green onions to the dressing. Toss until evenly combined.

▶ To serve, arrange the greens on salad plates or in shallow bowls. Top with mounds of the chicken salad and garnish with pepper, Parmesan cheese, and bunches of grapes.

TIP

When cooking pasta, be sure to use a large pot that is deeper than it is wide. (I use a Dutch oven.) This allows the pasta to move freely as it cooks and prevents sticking. Make sure the water is at a full boil before adding the pasta. Stir the pasta just once and begin timing, making certain to keep the water at a rapid boil throughout the cooking period. Cooking time will depend on the shape and thickness of the pasta. Perfectly cooked pasta should be al dente—firm but not hard, and evenly cooked so it offers some resistance to the teeth, yet is cooked through. Drain the pasta just as soon as it is done. There is no need to rinse pasta unless you must cool it quickly for use in a chilled pasta salad.

TEX-MEX CHICKEN SALAD WITH SOUTHWESTERN VINAIGRETTE

Makes **4** servings

It's hard to beat warmed flour tortillas as an accompaniment for this colorful salad with robust flavors of the Southwest.

For the vinaigrette:

¼	cup extra-virgin olive oil
2	tablespoons red wine vinegar
1	tablespoon fresh lemon juice
½	teaspoon Dijon mustard
½	teaspoon ground cumin
½	teaspoon sugar
	Salt and pepper to taste

For the salad:

1½	cups shredded rotisserie chicken, skin removed, cooled
1	(15-ounce) can black beans, drained and rinsed
1	cup frozen corn kernels, thawed
1	plum tomato, cut into ½-inch cubes
¼	cup coarsely chopped red onion
¼	cup coarsely chopped fresh cilantro
1	tablespoon finely chopped jalapeño chili, or to taste

To complete the recipe:

4	cups salad spinach
	Coarsely crumbled yellow corn tortilla chips for garnish

❍ Whisk together the vinaigrette ingredients in a large bowl. Add the salad ingredients and stir to combine.

❍ To serve, arrange the spinach on salad plates or in shallow bowls and top with the chicken mixture. Sprinkle with tortilla chips.

MAPLE-WALNUT CHICKEN SALAD

Makes **4** servings

The distinctive, seductively nutty flavor and fragrance of walnut oil is the essence of this warm salad. When company's coming, substitute a stylish mixture of signature greens such as endive, chicory, or escarole.

1	tablespoon olive oil
16	ounces chicken tenders, halved lengthwise and crosswise into strips
6	cups romaine lettuce torn into 2-inch pieces
2	green onions, coarsely chopped
4	plum tomatoes, each cut into 6 wedges
¼	cup finely chopped fresh flat-leaf parsley
1	tablespoon red wine vinegar
1	tablespoon minced fresh tarragon or 1 teaspoon dried tarragon
	Salt and pepper to taste
½	cup Maple-Walnut Vinaigrette (page 269)
	Toasted walnuts for garnish

❍ Heat the oil in a medium skillet over medium-high heat. Add the chicken; cook, stirring occasionally, for 5 minutes, or until lightly browned and thoroughly cooked.

❍ Meanwhile, mound the romaine lettuce onto plates; sprinkle with green onions. Arrange the tomato wedges around the edges.

❍ Remove the skillet from the heat; stir in the parsley, vinegar, tarragon, salt, and pepper.

◗ Arrange the warm chicken strips over the lettuce. Whisk the vinaigrette and drizzle about 2 tablespoons per salad over the chicken, lettuce, and tomato wedges. Garnish with walnuts. Serve immediately while the chicken is warm.

→ TIP ←

Toasting enhances the flavor and texture of most nuts. To toast nuts on the stovetop, toss them in a dry skillet over medium heat for 4 minutes or until golden brown. Or toast them in the microwave: Spread an even layer on a microwave-proof glass plate and microwave on HIGH for 2 minutes, stirring every 30 seconds. The nuts will become crisp, but they will not brown.

Because of their high fat content, nuts quickly become rancid at room temperature. Shelled nuts can be refrigerated in an airtight container for up to four months or frozen for up to six months. Toasting will freshen their flavor.

RED SWEET POTATO SALAD WITH CHICKEN

Makes **4** servings

The surprise addition of chicken to potato salad, plus the taste and color bonus of substituting red sweet potatoes for the customary white staple, gives this old-time favorite a new life of its own. For the best flavor—and appearance, too—select yams (or red sweet potatoes) with orange flesh rather than their yellow cousins. Present the salad in a large bowl, or assemble individual servings on beds of leaf lettuce.

3	cups yam (red sweet potatoes), peeled and cut into ¾-inch cubes (1 large or 2 medium-size yams)
1	tablespoon olive oil
8	ounces boneless, skinless chicken breasts, cut into ¾-inch squares
	Salt and pepper to taste
2	plum tomatoes, cut into ¾-inch cubes
2	green onions, coarsely chopped
¼	red bell pepper, cut into 1 x ¼-inch strips
¼	cup coarsely chopped fresh basil
½	cup Balsamic Vinaigrette (page 268), divided
	Freshly ground pepper and sprigs of fresh basil for garnish

◗ Put the yams in a medium microwave-proof dish; add ¼ cup water. Cover and microwave on HIGH for 5 minutes or until just tender. (Or cook the yams over simmering water in a stovetop steamer.) Drain and rinse with cold water.

◗ While the yams are cooking, heat the oil in a medium skillet over medium-high heat. Add the chicken; sprinkle with salt and pepper. Cook, stirring occasionally, for 5 minutes or until lightly browned and thoroughly cooked.

◗ Toss together the chicken, yams, tomatoes, green onions, bell pepper, and basil in a large bowl. Whisk the vinaigrette; add ¼ cup to the salad and toss again.

◗ Drizzle the salad with the remaining ¼ cup vinaigrette just before serving. Garnish with pepper and fresh basil sprigs.

CASHEW CHICKEN SALAD WITH CILANTRO VINAIGRETTE

Makes **4** servings

This is one of the most stunning salads in this book, especially when I serve it on my festive orange plates. And the blend of flavors is hard to beat, too. It's definitely a great choice for do-ahead summer entertaining when nectarines are at peak flavor. In the winter, I substitute oranges.

For the chicken:

12	ounces boneless, skinless chicken breasts
	Canola oil for brushing
	Dash of salt and pepper

For the vinaigrette:

¼	cup fresh orange juice
2	tablespoons canola oil
2	tablespoons red wine vinegar
1	teaspoon Dijon mustard
1	teaspoon sugar
¼	teaspoon Tabasco sauce, or to taste
¼	cup coarsely chopped fresh cilantro
	Salt and pepper to taste

To complete the recipe:

2	nectarines, cut into ½-inch cubes
1	red bell pepper, finely chopped
2	green onions, finely chopped
½	cup roasted, salted whole cashews
8	cups finely shredded romaine lettuce (1 medium head)

○ Heat a stovetop grill pan over high heat. Lightly brush both sides of the chicken breasts with oil. Reduce the heat to medium-high; cook for 5 minutes per side or until lightly browned and thoroughly cooked. Sprinkle with salt and pepper. Transfer to a plate and let cool.

○ While the chicken is cooking, whisk together the vinaigrette ingredients, except the cilantro, in a small bowl. Stir in the cilantro.

○ Cut the chicken into 1-inch squares. Toss together the chicken, nectarines, bell pepper, green onions, and cashews in a medium bowl. Add the vinaigrette and toss again.

○ To serve, arrange a layer of lettuce on large salad plates or in large, shallow bowls. Top with the chicken salad.

CHICKEN CAESAR SALAD

Makes **4** servings

Hail Caesar, the country's most popular salad! Well, a good thing just got better with the addition of chicken. I love the homemade Lemon Caesar Dressing, but you can use bottled dressing if you're in a time crunch.

12	ounces boneless, skinless chicken breasts
	Olive oil for brushing
	Salt and pepper to taste
8	cups romaine lettuce torn into 2-inch pieces (1 medium-size head)
¾	cup Lemon Caesar Dressing (page 269)
	Freshly ground pepper, freshly grated Parmesan cheese, and Garlic Croutons (page 280) or packaged garlic croutons for garnish

▶ Heat a stovetop grill pan over high heat. Lightly brush both sides of the chicken breasts with oil. Reduce the heat to medium-high; cook for 5 minutes per side or until lightly browned and thoroughly cooked. Transfer to a plate and sprinkle with salt and pepper. Cut into 2 x ½-inch strips.

▶ Toss the lettuce with the chicken in a large bowl. Add the dressing and toss again.

▶ Serve the salads in large, shallow salad bowls and garnish with pepper, Parmesan cheese, and croutons.

CHINESE CHICKEN SALAD WITH HOISIN DRESSING

Makes **4** servings

This dish is the star of many a restaurant menu, but it's amazingly easy to prepare at home. Actually, I like the salad even more if it stands for 30 minutes or so to allow the cabbage to wilt, but it's delicious served right away, too. To make the servings more substantial, when assembling the salad plates, add a layer of cooked thin Chinese egg noodles over the greens.

For the dressing:

½	cup white rice vinegar
¼	cup canola oil
3	tablespoons soy sauce
2	tablespoons hoisin sauce
1	tablespoon dark (Asian) sesame oil
3	tablespoons sugar
1	tablespoon finely chopped fresh ginger
1	teaspoon minced garlic
1	teaspoon mustard powder

For the salad:

2	cups coarsely shredded rotisserie chicken, skin removed, cooled
1	cup (3 ounces, about 24) Chinese pea pods, stems and strings removed
6	cups finely shredded Napa (Chinese) cabbage
4	ribs bok choy, coarsely chopped (including green tops)
4	green onions, finely chopped
¾	cup toasted slivered almonds, divided
1	(8-ounce) can Mandarin orange segments, drained

▶ Combine the dressing ingredients in a small bowl. Whisk until the sugar is dissolved.

▶ Toss together the chicken, pea pods, Napa cabbage, bok choy, green onions, and ½ cup of the almonds in a large bowl. Add the oranges and dressing; toss gently.

▶ Serve the salad in large, shallow bowls. Garnish with the remaining ¼ cup almonds.

--- TIP ---

Buy dark amber-colored Asian sesame oil, which is extracted from toasted (or roasted) sesame seeds. Light-colored sesame oils, which are extracted from untoasted seeds, lack the distinctive strong flavor. Because the flavor dissipates during cooking, sesame oil is usually added as one of the last steps in a recipe. It's a flavoring oil and is rarely used as a cooking oil.

CHICKEN AND RICE SALAD WITH MANGO CHUTNEY DRESSING

Makes **4** servings

Here is a classic chicken and rice salad, but there's no shadow of the "same old, same old" when it's tossed with a divine chutney dressing.

For the chicken:

1	tablespoon canola oil
8	ounces boneless, skinless chicken breasts, cut into ¾-inch pieces
½	teaspoon curry powder
¼	teaspoon salt
⅛	teaspoon pepper

For the dressing:

⅓	cup mango chutney
3	tablespoons white rice vinegar
2	tablespoons canola oil
1½	teaspoons curry powder

To complete the recipe:

2	cups cooked basmati rice
2	plum tomatoes, cut into ½-inch cubes
1	cup frozen corn kernels, thawed
¼	cup coarsely chopped fresh cilantro
	Salt to taste
4	cups salad spinach
	Toasted sliced almonds for garnish

● To prepare the chicken, heat the oil in a medium skillet over medium-high heat. Stir in the chicken, curry powder, salt, and pepper. Cook, stirring frequently, for 5 minutes or until the chicken is lightly browned and thoroughly cooked. Transfer to a plate and allow to cool slightly.

● While the chicken is cooking, combine all the dressing ingredients in a blender; purée until smooth.

● Toss together the chicken, rice, tomatoes, corn, and cilantro in a medium bowl. Add the dressing and toss again. Season with salt.

● Serve the salad on beds of spinach. Garnish with almonds.

TIP

Plum tomatoes are the same as Italian or Roma tomatoes. They have thick, meaty walls, small seeds, little juice, and a rich, sweet flavor. These tomatoes are the best choice for salads or other recipes that benefit from less juicy tomatoes; they will retain their shape after being chopped or sliced.

CANNELLINI BEAN AND CHICKEN SALAD WITH RED WINE VINAIGRETTE

Makes **4** servings

I love to make this satisfying main course salad on especially busy days because it stirs together in a flash, but who'd ever guess? No cooking is necessary, and there's only one bowl to clean.

For the vinaigrette:

¼	cup red wine vinegar
2	tablespoons extra-virgin olive oil

1	tablespoon fresh lemon juice
2	teaspoons Dijon mustard
1	teaspoon minced garlic
¼	teaspoon salt, or to taste
¼	teaspoon pepper, or to taste
¼	cup finely chopped fresh basil

For the salad:

2	cups coarsely chopped rotisserie chicken, skin removed, cooled
1	(15-ounce) can cannellini beans, drained and rinsed
1	tomato, coarsely chopped
½	cup thinly sliced red onion

◐ Whisk together the vinaigrette ingredients, except the basil, in a medium bowl. Stir in the basil. Add the salad ingredients and stir gently.

GAZPACHO SALAD WITH GRILLED CHICKEN

Makes **4** servings

This idea came to me one day when I had planned to make my favorite gazpacho soup—instead, why not a salad? It's uncomplicated, visually appealing, and perfect to enjoy as a light lunch on a steamy summer day. Top the salad with Garlic Croutons (page 280) or accompany with Crispy Pita Triangles (page 280).

For the chicken:

12	ounces boneless, skinless chicken breasts
	Olive oil for brushing
	Dash of salt and pepper

For the tomato vinaigrette:

⅓	cup extra-virgin olive oil
2	tablespoons red wine vinegar
2	tablespoons fresh lemon juice
1	tablespoon tomato paste
1	teaspoon minced garlic
¼	teaspoon Tabasco sauce, or to taste
¼	teaspoon pepper, or to taste
	Salt to taste

For the salad:

3	plum tomatoes, cut into ½-inch cubes
1	cucumber, seeded and coarsely chopped (about 2 cups)
½	green bell pepper, coarsely chopped
3	green onions, coarsely chopped
4	cups salad spinach
	Freshly ground pepper for garnish

◐ Heat a stovetop grill pan over high heat. Lightly brush both sides of the chicken breasts with oil. Reduce the heat to medium-high; cook for 5 minutes per side or until lightly browned and thoroughly cooked. Transfer to a plate and sprinkle with salt and pepper.

◐ While the chicken is cooking, whisk together the vinaigrette ingredients in a small bowl.

◐ Toss together the tomatoes, cucumber, bell pepper, and green onions in a medium bowl. Add ¼ cup of the vinaigrette and toss.

◐ To serve, spread a layer of the spinach on salad plates and top with the tomato mixture. Diagonally slice the chicken into ½-inch strips. Arrange over the salad and drizzle with the remaining vinaigrette. Garnish with pepper.

CHICKEN-ASPARAGUS SALAD WITH SESAME-ORANGE DRESSING

Makes **4** servings

Chinese wheat-flour noodles tossed with Sesame-Orange Dressing are a delectable foundation for vegetables and chicken, all flavored with an enticing hint of citrus. Add a dash of red pepper flakes if you'd prefer the dressing with a little kick to it.

For the dressing:

½	teaspoon orange zest
¼	cup fresh orange juice
2	teaspoons sugar
2	teaspoons soy sauce
2	teaspoons dark (Asian) sesame oil
1	teaspoon sesame seeds
⅛	teaspoon pepper, or to taste
⅛	teaspoon salt, or to taste

To complete the recipe:

4	cups asparagus in 2-inch pieces
4	ounces Chinese wheat-flour noodles
2	cups rotisserie chicken in ½-inch pieces, skin removed, cooled
4	green onions, coarsely chopped
	Orange slices for garnish

● Bring a medium saucepan of water to a boil over high heat.

● Whisk together the dressing ingredients in a small bowl.

● Put the asparagus into a microwave-proof dish; add ¼ cup water. Cover and microwave on HIGH for 3 minutes or until crisp-tender. (Or cook the asparagus over simmering water in a stovetop steamer.) Drain and rinse with cold water.

● While the asparagus is cooking, drop the noodles into the boiling water and cook according to package instructions. As the noodles cook, stir occasionally with a fork to separate. Drain well; rinse with cool water. Transfer the noodles to a medium bowl; add 2 tablespoons of the dressing and toss.

● When the asparagus is done, drain well. Transfer to a medium bowl. Add the chicken and green onions. Toss with the remaining dressing.

● To serve, spread the noodles on plates. Top with the chicken mixture and garnish with orange slices.

LEMON-TARRAGON CHICKEN SALAD

Makes **4** servings

During the summer months, my friends Nick and Karen Schmit, who live in a beautiful, wooded rural area in Wisconsin, welcome many out-of-town visitors to their home. Karen often makes this quick-to-prepare chicken salad, accompanied by ciabatta, to serve for al fresco dinners on warm, laid-back evenings, and it's always a big hit. "Delicious and refreshing" is the compliment she hears most often.

For the lemon dressing:

¼ cup mayonnaise

2 tablespoons finely chopped shallot

1 teaspoon lemon zest

1 tablespoon fresh lemon juice

1 teaspoon Dijon mustard

For the salad:

3 cups shredded rotisserie chicken, skin removed, cooled

2 ribs celery, finely chopped

2 tablespoons finely chopped fresh tarragon

Salt and pepper to taste

▶ Whisk together all the dressing ingredients in a medium bowl. Add the salad ingredients and stir gently until evenly combined.

CHICKEN AND MANGO SALAD WITH GINGERED ORANGE DRESSING

Makes **4** servings

Thanks to my travels through the South Pacific, mango has become one of my favorite fruits, and I always purchase several as I wander through the markets in Tahiti and Samoa. Here, combining mango with orange and ginger enhances its taste of the tropics. The peppery flavor of watercress contrasts nicely with the sweetness of the fruit and the tartness of the dressing. But if you prefer, substitute salad spinach for some or all of the watercress. Allow the chicken to cool or serve warm.

For the chicken:

16 ounces chicken tenders

Canola oil for brushing

Dash of salt and pepper

For the dressing:

½ cup thawed frozen orange juice concentrate

¼ cup canola oil

¼ cup white rice vinegar

2 tablespoons finely chopped crystallized ginger

Salt and pepper to taste

To complete the recipe:

2 large bunches watercress

1½ cups jarred mango in ½-inch slices

½ cup very thinly sliced red onion

▶ Heat a stovetop grill pan over high heat. Lightly brush both sides of the chicken with oil. Reduce the heat to medium-high; cook for 3 minutes per side or until lightly browned and thoroughly cooked. Transfer to a plate and sprinkle with salt and pepper.

▶ While the chicken is cooking, combine the dressing ingredients in a blender; purée until smooth.

▶ To assemble the salads, mound the watercress on 4 salad plates. Top with the chicken, mango, and onion. Drizzle with the dressing.

MANGO CHUTNEY CHICKEN SALAD

Makes **4** servings

Chutney, which is usually served as a condiment, is made with fruit, vinegar, sugar, and spices. Here, its sweet-sour flavor adds an unexpected element to this out-of-the-ordinary chicken salad. In place of rotisserie chicken, use grilled chicken, if you like.

½	cup mayonnaise
¼	cup mango chutney
2	teaspoons curry powder
4	cups coarsely chopped rotisserie chicken, skin removed, cooled
½	red bell pepper, finely chopped
2	green onions, finely chopped
	Salt and pepper to taste
2	heads Boston lettuce, leaves separated
	Whole roasted, salted cashews for garnish

► Stir together the mayonnaise and chutney in a large bowl. Add the remaining ingredients, except the lettuce and garnish, and stir until evenly combined.

► Arrange the lettuce on salad plates. Top with the chicken salad and garnish with cashews.

Soups

MODERN MOM'S CHICKEN NOODLE SOUP

Makes **4** servings (8 cups)

How would a mother cure her family's ills without it? This humble yet delectable soup is everybody's favorite. For variety, in place of the noodles you can add cheese-, mushroom-, or chicken-filled tortellini or ravioli to make a more filling entrée. For a lighter soup, I substitute orzo pasta.

1	tablespoon olive oil
3	ribs celery with green tops, thinly sliced
2	carrots, halved lengthwise and thinly sliced
¼	cup coarsely chopped onion
1	(49-ounce) can reduced-sodium chicken broth
8	ounces chicken tenders, cut into 1-inch pieces
4	ounces (about 3 cups) wide egg noodles
2	tablespoons finely chopped fresh flat-leaf parsley
2	teaspoons finely chopped fresh thyme or ½ teaspoon dried thyme
¼	teaspoon pepper, or to taste
	Salt to taste

► Heat the oil in a Dutch oven over medium-high heat. Add the celery, carrots, and onion; cook, stirring occasionally, for 2 minutes or until the carrots are crisp-tender and the onion is translucent but not browned.

► Stir in the chicken broth. Cover and increase the heat to high. When the broth comes to a boil, stir in the remaining ingredients, except the salt. When the liquid returns to a boil, reduce the heat to medium; cover and cook for 8 minutes or until the chicken is thoroughly cooked and the noodles are tender. Season with salt.

Modern Mom's
Chicken Noodle Soup

Shiitake mushrooms are also called Chinese black mushrooms, forest mushrooms, golden oak mushrooms, and Oriental mushrooms. These large, umbrella-shaped, brown-black mushrooms offer a rich and unique flavor. In forests, they grow on fallen or cut oak trees; in the United States, they are now cultivated on oak or artificial logs.

Choose plump mushrooms with edges that curl under; avoid broken or shriveled caps. Store shiitake mushrooms in the refrigerator in a dish covered with a damp cloth or paper towel rather than in a closed container. (Sprinkle the towel with water if it dries out.) The mushrooms will keep for only two or three days; beyond that, the flavor deteriorates. Shiitake mushroom stems are extremely tough and should be removed. (Rather than throwing them out, however, use them to add flavor to stocks and sauces; discard the stems after they have been used for flavoring.)

Dried shiitake mushrooms can be stored at room temperature in a sealed bag or a jar. They must be reconstituted before being used in recipes. To reconstitute, soak them in boiling water for about 5 minutes or for 30 minutes in lukewarm water, or until softened. Like fresh shiitake mushrooms, the stems are tough and must be removed.

SHIITAKE MUSHROOM SOUP

Makes **4** servings (6 cups)

For vegetarians, omit the chicken and substitute vegetable broth. Shiitake mushrooms can take the place of meat.

2	(14-ounce) cans reduced-sodium chicken broth
4	ounces fresh shiitake mushrooms, stems removed and discarded, caps cut into ¼-inch strips (1½ cups)
4	ounces boneless, skinless chicken breasts, cut into 1 x ¼-inch strips
1	cup Chinese pea pods, stems removed
½	cup coarsely shredded carrot
3	green onions, finely chopped
1	tablespoon cold water
1	tablespoon cornstarch
1	tablespoon soy sauce, or to taste
1	teaspoon finely minced chopped ginger
1	teaspoon dark (Asian) sesame oil, or to taste
1	teaspoon Chinese chili paste with garlic
	Ground white pepper to taste
	Black sesame seeds for garnish

◗ Pour the chicken broth into a Dutch oven and bring to a boil over high heat.

◗ Stir in the mushrooms, chicken, pea pods, carrot, and green onions. When the liquid returns to a boil, reduce the heat to medium; cover and cook for 10 minutes or until the chicken is thoroughly cooked and the vegetables are tender.

○ Stir together the water and cornstarch in a small bowl until smooth. Add to the soup, stirring constantly for 2 minutes or until slightly thickened and clear. Stir in the remaining ingredients, except the garnish.

○ Garnish the servings with sesame seeds.

EGG DROP SOUP

Makes **4** servings (6 cups)

A classic of Chinese cuisine, Egg Drop Soup is simplified here for speedy preparation. If you prefer, ¼ cup cholesterol-free egg product or 4 egg whites work just fine in place of whole eggs. Serve the aromatic soup with crispy sesame crackers.

2	(14-ounce) cans reduced-sodium chicken broth
1	tablespoon soy sauce
4	ounces chicken tenders, cut into ½-inch strips
1	red bell pepper, cut into ⅛-inch strips
1	cup frozen baby peas
¾	cup coarsely shredded carrot
3	green onions, finely chopped
1	teaspoon minced garlic
¼	teaspoon ground white pepper, or to taste
2	eggs
1	teaspoon dark (Asian) sesame oil, or to taste
	Salt to taste

○ Pour the chicken broth into a Dutch oven; stir in the soy sauce. Bring to a boil over high heat.

○ Stir in the chicken, bell pepper, peas, carrot, green onions, garlic, and white pepper. When the liquid returns to a boil, reduce the heat to medium; cover and cook for 6 minutes or until the chicken is thoroughly cooked and the vegetables are tender.

○ In a small bowl, lightly beat the eggs with a fork until they are light and lemon-colored.

○ Add the eggs to the soup, pouring slowly in a very thin stream; stir constantly until the eggs cook and form shreds. Stir in the sesame oil and salt.

--- TIP ---

Cholesterol-free egg products are made from real egg whites. The flavor is enhanced by the addition of a small amount of corn oil, and some yellow coloring is added to give the appearance of whole eggs.

Reduced-cholesterol egg products are made from whole eggs from which nearly all the cholesterol has been removed. Egg products are found both in the freezer and in the refrigerated sections of most supermarkets.

SHERRIED BLACK BEAN SOUP

Makes **4** servings (4 cups)

Serve bowls of sweet and juicy mango drizzled with fresh lime juice as a refreshing complement to the bold spicy flavors of this chunky bean soup.

1	tablespoon olive oil
1	cup finely chopped onion
½	cup coarsely shredded carrot
1½	teaspoons minced garlic
½	teaspoon ground cumin
½	teaspoon ground coriander
2	(14-ounce) cans reduced-sodium chicken broth
1	(15-ounce) can black beans, drained and rinsed
¼	teaspoon pepper, or to taste
⅛	teaspoon red pepper flakes, or to taste
2	tablespoons dry sherry
	Salt to taste
	Coarsely chopped fresh flat-leaf parsley for garnish

❍ Heat the oil in a Dutch oven over medium-high heat. Add the onion, carrot, and garlic; cook, stirring occasionally, for 5 minutes or until tender. Add the cumin and coriander; stir for about 30 seconds.

❍ Stir in the remaining ingredients, except the salt and garnish. Increase the heat to high and bring to a boil. Reduce the heat to low; cover and simmer for 5 minutes.

❍ Use an immersion blender to process until about half of the mixture is puréed but the soup remains chunky. (Or transfer 1 cup of the soup to a standing blender, purée, and stir back into the Dutch oven.) Season with salt.

❍ Garnish the servings with parsley.

TIP

Sherry is a fortified wine to which brandy or another spirit has been added to increase the flavor and boost the alcohol content. Sherries vary in color, flavor, and sweetness. Finos are dry and light; they include manzanillas, which are very dry and delicate with a hint of saltiness, and amontillados, which are aged and have a distinctively nutty flavor. Olorosos, often labeled cream or golden sherry, are darker and sweet. Avoid cooking sherry, which is overly salty and does not compare to sherry in flavor or aroma.

CURRIED CHICKEN AND RICE SOUP

Makes **4** servings (7 cups)

Comfort food with a touch of fusion, this jazzed-up version of good old-fashioned chicken and rice soup is one of my favorites for lunch on a cold winter day. In fact, I usually increase the curry powder to 2 teaspoons to add "heat."

3	(14-ounce) cans reduced-sodium chicken broth
1	(14-ounce) can diced tomatoes
8	ounces chicken tenders, cut into ½-inch pieces
½	cup rosamarina (small, rice–shaped pasta)
¼	cup finely chopped fresh flat-leaf parsley
1	teaspoon curry powder, or to taste
1	teaspoon minced garlic
2	teaspoons finely chopped fresh thyme or ½ teaspoon dried thyme
¼	teaspoon pepper, or to taste
	Salt to taste

● Stir together the chicken broth and tomatoes in a Dutch oven. Bring to a boil over high heat.

● Stir in the remaining ingredients, except the salt. When the liquid returns to a boil, reduce the heat to low; cover and cook for 10 minutes or until the chicken is thoroughly cooked and the rosamarina is tender. Season with salt.

CHICKEN SOUP SALSA VERDE

Makes **4** servings (5 cups)

My friend Karen Schmit has always been a creative cook known for entertaining during both summers in Wisconsin and winters in New Zealand. Sometimes she enjoys serving dishes that have simmered on the stove all day long, but she gets this delicious soup on the table in a flash. Karen warns that "hot" salsa verde may be overpowering. And she recommends accompanying the soup with a basket of crispy, lime-flavored tortilla chips. My son, Brett, whose favorite cuisine is Mexican, also likes to add a topping of shredded Mexican cheese blend.

3	cups shredded rotisserie chicken, skin removed
1	(15-ounce) can cannellini beans, drained and rinsed
1	(14-ounce) can reduced-sodium chicken broth
1	cup "medium" salsa verde
½	teaspoon ground cumin
	Sour cream and finely chopped fresh cilantro for garnish

● Combine all the ingredients, except the garnishes, in a medium saucepan over medium-high heat. When the liquid comes to a boil, reduce the heat to medium; cover and cook, stirring occasionally, for 5 minutes.

● Top each bowl with a generous dollop of sour cream, and sprinkle with cilantro.

ORANGE SOBA NOODLE SOUP

Makes **4** servings (7 cups)

The typical proportions of broth to solid ingredients are reversed in this hearty soup. Here, a large helping of noodles fills the bowls, with the spicy broth, chicken, and vegetables poured over. Make nothing else for dinner, and devour a large bowlful with chopsticks and a Chinese soup spoon.

1	(49-ounce) can reduced-sodium chicken broth
8	ounces chicken tenders, cut into ½-inch strips
8	ounces soba (buckwheat) noodles
1	cup coarsely shredded carrot
4	green onions, finely chopped
2	tablespoons soy sauce
1	teaspoon minced garlic
½	teaspoon red pepper flakes, or to taste
⅛	teaspoon ground white pepper, or to taste
2	teaspoons orange zest
¼	cup fresh orange juice
1	teaspoon dark (Asian) sesame oil, or to taste
	Coarsely chopped green onions for garnish

○ Pour the chicken broth into a Dutch oven and bring to a boil over high heat. Stir in the chicken, noodles, carrot, green onions, soy sauce, garlic, red pepper flakes, and white pepper. When the liquid returns to a boil, reduce the heat to medium; cover and cook for 6 minutes or until the chicken is thoroughly cooked and the noodles and vegetables are tender.

○ Stir in the orange zest, orange juice, and sesame oil.

○ To serve, use tongs to fill large soup bowls with the cooked noodles. Arrange chicken strips atop the noodles; pour the broth and vegetables over all. Garnish with green onions and serve piping hot.

> ──── · TIP · ────
>
> Soba noodles are made from buckwheat and wheat flours. They are a favorite in Japan, where I've seen soba masters meticulously roll the dough and cut the thin strands of noodles. The noodles are valued because of their nutty flavor and high nutritional value, including protein, B vitamins, minerals, and fiber. You'll find soba noodles in health-food stores and in the Asian section of most supermarkets.

TWO-POTATO CHICKEN SOUP WITH SPINACH

Makes **4** servings (8 cups)

A potato soup is all the better when it's made with chicken and two kinds of potatoes. The pleasing blend of flavors is enhanced by the sweetness of the yam.

1	(49-ounce) can reduced-sodium chicken broth
3	cups finely shredded salad spinach
1	large yam (red sweet potato), peeled and cut into ¾-inch cubes (about 2 cups)
1	large red-skinned potato, cut into ¾-inch cubes (about 1½ cups)
4	green onions, finely chopped

1	teaspoon dried rosemary, crushed
¼	teaspoon pepper, or to taste
8	ounces chicken tenders, cut into 1-inch pieces
	Salt to taste

▶ Pour the chicken broth into a Dutch oven and bring to a boil over high heat.

▶ Stir in the remaining ingredients, except the chicken and salt. When the liquid returns to a boil, reduce the heat to medium; cover and cook for 5 minutes. Add the chicken; continue to cook for 5 more minutes or until the chicken is thoroughly cooked and the potatoes are tender. Season with salt.

RAMEN NOODLE SOUP WITH SPINACH AND CORN

Makes **4** servings (8 cups)

This Asian soup was inspired by a satisfying lunch my son and I enjoyed in a charming San Francisco noodle restaurant recommended by some "'foodie" insiders of the city. The flavor is at its best when fresh corn is available, but in the winter, frozen corn will do. I provide togarashi powder or red pepper flakes at the table so guests can personalize the amount of hotness.

1	(49-ounce) can reduced-sodium chicken broth
2	tablespoons soy sauce
⅛	teaspoon ground white pepper, or to taste
2	cups fresh corn (cut from about 4 ears) or frozen corn kernels
6	ounces ramen noodles (discard flavoring packets)

8	cups coarsely chopped salad spinach
⅛	teaspoon red pepper flakes, or to taste
4	teaspoons salted butter
	Togarashi powder or red pepper flakes for topping

▶ Pour the chicken broth into a Dutch oven; stir in the soy sauce and white pepper. Cover and bring to a boil over high heat. Stir in the corn and drop in the noodles. Reduce the heat to medium-high; cover and cook for 2 minutes or until the noodles begin to soften. As the noodles cook, stir occasionally with a fork to separate.

▶ Reduce the heat to medium. Stir in the spinach and red pepper flakes. Cover and cook, stirring occasionally, for 1 minute or until the spinach is wilted and the noodles are tender.

▶ To serve, use tongs to transfer generous amounts of noodles, spinach, and corn to deep soup bowls; use a ladle to add the broth. Top each steaming bowl of soup with 1 teaspoon butter. Place togarashi powder or red pepper flakes on the table for topping.

——— TIP ———

Togarashi is a small, hot, red Japanese chili that is available in several dried forms, which you'll find in Asian markets. "Ichimi" togarashi contains only the chili powder. "Nanomi" togarashi contains the chili powder plus additional ingredients, such as sesame seeds, seaweed, and orange peel. Either makes a delicious flavor enhancement for this recipe.

CURRIED PUMPKIN AND BLACK BEAN SOUP

Makes **4** servings (6½ cups)

Welcome fall with this fabulous soup that is as colorful as it is tasty. Another bonus: It's substantial enough to stand on its own with a basket of warm flour tortillas.

1	tablespoon olive oil
½	cup finely chopped red onion
½	red bell pepper, finely chopped
1½	teaspoons minced garlic
2	tablespoons curry powder
2	(14-ounce) cans reduced-sodium chicken broth
1	(15-ounce) can pumpkin
1	(15-ounce) can black beans, drained and rinsed
½	cup half-and-half
¼	cup dry sherry
1	teaspoon packed brown sugar
	Salt and pepper to taste
	Sour cream and roasted pumpkin seeds for garnish

◗ Heat the oil in a Dutch oven over medium-high heat. Add the onion and bell pepper; cook, stirring occasionally, for 5 minutes or until tender. Add the garlic and curry powder; stir for 30 seconds.

◗ Stir in the remaining ingredients, except the garnish. Cook, stirring frequently, for 3 minutes or until heated through.

◗ Garnish the servings with sour cream and pumpkin seeds.

TOMATO-FENNEL SOUP

Makes **4** servings (6 cups)

My friend Judy Tills discovered this wonderful soup at one of her favorite Minneapolis restaurants. She developed this version, which she keeps on hand in the freezer for serving friends at impromptu lunchtime get-togethers. The dish always gets raves, and those who request the recipe are surprised by the secret ingredient, Pernod. Judy says this licorice-flavored French liqueur is essential to the flavor of the soup, and it's a perfect match with fennel, which adds its own hint of licorice.

2	large fennel bulbs
¼	cup unsalted butter
1	cup finely chopped onion
1½	teaspoons minced garlic
2	(14-ounce) cans diced tomatoes
1½	cups reduced-sodium chicken broth
½	teaspoon salt, or to taste
¼	teaspoon pepper, or to taste
¼	cup Pernod
	Garlic Croutons (page 280) or packaged croutons for garnish

◗ Cut the tops from the fennel bulbs and reserve a few sprigs for garnishing. Finely chop the bulbs.

◗ Melt the butter in a large skillet over medium-high heat. Add the chopped fennel, onion, and garlic. Reduce the heat to low; cover and cook, stirring occasionally, for 12 minutes or until tender.

◗ Meanwhile, combine the tomatoes, chicken broth, salt, and pepper in a medium saucepan. Bring to a boil over high heat, stirring occasionally. Reduce the heat to low; cover and simmer for 5 minutes.

⊙ Stir the cooked vegetables and Pernod into the tomato mixture; heat for 1 minute. Use an immersion blender to purée until nearly smooth.

⊙ Serve the soup sprinkled with croutons, and garnish with the reserved fennel sprigs.

> ──── · TIP · ────
>
> Fresh fennel (also known as finocchio) looks like a flattened bunch of celery with a broad, white, bulbous base and feathery fronds. To use the bulb, cut off the stalks and discard the bottom end. Cut the bulb in half lengthwise and slice it crosswise into crescent-shaped slices, which can be eaten raw in salads or cooked. The stalks are fibrous, with little use other than adding to stocks. The bright green feathery foliage can be used as a garnish or snipped like dill to use for flavoring. Fennel's distinct licorice flavor and aroma becomes milder when the vegetable is cooked.

ASIAN NOODLE SOUP WITH CHARD, GINGER, AND CILANTRO

Makes **4** servings (8 cups)

Perhaps you've seen chard, a robust vegetable with colorful leaves, in the produce section of your supermarket and wondered how to use it. This meal-sized soup, in which you liven the leaves with ginger and curry paste, makes the perfect introduction. For some dishes, the stems are chopped and added, but not here. I like this soup fiery and always add 1 teaspoon or more of the curry paste. So taste first and judge for yourself.

1	(49-ounce) can reduced-sodium chicken broth
12	ounces chicken tenders, cut into ½-inch pieces
4	cups firmly packed Swiss chard leaves in ½-inch strips
1	cup coarsely shredded carrots
2	tablespoons finely chopped fresh ginger
3	ounces thin Chinese wheat-flour noodles
½	teaspoon red curry paste or ¼ teaspoon red pepper flakes, or to taste
¼	cup coarsely chopped fresh cilantro
8	lime wedges

⊙ Pour the chicken broth into a Dutch oven and bring to a boil over high heat. Add the chicken, chard, carrots, and ginger. When the liquid returns to a boil, reduce the heat to medium and cook, stirring occasionally, for 2 minutes or until the chard is wilted.

⊙ Add the noodles and continue to cook for 3 minutes or until the chicken is thoroughly cooked and the noodles are tender. (Separate the noodles with a fork as they cook.)

⊙ Stir in the curry paste.

⊙ To serve, use tongs to transfer the noodles to soup bowls. Ladle the broth, chicken, and vegetables over the noodles. Sprinkle with cilantro. Accompany with lime wedges for squeezing into the soup at the table.

SANGIOVESE TOMATO SOUP WITH CHICKEN

Makes **4** servings (8 cups)

Red wine transforms ordinary and easy-to-prepare tomato soup into something truly wonderful. The full flavors call for a substantial salad and toothsome bread as accompaniments.

1	(28-ounce) can crushed tomatoes
2	(14-ounce) cans reduced-sodium beef broth
½	cup Sangiovese, or other medium-bodied, high-acid red wine
2	tablespoons finely chopped fresh flat-leaf parsley
¼	teaspoon pepper, or to taste
1	tablespoon olive oil
8	ounces chicken tenders, cut into 1-inch pieces
¾	cup finely chopped onion
½	green bell pepper, finely chopped
2	teaspoons minced garlic
1	cup coarsely chopped salad spinach
¼	cup finely chopped fresh basil
	Salt to taste
½	cup crumbled feta cheese

⦿   Combine the tomatoes, beef broth, wine, parsley, and pepper in a Dutch oven over high heat. When the liquid comes to a boil, reduce the heat to low; cover and simmer for 8 minutes.

⦿   Meanwhile, heat the oil in a large skillet over medium-high heat. Add the chicken, onion, bell pepper, and garlic; cook, stirring frequently, for 5 minutes or until the chicken is thoroughly cooked and the vegetables are tender.

⦿   Stir the chicken mixture, spinach, and basil into the Dutch oven. Cook over medium heat, stirring occasionally, for 2 minutes or until the spinach is wilted and the soup is heated through. Season with salt.

⦿   Ladle the soup into bowls and top with feta cheese.

TIP

As the author of *The Spirited Vegetarian: Over 100 Recipes Made Lively with Wine and Spirits*, I developed many recipes cooked with wine. My most important guideline is simple: If you can't drink it, don't cook with it. But cooking doesn't require that you invest in a fine vintage. There are many excellent, reasonably priced wines perfect for cooking. I also see cooking as an opportunity to use up wine opened the night before or several days earlier. Opened bottles of wine will keep in the refrigerator for up to a week while retaining quality adequate for cooking. (Removing air from the bottle with a vacuum wine saver, a gadget available in wine and gourmet shops, is beneficial.) For longer storage of wine destined for cooking, you can freeze it in ice cube trays. Most important is not to use any wines labeled "cooking wine" because they contain additives and are overly salty.

Note: The exceptions to these storage tips are fortified wines, such as port and sherry. Because they are partially oxidized to begin with, these wines have a longer life once opened and can be stored either in or out of the refrigerator.

ROASTED CHICKEN STEW PROVENÇAL

Makes **4** servings (6 cups)

The secret to the flavor and aroma of this thick rustic stew is herbes de Provence, a mixture of herbs traditionally grown and used in the south of France, where I always purchase it as I meander through Cours Saleya, the colorful outdoor market in Nice. The blend, which usually contains basil, fennel seed, marjoram, rosemary, sage, summer savory, thyme, (and sometimes lavender), can also be found in many gourmet shops and in the spice section of some supermarkets.

1	tablespoon olive oil
1	carrot, halved lengthwise and cut into very thin slices
½	cup finely chopped onion
1	teaspoon minced garlic
1	(15-ounce) can cannellini beans, drained and rinsed
1	(14-ounce) can reduced-sodium chicken broth
1	(14-ounce) can diced tomatoes with balsamic vinegar, basil, and olive oil
2	cups small red-skinned potatoes in ⅜-inch cubes
1	teaspoon herbes de Provence
2	cups coarsely shredded rotisserie chicken, skin removed
½	teaspoon pepper, or to taste
	Salt to taste
	Freshly ground pepper and freshly shredded Parmesan cheese for garnish

❍ Heat the oil in a Dutch oven over medium-high heat. Add the carrot, onion, and garlic; cook, stirring occasionally, for 4 minutes or until the carrot is crisp-tender.

❍ Stir in the beans, chicken broth, tomatoes, potatoes, and herbes de Provence. Increase the heat to high; when the liquid comes to a boil, reduce the heat to medium. Cover and cook for 5 minutes or until the carrot and potatoes are tender. Add the chicken, pepper, and salt. Stir gently until warm.

❍ Serve the stew in large soup bowls and garnish with pepper and Parmesan cheese.

--- · TIP · ---

New potatoes are young red-skinned potatoes that are harvested before maturity. They are small, thin-skinned, low in starch, and sweet in flavor. They become tender rapidly compared to mature potatoes and hold their shape as they cook.

Like all potatoes, store new potatoes at room temperature in a dark place, where they will keep for up to two weeks. Do not store potatoes in the refrigerator because the cold will cause their starch to convert to sugar and they will darken when cooked.

MEXICAN TACO SOUP

Makes **4** servings (8 cups)

Who doesn't love tacos? This zesty soup corrals all
those favorite flavors and wrangles them into a soup
pot, where aromas fill the kitchen and announce that
"Soup's on!"

1	tablespoon olive oil
8	ounces boneless, skinless chicken breasts, cut into 1 x ½-inch strips
½	red bell pepper, finely chopped
½	cup finely chopped onion
2	teaspoons minced garlic
1	(14-ounce) can reduced-sodium chicken broth
1	(14-ounce) can diced tomatoes
1	(14-ounce) can black beans or pinto beans, drained and rinsed
1	(4-ounce) can diced jalapeño chilies, drained
½	cup frozen corn kernels
½	teaspoon ground cumin
2	tablespoons finely chopped fresh cilantro
½	teaspoon pepper, or to taste
	Salt to taste
	Finely shredded Cheddar or Monterey Jack cheese and coarsely crumbled yellow corn tortilla chips for garnish

▶ Heat the oil in a Dutch oven over medium-high
heat. Add the chicken; cook, stirring occasionally, for
3 minutes or until lightly browned but not thoroughly
cooked. Stir in the bell pepper, onion, and garlic.
Cook, stirring occasionally, for 5 minutes or until
the chicken is thoroughly cooked and the vegetables
are tender.

▶ Stir in the chicken broth, tomatoes, beans,
chilies, corn, and cumin. Increase the heat to high.
When the liquid comes to a boil, reduce the heat
to medium; cover and cook for 2 minutes or until
warm. Stir in the cilantro and season with pepper
and salt.

▶ Garnish the servings with cheese and tortilla chips.

WHITE BEAN CHICKEN CHILI

Makes **4** servings (7 cups)

Rather than the customary red kidney beans and
tomatoes, this chili is updated with white kidney
beans and cream. Chicken thighs offer a richer
flavor, but if you prefer, substitute boneless, skinless
chicken breasts.

For the chicken:

2	tablespoons olive oil
12	ounces boneless, skinless chicken thighs, cut into 1-inch pieces
1	large onion, finely chopped
2	teaspoons minced garlic
1	tablespoon minced fresh oregano or 1 teaspoon dried oregano
1	teaspoon ground cumin
¼	teaspoon red pepper flakes, or to taste
¼	teaspoon salt, or to taste
⅛	teaspoon pepper, or to taste

To complete the recipe:

2½	cups reduced-sodium chicken broth
2	(15-ounce) cans cannellini beans, drained and rinsed
1	(4-ounce) can diced green chilies, drained

½ cup half-and-half

Finely shredded mild Cheddar cheese and coarsely chopped fresh cilantro for garnish

● Heat the oil in a Dutch oven over medium-high heat. Add all the chicken ingredients. Cook, stirring occasionally, for 5 minutes or until the chicken is lightly browned and thoroughly cooked.

● Meanwhile, combine the chicken broth, beans, and chilies in a medium saucepan. Bring to a boil over high heat. Reduce the heat to medium-low; cover and simmer for 3 minutes.

● Reduce the heat under the Dutch oven to low. Stir in the chicken broth mixture. Gradually stir in the half-and-half; heat gently until thoroughly warm.

● Garnish the servings with cheese and cilantro.

CURRIED WINTER SQUASH SOUP

Makes **4** servings (5 cups)

This fragrant, creamy winter squash soup invites you to stay inside rather than venture out on a cold night. Yet using frozen squash means that you can easily and quickly enjoy the luscious flavors all year round. I like to pair this soup with Mushroom and Red Beet Salad with Honey-Mustard Dressing (page 224) for a colorful meal.

2 (10-ounce) packages frozen winter squash
1 tablespoon olive oil
½ cup finely chopped onion
1 teaspoon minced garlic
1 tablespoon curry powder

1 (14-ounce) can reduced-sodium chicken broth
¼ cup dry sherry
1 tablespoon packed brown sugar
2 teaspoons minced fresh oregano or ½ teaspoon dried oregano
½ cup half-and-half or whole milk
½ teaspoon pepper, or to taste
Salt to taste
Coarsely chopped fresh flat-leaf parsley for garnish

● Thaw the squash in the microwave according to package instructions.

● Meanwhile, heat the oil in a Dutch oven over medium-high heat. Add the onion and garlic; cook, stirring occasionally, for 3 minutes or until tender. Add the curry powder and stir for about 30 seconds.

● Stir in the squash, chicken broth, sherry, brown sugar, and oregano. Cook, stirring occasionally, for 5 minutes. Reduce the heat to low. Stir in the half-and-half; stir for 1 minute or until warm. Season with pepper and salt.

● Garnish the servings with parsley.

MINESTRONE SOUP

Makes **4** servings (8 cups)

This hearty Italian soup is a contemporary version of my original minestrone soup, which simmered all day. What a pleasant surprise to find that the transformation is equally good—and ready to serve in a fraction of the time.

1	tablespoon olive oil
1	carrot, cut into ⅛-inch slices
½	cup finely chopped onion
2	teaspoons minced garlic
2	(14-ounce) cans reduced-sodium chicken broth
1	(14-ounce) can fire-roasted tomatoes
1	(14-ounce) can cannellini beans, drained and rinsed
8	ounces boneless, skinless chicken breasts, cut into ½-inch squares
1	zucchini, halved lengthwise, halved again, and cut into ¼-inch slices
⅓	cup elbow macaroni
2	tablespoons finely chopped fresh basil or ½ teaspoon dried basil
1	tablespoon finely chopped fresh oregano or ½ teaspoon dried oregano
¼	teaspoon pepper, or to taste
	Salt to taste
	Freshly grated Parmesan cheese and Garlic Croutons (page 280) for garnish

❍ Heat the oil in a Dutch oven over medium-high heat. Add the carrot, onion, and garlic; cook, stirring occasionally, for 4 minutes or until the carrot is crisp-tender.

❍ Stir in the chicken broth and tomatoes; bring to a boil over high heat. Stir in the remaining ingredients, except the garnish. When the liquid returns to a boil, reduce the heat to medium; cover and cook for 10 minutes, or until the chicken is thoroughly cooked and the pasta and vegetables are tender.

❍ Serve the soup in large shallow bowls and garnish with Parmesan cheese and croutons.

HERBED PASTA AND BEAN SOUP

Makes **4** servings (7 cups)

The ingredients are waiting right in your pantry and refrigerator to create this yummy meal-in-a-bowl. Vary the recipe by using different beans, such as garbanzo, kidney, Great Northern, or cannellini, and a variety of pastas, such as medium shells or spaghetti broken into 2-inch lengths.

2	tablespoons olive oil
½	green bell pepper, coarsely chopped
½	cup coarsely chopped onion
1	teaspoon minced garlic
1	(14-ounce) can diced tomatoes
1	(14-ounce) can reduced-sodium chicken broth
1	teaspoon finely chopped fresh thyme or ½ teaspoon dried thyme
½	teaspoon pepper, or to taste
½	cup elbow macaroni
1	(15-ounce) can pinto beans, drained and rinsed
¼	cup finely chopped fresh flat-leaf parsley
	Salt and pepper to taste
	Freshly shredded Cheddar cheese for garnish

❍ Heat the oil in a Dutch oven over medium-high heat. Add the bell pepper, onion, and garlic; cook, stirring occasionally, for 4 minutes or until tender. Stir in the tomatoes, chicken broth, thyme, and pepper. Cover and increase the heat to high.

❍ When the liquid comes to a boil, stir in the macaroni. When it returns to a boil, reduce the heat to medium-high; cover and cook, stirring occasionally, for 5 minutes or until the macaroni is al dente.

❍ Add the beans and parsley; stir gently for 1 minute or until heated through. Season with salt and adjust the pepper.

❍ Sprinkle the servings with cheese.

Sandwiches and Tortillas

LEMON-BASIL CHICKEN IN PITA POCKETS

Makes **4** servings

When you prefer a chicken salad, cook the chicken without flattening and cut it into cubes. Or plan ahead and use leftovers from last night's dinner. Toss with about half the chutney sauce and serve on a bed of greens.

For the chicken:

4	boneless, skinless chicken breasts
1	tablespoon olive oil
	Salt and pepper

For the chutney sauce:

½	cup mayonnaise or plain yogurt
½	cup mango chutney
3	tablespoons fresh lemon juice
2	teaspoons grated lemon rind

To complete the recipe:

4	pita bread rounds, halved to form 8 pockets
8	leaves soft leaf lettuce
16	large fresh basil leaves
16	thin cucumber slices

❍ Place the chicken breasts between 2 sheets of plastic wrap or place in a plastic bag; flatten to an even ¼-inch thickness.

❍ Heat the oil in a large skillet over medium-high heat. Add the chicken; sprinkle with salt and pepper. Cook for 4 minutes or until lightly browned. Turn the chicken and sprinkle with salt and pepper. Cook for 4 minutes or until lightly browned and thoroughly cooked. Transfer to a plate and cover to keep warm.

❍ While the chicken is cooking, stir together the sauce ingredients in a small bowl.

❍ For each sandwich, open 2 pita pockets; line with lettuce leaves. Slice each chicken breast in half. Place 1 chicken breast half, 2 basil leaves, and 2 cucumber slices in each pita pocket. Drizzle with 2 tablespoons sauce.

❍ Serve immediately while warm.

— TIP —

Lebanese pita bread is flat with no opening in the middle. Mediterranean or Greek pita bread splits horizontally to form a pocket for stuffing; this is the type of pita needed for this recipe.

Turkey, Apple, and Brie Panini

TURKEY, APPLE, AND BRIE PANINI

Makes **4** servings

I like to use green-skinned Granny Smith apples for these Italian-style sandwiches. Their tart flavor makes a delicious contrast with the sweet chutney and creamy Brie.

8	slices light rye bread
2	tablespoons unsalted butter
¼	cup mango chutney
8	ounces thinly sliced deli-roasted turkey
1	apple, cored and thinly sliced
4	ounces Brie cheese, cut into ½-inch chunks
	Canola oil for brushing

▶ For each sandwich, spread 1 slice of bread with butter and 1 slice with chutney. Place a layer of turkey slices and apple slices over the butter. Dot with chunks of Brie cheese. Close the sandwich with the other slice of bread, chutney side down. Lightly brush the outside of the sandwich with oil.

▶ Toast the sandwiches in a preheated panini grill for 3 minutes or until the bread is golden brown and the cheese is melted.

▶ Or toast both sides of the sandwiches in a skillet or stovetop grill pan over medium heat. Place another heavy skillet, bottom down, on top of the sandwiches and press gently for even browning.

▶ Depending on the size of your panini grill or skillet, you may need to toast the sandwiches in two batches.

TURKEY–PEPPER JACK PANINI

Makes **4** servings

Panini are simply grilled sandwiches given a boost in charisma by an Italian name. They're like your mom's grilled cheese sandwiches—only better. If you don't have a panini grill, the sandwiches can be toasted in a skillet on the stovetop.

8	slices multigrain bread
4	tablespoons unsalted butter
8	thin slices pepper Jack cheese
8	ounces thinly sliced deli-smoked turkey
1	tomato, cut into 8 thin slices
¼	cup fresh cilantro leaves
	Olive oil for brushing

▶ Lightly butter one side of each slice of bread. Place the slices on the counter butter side up.

▶ For each sandwich, layer 1 slice of bread with 2 slices of cheese, turkey, 2 tomato slices, and 1 tablespoon of the cilantro. Top each with a second slice of bread, butter side down. Lightly brush the outside of the sandwich with olive oil.

▶ Toast the sandwiches in a preheated panini grill for 3 minutes or until the bread is golden brown and the cheese is melted.

▶ Or toast both sides of the sandwiches in a skillet or stovetop grill pan over medium heat. Place another heavy skillet, bottom down, on top of the sandwiches and press gently for even browning.

▶ Depending on the size of your panini grill or skillet, you may need to toast the sandwiches in two batches.

CHICKEN FAJITAS

Makes **4** servings

Fajitas, a dish from the Tex-Mex border, are served in many variations, and each scrumptious twist is endlessly delicious. Diners can play a starring role in their assembly, layering their tortillas as they choose. When time permits, I add bowls of finely shredded lettuce, chopped tomatoes, and shredded Cheddar or Monterey Jack cheese to serve as accompaniments. To cut the chicken into thin strips, I find it's easiest to use kitchen shears.

¼	cup fresh lime juice
2	teaspoons chili powder
2	teaspoons minced garlic
1½	teaspoons ground cumin
½	teaspoon salt, or to taste
½	teaspoon pepper, or to taste
16	ounces chicken tenders, cut into 2 x ⅜-inch strips
1	tablespoon olive oil
1	red bell pepper, cut into 2 x ¼-inch strips
1	green bell pepper, cut into 2 x ¼-inch strips
1	cup thinly sliced yellow onion
¼	cup tomato salsa
¼	cup finely chopped fresh cilantro
8	(7-inch) flour tortillas

❍ Combine the lime juice, chili powder, garlic, cumin, salt, and pepper in a medium bowl. Add the chicken and toss; set aside for 5 minutes, stirring occasionally.

❍ Meanwhile, heat the oil in a large sauté pan over medium-high heat. Add the bell peppers and onion; cook, stirring occasionally, for 3 minutes or until the peppers are crisp-tender. Add the chicken with lime juice marinade; cook, stirring occasionally, for 4 minutes or until the chicken is thoroughly cooked and the vegetables are softened. Stir in the salsa and cilantro.

❍ While the fajita filling is cooking, stack the tortillas between 2 paper towels. Microwave on HIGH for 1 minute or until moist and warm.

❍ To serve, stack the tortillas on a plate and cover to keep warm. Spoon the chicken-vegetable mixture into a bowl. Assemble the fajitas as you eat by spooning some of the chicken mixture into the center third of each tortilla and fold the sides over the filling.

BLACKENED CHICKEN PITAS

Makes **4** servings

The magic of this recipe comes from playing the assertive spiciness of the seasonings against the subtle tartness of the sour cream and yogurt sauce. I like to garnish the servings with large bunches of seedless red grapes or fresh orange wedges. For variety, serve the chicken on toasted sandwich buns. Or cut the cooked chicken into cubes and toss with the seasoned sauce for a chilled chicken salad.

For the seasoning mixture:

3	tablespoons extra-virgin olive oil
1	tablespoon minced garlic
1	teaspoon paprika
½	teaspoon pepper
½	teaspoon cayenne pepper
½	teaspoon ground cumin
½	teaspoon salt

To complete the recipe:

½   cup sour cream

½   cup plain yogurt

1   teaspoon sugar

4   boneless, skinless chicken breasts

4   pita bread rounds, halved to form 8 pockets

8   leaves soft leaf lettuce (such as Bibb, Boston, green leaf, or red leaf)

8   thin (⅛-inch) tomato slices

8   thin (⅛-inch) red onion slices

◗ Stir together the seasoning mixture ingredients in a small bowl.

◗ Combine the sour cream and yogurt in a separate small bowl. Add 1 tablespoon of the seasoning mixture and the sugar; stir until the sugar is dissolved.

◗ Place the chicken breasts between 2 sheets of plastic wrap or place in a plastic bag; flatten to a ¼-inch uniform thickness. Spread the seasoning mixture on both sides of the chicken breasts.

◗ Heat a stovetop grill pan over high heat. Cook the chicken, turning once, for 8 minutes or until well browned (and somewhat blackened) and thoroughly cooked. Transfer to a plate and cover to keep warm.

◗ For each serving, open 2 pita pockets; line with lettuce leaves. Cut each chicken breast in half. Insert 1 chicken breast half, 1 tomato slice, and 1 onion slice (separated into rings) into each pocket. Drizzle the contents of each pocket with 2 tablespoons of the sour cream sauce mixture.

◗ Serve warm or at room temperature.

CHICKEN TORTILLA SANDWICHES WITH JALAPEÑO MAYONNAISE

Makes **4** servings

When time is short but you want to serve something unusual for lunch, here's a sensational chicken sandwich to make folks sit up and take notice. If you prefer, you can stuff the ingredients into pita bread pockets. Or transform the sandwich filling into chicken salad by stirring the mayonnaise mixture into the chicken. Juicy orange segments as a garnish on the plates add a nice balance to the hint of hotness in the mayonnaise.

For the mayonnaise:

½   cup mayonnaise

1   large plum tomato, cut into ¼-inch cubes

2   tablespoons finely chopped shallot

1   tablespoon finely chopped chili, such as jalapeño or Anaheim, or to taste

1   tablespoon fresh lime juice
    Salt and pepper to taste

To complete the recipe:

4   (10-inch) flour tortillas

2   cups finely shredded lettuce

3½ cups shredded rotisserie chicken, skin removed (both light and dark meat from a whole rotisserie chicken)

◗ Stir together all the mayonnaise ingredients in a small bowl.

◗ To assemble each sandwich, spread the center 2 inches of a tortilla with about ¼ cup mayonnaise mixture; top with ½ cup lettuce and about 1 cup chicken. Fold the edges of the tortilla over the chicken, overlapping at the center.

CHICKEN BURGERS

Makes **4** servings

Where's the beef? Well, who cares? Nobody when these juicy, flavorful burgers are on the menu. The procedure for each version is the same; however, the seasonings give each a totally different personality. Each recipe makes 4 servings.

Some supermarkets sell ground chicken, but it takes only seconds to produce at home. To grind the chicken, quarter the uncooked boneless, skinless breasts and drop into the bowl of a food processor fitted with a steel blade. Process with the on-off button to chop; the chicken will be ready in a flash. (Or you can substitute readily available ground turkey.)

General procedure:

● Transfer the ground chicken to a medium mixing bowl; stir in the remaining ingredients. Form each mixture into 4 patties, each 4 inches in diameter and about ½ inch thick.

● Heat the oil in a medium skillet over medium-high heat. Then cook the patties for 5 minutes per side or until lightly browned and thoroughly cooked. (If you prefer, the burgers can be broiled or cooked on either a stovetop grill pan or outdoor grill.)

● Serve the patties atop frills of leaf lettuce or on toasted buns with the suggested spread and your choice of accompaniments.

Asian Chicken Burgers

This recipe is simple, but the flavors are complex and satisfying.

16	ounces boneless, skinless chicken breasts, ground
½	cup cooked white, brown, or basmati rice
3	green onions, finely chopped
2	tablespoons finely chopped fresh cilantro
2	tablespoons soy sauce
1	teaspoon finely chopped fresh ginger
¼	teaspoon ground white pepper
	Dash of salt
1	tablespoon canola oil for cooking

● Follow the general procedure for Chicken Burgers. Serve the Asian Chicken Burgers on toasted buns spread with Spicy Peanut Sauce (page 265) or Chinese plum sauce. Add a layer of lettuce.

Mexican Chicken Burgers

Beans and rice—those treasured Mexican staples—add taste and texture to this south-of-the-border variation. Serve with Fresh Corn Salsa (page 275) or Vegetable Salsa (page 274) on the side.

16	ounces boneless, skinless chicken breasts, ground
½	cup cooked white or brown rice
⅓	cup canned black beans, drained and rinsed
¼	cup finely chopped onion
2	tablespoons tomato salsa
1½	teaspoons chili powder
1	teaspoon minced garlic
½	teaspoon pepper
¼	teaspoon salt
1	tablespoon olive oil for cooking

● Follow the general procedure for Chicken Burgers. Serve the Mexican Chicken burgers on toasted buns spread with Guacamole (page 272) and taco sauce. Add tomato slices and lettuce.

Italian Chicken Burgers

For those who love all things Italian—and who doesn't—these vibrantly seasoned burgers convey those popular flavors.

16	ounces boneless, skinless chicken breasts, ground
½	cup cooked white or brown rice
¼	cup finely chopped onion
2	tablespoons tomato paste
2	tablespoons finely chopped fresh basil
1	teaspoon minced garlic
½	teaspoon pepper
¼	teaspoon salt
1	tablespoon olive oil for cooking

● Follow the general procedure for Chicken Burgers. Serve the Italian Chicken Burgers on toasted buns, slices of Italian bread, or foccacia spread with Basil Pesto (page 274)—or pesto mixed with mayonnaise—and layer with tomato slices and lettuce.

TURKEY SOFT TACOS
Makes **4** servings

Ancho chilies—the sweetest of the dried chilies—have a fruity flavor, so the powder offers these same alluring elements. But if you don't have ancho chili powder on hand, you can substitute regular chili powder. Personalize the dish by using medium or hot salsa, depending on your craving for heat.

12	ounces ground lean turkey breast
½	cup finely chopped red onion
2	teaspoons minced garlic
1	(16-ounce) jar thick, chunky tomato salsa
1	tablespoon ancho chili powder
8	(7-inch) flour tortillas
1	cup finely shredded Monterey Jack cheese
1	avocado, cut into ¼-inch cubes
¼	cup coarsely chopped fresh cilantro
	Sour cream for garnish

● Heat a large sauté pan over medium-high heat. Add the turkey, onion, and garlic. Cook the mixture, stirring occasionally while crumbling the turkey, for 5 minutes or until it is lightly browned and the onion is tender. Stir in the salsa and chili powder. Reduce the heat to low; cover and simmer for 5 minutes.

● Meanwhile, stack the tortillas between 2 paper towels. Microwave on HIGH for 1 minute or until moist and warm.

● To assemble each taco, spoon a heaping ⅓ cup turkey mixture down the center of a tortilla. Top with 2 tablespoons cheese and 1 tablespoon avocado; sprinkle with cilantro. Fold the sides of the tortilla to the center to overlap.

● Garnish the servings with sour cream.

SAUSAGE AND BELL PEPPER CIABATTA SANDWICHES

Makes **4** servings

Ciabatta, Italian for "slipper," is a long, wide Italian bread with a soft interior and crisp, thin crust. The individual ciabatta rolls are well-suited to hold heaps of the sausage-and-sweet-pepper combination Italians love so well. These hearty sandwiches will satisfy even the hungriest men at your table. And for those weekends when they're glued to football on the screen, these fill the bill as half-time fare.

For the bell pepper sauce:

1	tablespoon olive oil
1	red bell pepper, cut into 1-inch pieces
1	green bell pepper, cut into 1-inch pieces
¼	cup onion in ¼-inch slices
1½	cups cheese-flavored tomato pasta sauce
⅓	cup Burgundy or other medium-bodied red wine

To complete the recipe:

1	tablespoon olive oil
4	(about 9 ounces) fully cooked sun-dried-tomato-flavored chicken sausage links, cut diagonally into ¼-inch slices
¼	cup finely chopped fresh basil
4	Italian ciabatta rolls (about 4 x 4 inches), halved horizontally
¼	cup shredded Asiago cheese

▶ To prepare the sauce, heat the oil in a large sauté pan over medium-high heat. Add the bell peppers and onion; cook, stirring frequently, for 5 minutes or until softened and lightly browned. Stir in the pasta sauce and wine. When the liquid comes to a boil, reduce the heat to low; simmer, stirring occasionally, for 5 minutes.

▶ Meanwhile, to cook the sausage, heat the oil in a medium skillet over medium-high heat. Add the sausage; cook, stirring occasionally, for 5 minutes or until just beginning to brown.

▶ Stir the sausage slices into the bell pepper sauce. Stir in the basil.

▶ Spoon the sausage mixture onto the bottom halves of the ciabatta rolls; sprinkle with the Asiago cheese. Close the sandwiches with the tops of the rolls.

TURKEY WRAPS WITH CHUTNEY AND PEANUTS

Makes **4** servings

Olé for tortillas! They've revolutionized the sandwich world. For another tasty wrap sandwich, substitute about 2 cups shredded rotisserie chicken for the deli turkey.

½	cup mayonnaise
½	cup mango chutney
1	tablespoon curry powder
	Salt and pepper to taste
4	(10-inch) flour tortillas or spinach flour tortillas
8	ounces (16 thin slices) deli turkey, coarsely chopped
½	cup coarsely chopped fresh cilantro
½	cup coarsely chopped lightly salted peanuts
2	cups coleslaw

❍ Stir together the mayonnaise, chutney, curry powder, salt, and pepper in a small bowl.

❍ For each wrap, spread ¼ cup mayonnaise mixture on a tortilla. In a 2-inch-wide strip down the center of each tortilla, layer 4 slices turkey, 2 tablespoons cilantro, 2 tablespoons peanuts, and ½ cup coleslaw.

❍ Fold the sides of the tortillas over the ends of the filling, and then roll up burrito-style to enclose the filling. Slice in half diagonally.

CHICKEN PESTO BAGUETTES

Makes **4** servings

This tasty sandwich filling does double duty as a salad when mounded over greens and garnished with tomato wedges.

¼	cup Basil Pesto (page 274)
¼	cup mayonnaise
2	tablespoons fresh lemon juice
½	cup golden raisins
3	cups shredded rotisserie chicken, skin removed, cooled
	Salt and pepper to taste
4	(6-inch) individual baguettes (or 6-inch pieces of 2 long baguettes), preferably whole grain
2	tomatoes, thinly sliced
4	romaine lettuce leaves

❍ Stir together the pesto, mayonnaise, lemon juice, and raisins in a medium bowl. Add the chicken and stir until evenly combined. Season with salt and pepper.

❍ To assemble the sandwiches, slice the baguettes in half horizontally. Spread the bottom of each half with ⅔ cup of the chicken mixture. Top with overlapping tomato slices, the lettuce leaves, and the top halves of the baguettes.

Pasta and Noodles

PASTA SHELLS WITH TOMATOES AND CHÈVRE

Makes **4** servings

The fresh, tangy taste of goat cheese and its creamy texture combine beautifully with tomatoes and herbs, creating elegant simplicity at its best. If you'd like, before adding the chicken broth mixture, toss cooked shrimp with the pasta shells. (Peel, devein, and poach fresh shrimp or use frozen shrimp that have been thawed.)

12	ounces medium (½- to 1-inch) pasta shells (about 4½ cups)
1	tablespoon olive oil
½	cup finely chopped onion
1½	teaspoons minced garlic
3	tomatoes, cut into 1-inch cubes
1	cup reduced-sodium chicken broth
1	tablespoon finely chopped fresh thyme
2	teaspoons finely chopped fresh rosemary
½	teaspoon pepper
½	cup (4 ounces) chèvre cheese
	Salt to taste
	Freshly ground pepper and sprigs of fresh thyme or rosemary for garnish

◗ Cook the pasta shells according to package instructions.

◗ Meanwhile, heat the oil in a large sauté pan over medium-high heat. Add the onion and garlic; cook, stirring occasionally, for 3 minutes or until tender. Add the tomatoes; stir for 2 minutes or until softened. Stir in the chicken broth, thyme, rosemary, and pepper; cook, stirring occasionally, for 2 minutes or until heated through. Remove from the heat and cover to keep warm.

◗ When the shells are done, drain well; return to the pasta pan. Add the chicken broth mixture and toss over medium heat until heated through. Remove from the heat. Add the chèvre cheese, and stir gently until melted. Season with salt.

◗ Garnish the servings with pepper and thyme or rosemary sprigs.

─── TIP ───

Chèvre and Montrachet are tangy, creamy cheeses made from goat's milk. Domestic goat cheese is a fine substitute for the more expensive, imported brands. Once opened, wrap tightly in plastic wrap and store in the refrigerator for up to one week. (Do not confuse chèvre and Montrachet with feta cheese or caprini, Italian goat cheese, which is drier, less creamy, and more acidic.)

CHICKEN AND MORELS WITH HONEY-MUSTARD SAUCE

Makes **4** servings

Fresh morels are generally available in April; depending on growing conditions, the season may last into June. The demand and price for these prized mushrooms are high, but nothing quite compares to morels' earthy flavor and aroma. To savor this recipe at any time of the year, dried morels may be substituted if necessary.

For the ideal menu to welcome spring, mound this aromatic mixture atop egg noodles or rice, and drizzle some of the sauce over steamed, fresh, slender asparagus on the side. Serve with a fruity, slightly acid Pinot Noir to balance nicely with the tang of Dijon mustard.

For the sauce:

¼ cup Dijon mustard

3 tablespoons honey

½ cup half-and-half

2 tablespoons finely chopped fresh tarragon

¼ teaspoon pepper

Salt to taste

To complete the recipe:

1 tablespoon olive oil

16 ounces chicken tenders, cut into ½-inch strips

4 ounces (about 16) fresh morel mushrooms, stems trimmed and discarded, caps halved if very large

¼ cup finely chopped shallots

Freshly ground pepper and sprigs of fresh tarragon for garnish

▶ To prepare the sauce, combine the mustard and honey in a small bowl. Stir in the remaining sauce ingredients.

▶ Heat the oil in a large sauté pan over medium-high heat. Add the chicken; cook, stirring occasionally, for 2 minutes or until lightly browned but not thoroughly cooked. Reduce the heat to medium; add the mushrooms and shallots. Continue cooking, stirring constantly, for 4 more minutes or until the mushrooms are tender and the chicken is thoroughly cooked.

▶ Reduce the heat to low. Pour the sauce over the chicken and mushrooms. Stir gently until warm and evenly distributed.

Variation: In place of 4 ounces fresh morels, you can substitute 1 ounce dried morels. Before adding to the recipe, the dried mushrooms must be rehydrated. In a small bowl, pour 1 cup warm water over the mushrooms and soak for 30 minutes (for added flavor, soak the mushrooms in warm sherry, brandy, or broth); or blanch the mushrooms in boiling water for 2 to 5 minutes. As the water is absorbed, turn the mushrooms occasionally and add more water if necessary. For maximum flavor, use only as much water as the mushrooms will absorb. Drain well before adding to the recipe.

⊢ TIP ⊣

Morels are edible wild mushrooms belonging to the same fungus species as the truffle. The flavor is smoky, earthy, and nutty; in general, the darker the mushroom, the stronger the flavor. Choose fresh mushrooms with a firm yet spongy texture. Refrigerate them in a single layer covered with a damp towel; avoid airtight plastic bags. Do not eat raw morels; they must be cooked.

Dried morels, available year-round, have a more intense, smokier flavor than fresh; they can be substituted in recipes after being rehydrated. To remove traces of sand, both fresh and dried morels should be rinsed before use.

CHICKEN PENNE WITH CREAMY TOMATO SAUCE

Makes **4** servings

Here's the perfect excuse to bring together a group of friends. It's one of my favorite dishes for easy entertaining, and it always receives praise. I accompany the pasta with artisan bread and Basil Pesto Butter (page 274) for spreading, along with a fresh green salad tossed with Balsamic Vinaigrette (page 268) and topped with Garlic Croutons (page 280). For wine, the fresh berry fruit flavor of French Beaujolais-Villages mingles nicely with the creamy texture of the sauce.

8	ounces penne
1	tablespoon olive oil
12	ounces chicken tenders, cut into 1-inch pieces
	Salt and pepper to taste
1	(14-ounce) can tomatoes with Italian herbs
½	cup jarred roasted red bell peppers, drained and cut into ¼-inch strips
1	teaspoon minced garlic
1	cup arugula leaves, stems removed and discarded
½	cup coarsely chopped fresh basil
¼	cup heavy cream
2	teaspoons balsamic vinegar
¼	teaspoon red pepper flakes, or to taste
	Sprigs of fresh basil for garnish

● Cook the penne according to package instructions.

● Meanwhile, heat the oil in a large sauté pan over medium-high heat. Add the chicken and a dash of salt and pepper; cook, stirring occasionally, for 5 minutes or until lightly browned and thoroughly cooked. Stir in the tomatoes, bell peppers, and garlic. When the liquid begins to bubble, reduce the heat to low. Stir in the arugula and basil. When they are wilted, stir in the cream, vinegar, and red pepper flakes. (Do not let the mixture come to a boil.)

● When the penne is done, drain well and return to the pasta pan. Add the sauce and stir until evenly combined. Season with salt and pepper.

● Garnish the servings with basil sprigs.

ROTINI WITH CREAMY THREE-HERB PESTO AND CHICKEN

Makes **4** servings

Consider planting herbs in your garden or in pots on your deck. The midsummer results of my efforts inspired this aromatic blend of flavors. The ingredient list looks long, but the pesto takes just seconds to prepare. And you can make it up to two days in advance.

For the pasta:

12	ounces rotini
1	tablespoon olive oil
16	ounces chicken tenders, cut into 1-inch pieces
	Dash of salt and pepper

For the pesto:

½	cup (4 ounces) chèvre cheese
½	cup fresh flat-leaf parsley sprigs
½	cup fresh basil leaves
½	cup reduced-sodium chicken broth
¼	cup coarsely chopped shallots
1	tablespoon extra-virgin olive oil
2	teaspoons minced garlic
2	teaspoons coarsely chopped fresh rosemary

½ teaspoon pepper, or to taste

¼ teaspoon salt, or to taste

To complete the recipe:

Sprigs of fresh herbs, plum tomato slices, and freshly shredded Romano cheese for garnish

○ Cook the rotini according to package instructions.

○ Meanwhile, heat the oil in a large skillet over medium-high heat. Add the chicken; sprinkle with salt and pepper. Cook, stirring occasionally, for 5 minutes or until lightly browned and thoroughly cooked.

○ At the same time, process all the pesto ingredients in a food processor until nearly smooth.

○ When the pasta is done, drain well. Return to the pasta pan. Add the pesto and toss. Add the chicken and toss again.

○ Garnish the servings with sprigs of fresh herbs, tomato slices, and Romano cheese.

WALNUT CHICKEN WITH SHERRY SAUCE

Makes **4** servings

Walnuts contribute both crunch and elegance to this chicken and green bean medley, further enhanced by the nutty nuance of the sherry. Serve this over wide noodles, rice, mashed potatoes, or lightly browned polenta slices.

For the sauce:

1 tablespoon cold water

2 teaspoons cornstarch

¾ cup reduced-sodium chicken broth

¼ cup soy sauce

2 tablespoons dry sherry

1 teaspoon finely chopped fresh ginger

1 teaspoon minced garlic

⅛ teaspoon ground white pepper

To complete the recipe:

2 tablespoons canola oil, divided

16 ounces chicken tenders, halved lengthwise and crosswise

3 cups green beans in 2-inch pieces

4 green onions, cut into 2-inch lengths

½ cup coarsely chopped walnuts

1 tablespoon walnut oil

Sprigs of fresh flat-leaf parsley for garnish

○ Stir together the water and cornstarch in a medium bowl until smooth. Stir in the remaining sauce ingredients.

○ Heat 1 tablespoon oil in a large sauté pan over medium-high heat. Add the chicken; cook, stirring occasionally, for 5 minutes or until lightly browned and thoroughly cooked. Remove from the heat.

○ While the chicken is cooking, heat the remaining 1 tablespoon oil in another large skillet. Add the green beans; cook, stirring occasionally, for 5 minutes or until crisp-tender. Reduce the heat to medium. Add the sauce and stir gently for 2 minutes or until thickened and clear.

○ Reduce the heat to low; stir in the cooked chicken, green onions, walnuts, and walnut oil. Heat until warmed through.

○ Garnish the servings with parsley sprigs.

GINGERED CHICKEN AND PINEAPPLE STIR-FRY

Makes **4** servings

This quick stir-fry may earn its way as a family favorite; kids particularly love the hint of sweetness from the fruit. Serve it over slender Chinese wheat-flour noodles, another youngsters' favorite.

For the sauce:

½	cup pineapple juice (from 20-ounce can of pineapple chunks)
½	cup fresh orange juice
2	tablespoons soy sauce
1	tablespoon hoisin sauce
1	tablespoon Chinese chili paste with garlic
1	tablespoon grated orange peel
2	teaspoons cornstarch

For the stir-fry:

2	tablespoons canola oil, divided
16	ounces chicken tenders, cut into ½-inch strips
1	cup fresh snow peas
2	tablespoons finely chopped fresh ginger
2	teaspoons minced garlic
4	cups Napa (Chinese) cabbage in ½-inch slices
1	(20-ounce) can pineapple chunks in pineapple juice, drained; ½ cup juice reserved for sauce

● Combine all the sauce ingredients in a small bowl; whisk to dissolve the cornstarch.

● Heat 1 tablespoon oil over high heat in a large sauté pan. Add the chicken; cook, stirring occasionally, for 5 minutes or until thoroughly cooked. Transfer to a bowl and cover to keep warm.

● Add the remaining 1 tablespoon oil to the same skillet. Add the snow peas, ginger, and garlic; cook, stirring frequently, over high heat for 2 minutes or until the vegetables are crisp-tender.

● Stir in the cooked chicken, cabbage, pineapple, and the sauce mixture. Cook, stirring constantly, over medium-high heat for 2 minutes or until the sauce thickens slightly and the chicken, pineapple, and vegetables are heated through.

TIP

Napa cabbage, also called Chinese cabbage or celery cabbage, is recognized by its solid oblong heads of long, smooth stalks with crinkly, thick-veined, pale-green leaves. Unlike the strong flavor of head cabbage, Chinese cabbage is delicately mild; it can be used raw or in stir-fries. In most supermarkets, it is available year-round. Refrigerate, tightly wrapped, for up to three days.

MEDITERRANEAN CHICKEN WITH PENNE

Makes **4** servings

This recipe was born of happy memories of al fresco feasts I have enjoyed during my travels throughout southern Europe. The dish makes a warm, hearty dinner. And the leftovers, served chilled or at room temperature, become a deluxe lunch the next day. (I suggest tossing the pasta with the chicken and zucchini topping when serving the dish chilled.) If you have some dry red or white wine left from last night's dinner, substitute it for the chicken broth.

12	ounces penne
3	tablespoons olive oil, divided
12	ounces chicken tenders, cut into 1-inch pieces
1	teaspoon minced garlic
	Salt and pepper to taste
2	small zucchini, cut into ¾-inch slices
2	plum tomatoes, cut into ¾-inch cubes
1	cup packed coarsely shredded salad spinach
¼	cup reduced-sodium chicken broth, dry red wine, or dry white wine
1	tablespoon finely chopped fresh oregano
	Freshly ground pepper and coarsely crumbled feta cheese for garnish

▶ Cook the penne according to package instructions.

▶ Meanwhile, heat 1 tablespoon oil in a large sauté pan over medium-high heat. Add the chicken, garlic, and a dash of salt and pepper; cook, stirring occasionally, for 5 minutes or until the chicken is lightly browned and thoroughly cooked. Transfer to a plate and cover to keep warm.

▶ Heat 1 tablespoon oil in the skillet over medium-high heat. Add the zucchini; cook, stirring occasionally, for 2 minutes or until crisp-tender. Stir in the tomatoes, spinach, chicken broth, and oregano. Reduce the heat to medium. Cover and cook for 3 minutes or until the zucchini is tender and the spinach is wilted. Add the chicken; stir gently for 1 minute or until warm. Season with additional salt and pepper.

▶ When the penne is done, drain well and return to the pasta pan. Add the remaining 1 tablespoon oil and toss.

▶ To serve, spoon the penne into shallow pasta bowls. Top with the chicken-vegetable mixture and garnish with pepper and feta cheese.

BELL PEPPER–ROSEMARY CHICKEN

Makes **4** servings

A colorful array of bell peppers displayed at my local farmers' market inspired this recipe. All bell peppers are sweet and mild with subtle variations in flavor, so don't hesitate to substitute others, such as purple or orange bell peppers. Serve this eye-catching dish over egg noodles or rice.

2	tablespoons olive oil, divided
12	ounces boneless, skinless chicken breasts, cut into 2 x ⅜-inch strips
1	red bell pepper, cut into 3 x ⅜-inch strips
1	yellow bell pepper, cut into 3 x ⅜-inch strips
¾	cup yellow onion in ¼-inch strips
¼	cup fresh lemon juice
1	tablespoon soy sauce
1½	teaspoons finely chopped fresh rosemary or ½ teaspoon dried rosemary, crushed
½	teaspoon pepper, or to taste
	Salt to taste

○ Heat 1 tablespoon oil in a large skillet over medium-high heat. Add the chicken; cook, stirring occasionally, for 5 minutes or until lightly browned and thoroughly cooked. Transfer to a bowl and cover to keep warm.

○ Heat the remaining 1 tablespoon oil in the skillet. Add the bell peppers and onion; cook, stirring occasionally, for 5 minutes or until tender. Reduce the heat to medium; add the cooked chicken, lemon juice, soy sauce, and rosemary. Season with pepper and salt. Stir gently for 1 minute or until heated through.

CHICKEN WITH LINGUINE AND TOMATO-BASIL SAUCE

Makes **4** servings

The secret to the success of this simple recipe is using top-quality ingredients. Canned diced tomatoes are a time-saver and a far better choice than mediocre fresh tomatoes. Use fresh garlic, fresh basil, freshly ground pepper, and extra-virgin olive oil, and their flavors will shine.

For the pasta:

8	ounces linguine

For the sauce:

1	(14-ounce) can diced tomatoes
2	teaspoons minced garlic
½	teaspoon pepper, or to taste
¼	teaspoon salt, or to taste

To complete the recipe:

3	tablespoons all-purpose flour
⅛	teaspoon salt
⅛	teaspoon pepper
12	ounces chicken tenders
2	tablespoons extra-virgin olive oil, divided
¼	cup finely chopped fresh basil
	Freshly ground pepper, freshly grated Parmesan cheese, and toasted pine nuts for garnish

○ Cook the linguine according to package instructions.

○ Stir together the sauce ingredients in a medium bowl.

○ Combine the flour, salt, and pepper in a flat-bottomed shallow bowl. Press both sides of the chicken into the mixture to lightly coat.

◗　Heat 1 tablespoon oil in a large sauté pan over medium-high heat. Add the chicken; cook for 2 minutes per side or until lightly browned but not thoroughly cooked.

◗　Reduce the heat to medium; pour the sauce over the chicken. Cover and cook for 6 minutes or until the chicken is thoroughly cooked. Stir in the basil.

◗　When the linguine is done, drain well. Return to the pasta pan and toss with the remaining 1 tablespoon oil.

◗　To serve, transfer the linguine to large shallow bowls. Arrange a layer of chicken strips and top with the sauce. Garnish with pepper, Parmesan cheese, and pine nuts.

Stovetop Dishes

CUMIN-SCENTED CHICKEN BREASTS WITH LATIN CITRUS SAUCE

Makes **4** servings

This quickly cooked sauce offers a surprising depth of flavors accented by a bright citrus note. To continue the Latin theme, serve the chicken with black beans and rice.

For the chicken:

2	teaspoons packed brown sugar
1	teaspoon ground cumin
½	teaspoon salt
⅛	teaspoon cayenne pepper (ground red pepper)
4	boneless, skinless chicken breasts
1	tablespoon olive oil

For the sauce:

1	tablespoon minced garlic
⅓	cup fresh lime juice
⅓	cup fresh orange juice
3	tablespoons honey
3	tablespoons finely chopped fresh cilantro
3	tablespoons finely chopped fresh mint
	Salt to taste

For the garnish:

Sprigs of fresh mint and orange slices

◗　Combine the brown sugar, cumin, salt, and cayenne pepper in a small bowl. Rub over all surfaces of the chicken.

◗　Heat the oil in a large skillet over medium-high heat. Add the chicken; cook for 5 minutes per side or until golden brown and thoroughly cooked. Transfer to a plate and cover to keep warm.

◗　To make the sauce, add the garlic to the same skillet over medium-high heat; cook, stirring constantly, for 15 seconds. Stir in the lime juice, orange juice, and honey; cook, stirring frequently, for 2 minutes or until slightly thickened. Stir in the cilantro and mint. Season with salt.

◗　To serve, spoon the sauce over the chicken. Garnish with mint sprigs and orange slices.

Chicken in Parsley Pesto Broth

CHICKEN IN PARSLEY PESTO BROTH

Makes **4** servings

These chicken breasts are partnered with an aromatic broth and vegetables. Although this dish isn't a soup, serve it in shallow bowls for an artful presentation. To make the rustic meal more substantial, I usually include a small mound of rice in the bowl.

For the chicken:

1	tablespoon olive oil
16	ounces boneless, skinless chicken breasts
	Dash of salt and pepper

For the pesto:

½	cup fresh flat-leaf parsley sprigs
¼	cup coarsely chopped fresh chives
¼	cup fresh thyme leaves
3	tablespoons extra-virgin olive oil
1	tablespoon fresh lemon juice
2	teaspoons minced garlic
¼	teaspoon salt, or to taste

To complete the recipe:

1	(14-ounce) can reduced-sodium chicken broth
½	cup frozen corn kernels
½	cup frozen baby peas
	Salt and pepper to taste
	Freshly ground pepper for garnish

◗ Heat the oil in a large sauté pan over medium-high heat. Add the chicken; cook for 4 minutes per side or until lightly browned and almost cooked. Lightly sprinkle with salt and pepper.

◗ While the chicken is cooking, combine the pesto ingredients in a blender and purée until nearly smooth. Stir in the chicken broth.

◗ Pour the pesto-broth mixture over the chicken. Add the corn and peas. Season with salt and pepper. Increase the heat to high and bring the liquid to a boil.

◗ To serve, cut the chicken breasts into ½-inch slices and transfer to shallow bowls. Ladle the broth and vegetables over the chicken. Garnish with pepper.

TIP

Fresh herbs, which come from the leafy part of plants, contain more moisture and therefore are milder than dried herbs. When substituting, the conversion is about 3 to 1 for fresh to dried, depending on the recipe and herb being used.

When stored in a tightly closed tin or glass container in a dark, dry place, dried herbs will remain flavorful for about a year; it's a good idea to date them. They should resemble the color they were when fresh and should not be dull or brownish green.

To get the most flavor out of dried herbs, crumble them between your fingers as you add them to your recipes.

THAI CHICKEN WITH BASIL

Makes **4** servings

Fragrant Thai basil has pointy, slightly serrated, dark green leaves on reddish purple stems. It's valued for its intense anise scent and licorice flavor. This specialty herb is usually found in Asian markets, but if necessary you can substitute the more commonly available sweet basil.

Thais serve this deliciously simple stir-fry over a plate of steaming jasmine rice. You also could toss the heady mixture with rice noodles.

3	tablespoons water
2	tablespoons Thai fish sauce
2	tablespoons soy sauce
2	teaspoons sugar
2	tablespoons canola oil
16	ounces boneless, skinless chicken breasts or thighs, or a combination, cut into 1-inch strips
½	cup thinly sliced onion
1½	teaspoons minced garlic
1½	cups snow peas, stems removed
½	cup coarsely chopped fresh Thai basil or sweet basil
1	tablespoon coarsely chopped jalapeño, serrano, or Thai chilies, or to taste

❍ Combine the water, fish sauce, soy sauce, and sugar in a small bowl; stir until the sugar is dissolved.

❍ Heat the oil in a large sauté pan over medium-high heat. Add the chicken, onion, and garlic; cook, stirring occasionally, for 5 minutes or until the chicken is lightly browned but not thoroughly cooked.

❍ Stir in the fish sauce mixture and snow peas; cook, stirring occasionally, for 2 minutes or until the snow peas are crisp-tender and the chicken is thoroughly cooked. Stir in the basil and chilies.

LEMON CHICKEN WITH ARTICHOKES

Makes **4** servings

Adding lemon slices in addition to the juice imparts a deep flavor to this fresh spring dish. I like to serve it over basmati rice or couscous. My son prefers bow-tie pasta. You decide.

2	tablespoons olive oil, divided
16	ounces chicken tenders, cut into ½-inch strips
	Salt and pepper to taste
½	red bell pepper, finely chopped
½	cup finely chopped shallots
1	tablespoon finely chopped fresh thyme
8	(½-inch) lemon slices
1	(14-ounce) can artichoke hearts packed in water, drained
2	tablespoons fresh lemon juice

❍ Heat 1 tablespoon oil in a large skillet over medium-high heat. Add the chicken; cook, stirring occasionally, for 5 minutes or until lightly browned and thoroughly cooked. Transfer to a plate, sprinkle with salt and pepper, and cover to keep warm.

❍ Heat the remaining 1 tablespoon oil in the skillet; add the bell pepper, shallots, and thyme. Cook, stirring occasionally, for 2 minutes. Add the lemon slices; cook, turning occasionally, for 1 minute or until darkened and tender.

○ When the bell pepper is tender, return the chicken to the pan. Stir in the artichoke hearts and lemon juice. Stir gently for 30 seconds or until warm.

CHICKEN MOLE WITH CILANTRO AND PEPITAS

Makes **4** servings

This ever-popular Mexican dish takes hours to prepare the traditional way, grinding the mole's spices by hand. Using prepared mole paste, however, means it's ready to enjoy in mere minutes. This shortcut is used in Mexico, too; I saw buckets and mounds of the paste for sale in the crowded Acapulco market where the locals shop daily. Serve this dish over rice, and complete the meal with Fresh Corn Salsa (page 275) or roasted corn on the cob. Pepitas are a must for garnishing the dish. You'll find them in health-food stores, in Mexican markets, and in the Hispanic section of many supermarkets.

1	teaspoon ancho or chipotle chili powder
1	teaspoon ground cumin
½	teaspoon salt
20	ounces boneless, skinless chicken thighs
1	tablespoon olive oil
¾	cup reduced-sodium chicken broth
3	tablespoons mole paste
½	cup finely chopped onion
1	tomato, coarsely chopped
	Finely chopped fresh cilantro and pepitas (roasted and salted pumpkin seeds) for garnish

○ Combine the chili powder, cumin, and salt in a small bowl. Rub over all surfaces of the chicken.

○ Heat the oil in a large sauté pan over medium-high heat. Add the chicken; cook for 2 minutes per side or until well browned but not thoroughly cooked. Transfer to a plate and cover to keep warm.

○ While the chicken is cooking, whisk the chicken broth and mole paste together.

○ Add the onion to the skillet; cook, stirring constantly, for 2 minutes or until tender.

○ Return the chicken to the skillet. Pour the chicken broth mixture over the chicken and sprinkle with the tomato. Reduce the heat to low; cover and simmer, stirring occasionally, for 8 minutes or until the chicken is thoroughly cooked.

○ Top the servings with cilantro and pepitas.

— TIP —

Mole paste is a thick, reddish brown paste made from chilies, onion, garlic, ground sesame or pumpkin seeds, and a small amount of Mexican chocolate, which is the most distinctive ingredient. You'll find jars in the Hispanic/Mexican section of the supermarket.

CHICKEN, CORN, AND TOMATO SKILLET

Makes **4** servings

This is pure and simple "comfort food"—a nourishing, one-dish family meal that will fill your kitchen with enticing aromas just as if you'd been cooking all day. Be sure to use white basmati rice, which cooks more quickly than brown basmati.

1	cup reduced-sodium chicken broth
1	(14-ounce) can diced tomatoes
8	ounces boneless, skinless chicken breasts, cut into ½-inch squares
⅔	cup uncooked white basmati rice
1	cup frozen corn kernels
2	tablespoons finely chopped fresh basil or 1 teaspoon dried basil
½	teaspoon pepper, or to taste
	Salt to taste
	Sprigs of fresh basil for garnish

○ Stir together the chicken broth and tomatoes in a large sauté pan. Bring to a boil over high heat.

○ Stir in the chicken, rice, corn, dried basil (if using), and pepper. When the liquid returns to a boil, reduce the heat to medium; cover and cook for 12 minutes or until the chicken is thoroughly cooked and the rice is tender. Stir in the fresh basil (if using). Season with pepper and salt.

○ Garnish the servings with basil sprigs.

JAMAICAN CHICKEN WITH BLACK BEANS

Makes **4** servings

Spices have played an important role in the history of the Caribbean islands beginning with Columbus, who came looking for spices when he sailed from Spain. Allspice, also known as Jamaican pepper, comes from a berry that grows on the indigenous pimento tree. Serve this aromatic dish with basmati rice. My friends Unni and Conrad Farinola suggest Jamaican Red Stripe Beer for the perfect beverage accompaniment.

1	tablespoon olive oil
12	ounces boneless, skinless chicken breasts, cut into 1-inch squares
1	cup finely chopped onion
2	teaspoons curry powder
1½	teaspoons minced garlic
1	(15-ounce) can black beans, drained and rinsed
1	(14-ounce) can diced tomatoes
1	tablespoon finely chopped fresh thyme
½	teaspoon ground allspice
½	teaspoon red pepper flakes, or to taste
½	teaspoon pepper, or to taste
	Salt to taste
	Coarsely chopped fresh cilantro for garnish

○ Heat the oil in a large sauté pan over medium-high heat. Add the chicken, onion, curry powder, and garlic; cook, stirring occasionally, for 5 minutes or until the chicken is thoroughly cooked and the onions are tender.

○ Stir in the remaining ingredients. Reduce the heat to low; cover and simmer for 5 minutes or until heated through.

○ Garnish the servings with cilantro.

Jamaican Chicken
with Black Beans

JAMAICAN COCONUT MILK CHICKEN

Makes **4** servings

Thanks to the East Indian influence on this Caribbean island, curry powder is an important part of Jamaican cooking, where it often enlivens chicken, seafood, or goat. This curry is great with basmati rice, even better if it is coconut flavored. So if you use a 5-ounce can of coconut milk for the chicken, stir the remaining milk into the water used for cooking the rice.

½	cup "lite" coconut milk
½	cup apple juice
2	tablespoons canola oil
1	tablespoon curry powder
16	ounces chicken tenders, cut into ½-inch strips
1	red bell pepper, cut into ¼-inch strips
½	cup onion in ¼-inch strips
⅛	teaspoon salt, or to taste
⅛	teaspoon pepper, or to taste

◐ Stir together the coconut milk and apple juice in a small bowl. Set aside.

◐ Heat the oil in a large sauté pan over medium-high heat. Add the curry powder and stir for 30 seconds.

◐ Add the chicken, bell pepper, and onion. Cook, stirring occasionally, for 5 minutes or until the chicken is lightly browned and thoroughly cooked.

◐ Reduce the heat to low. Add the coconut milk mixture. Simmer, stirring occasionally, for 5 minutes. Season with salt and pepper.

— TIP —

Do not confuse canned unsweetened coconut milk with "cream of coconut," which is used mainly for desserts and mixed drinks. Coconut milk is made from the firm, white meat found inside brown, hairy coconuts, and it is different from the thin, clear liquid naturally found inside a coconut. "Lite" or low-fat coconut milk, available in Asian markets and many supermarkets, contains about half the calories and fat of regular coconut milk. To reduce the fat when using regular coconut milk, combine it with an equal amount of water. In both low-fat and regular products, the coconut fat naturally separates from the coconut milk, so shake well before using. Leftover coconut milk can be frozen.

CHICKEN WITH TOMATO-PEANUT SAUCE

Makes **4** servings

My friend Nancy Bundt, the esteemed photographer for this cookbook, lives in Oslo, where she enjoys getting together with other international people residing in Norway. One day when Nancy prepared American barbecued ribs with the works at one of her backyard parties, a guest from Ghana shared this delicious—and amazingly easy to prepare—chicken recipe that pairs nicely with couscous or rice.

1	(14-ounce) can diced tomatoes
½	cup smooth or chunky natural peanut butter
1	teaspoon minced garlic
1	tablespoon canola oil
½	cup coarsely chopped onion
12	ounces boneless, skinless chicken breasts, cut into 1-inch squares
2	tablespoons fresh lemon juice
	Salt and pepper to taste
	Freshly ground pepper and sprigs of fresh cilantro for garnish

▶ Combine the tomatoes, peanut butter, and garlic in a small bowl. Stir until smooth.

▶ Heat the oil in a large sauté pan over medium-high heat. Add the onion; cook, stirring constantly, for 3 minutes or until tender. Add the chicken; continue to cook, stirring occasionally, for 5 minutes or until thoroughly cooked.

▶ Reduce the heat to low. Add the tomato mixture and lemon juice. Season with salt and pepper. Cover and cook for 5 minutes.

▶ Garnish the servings with pepper and cilantro sprigs.

TIP

Spices are aromatic seasonings obtained from the bark, buds, fruit, roots, seeds, or stems of various plants. Herbs usually come from the leafy part of a plant.

MAPLE-ORANGE CHICKEN STIR-FRY

Makes **4** servings

Delicious! I love these flavors—slightly orangey, with a sweet vinegary finish. And talk about beautiful—the ingredients glisten orange, red, and green in the glossy brown sauce. This stir-fry definitely needs rice, and maybe a fortune cookie or an almond cookie for dessert (perhaps with some green tea ice cream).

1	tablespoon olive oil
16	ounces chicken tenders, cut into 1-inch pieces
1½	cups green beans in 2-inch pieces
1	red bell pepper, cut into ¼-inch strips
⅓	cup pure maple syrup
3	tablespoons frozen orange juice concentrate, thawed
3	tablespoons soy sauce
3	tablespoons cider vinegar
2	teaspoons cornstarch
1	(11-ounce) can Mandarin oranges in light syrup, drained

▶ Heat the oil in a large sauté pan over high heat. Add the chicken, green beans, and bell pepper; cook, stirring frequently, for 6 minutes or until the chicken is thoroughly cooked and the vegetables are crisp-tender.

▶ Meanwhile, whisk together the maple syrup, orange juice concentrate, soy sauce, vinegar, and cornstarch until smooth. Add to the sauté pan. Reduce the heat to low; cook, stirring constantly, for 2 minutes or until thickened and glossy. Add the Mandarin oranges and stir gently until heated through.

CASHEW CHICKEN STIR-FRY

Makes **4** servings

Here's a Chinese takeout classic that's super-easy to prepare at home whenever your family craves its longtime favorite. Make the sauce spicy, or keep it mild by adjusting the amount of red pepper flakes. These are the seeds of fiery hot chilies, so a little can go a long way. Refrigerate the seeds to preserve their color and flavor.

For the chicken:

2	tablespoons canola oil, divided
12	ounces chicken tenders, cut in half crosswise

For the sauce:

1	tablespoon cold water
1	tablespoon cornstarch
1	cup reduced-sodium chicken broth
2	tablespoons soy sauce
2	teaspoons minced garlic
½	teaspoon red pepper flakes, or to taste
½	teaspoon turmeric
⅛	teaspoon ground white pepper, or to taste

To complete the recipe:

4	cups small broccoli florets
1	red bell pepper, cut into 2 x ¼-inch strips
3	green onions, cut into 1½-inch strips
¼	cup whole raw cashews

▶ Heat 1 tablespoon oil in a large sauté pan over medium-high heat. Add the chicken and cook, stirring occasionally, for 6 minutes or until lightly browned and thoroughly cooked. Transfer to a bowl and cover to keep warm.

▶ While the chicken cooks, prepare the sauce. Stir together the water and cornstarch in a small bowl until smooth. Stir in the remaining sauce ingredients.

▶ Heat the remaining 1 tablespoon oil in a skillet or wok. Add the broccoli; stir-fry for 2 minutes. Add the bell pepper and green onions; continue to stir-fry for 4 minutes or until the broccoli and bell pepper are crisp-tender.

▶ Reduce the heat to medium. Stir the sauce and pour it over the vegetables. Stir constantly for 2 minutes or until it thickens to a maple-syrup consistency and becomes clear. Stir in the chicken and cashews.

> — **TIP** —
>
> For cooking, raw cashews are often preferable to roasted and salted cashews. Having no added salt or fat, raw cashews will absorb the other flavors in your recipe, and they'll soften and plump up slightly to a pleasing consistency.

CHICKEN WITH CURRIED PEACHES

Makes **4** servings

Curry makes a flavor statement here; it's a natural mate to chicken and fruit. Because there is a wide variation in the intensity of curry powders, adjust the amount to suit your taste. I like to serve this with basmati rice, steamed vegetables, a green salad, and crusty bread.

¼	cup water
1	tablespoon canola oil
1	tablespoon curry powder, or to taste
16	ounces chicken tenders, cut into 1-inch strips
½	cup fresh orange juice

1	tablespoon packed brown sugar
1	tablespoon finely chopped fresh ginger
3	peaches, peeled and cut into ½-inch wedges
	Salt and pepper to taste
	Toasted chopped walnuts for garnish

▶ Heat the water and oil in a large sauté pan over medium-high heat until bubbly. Add the curry powder; stir for about 30 seconds.

▶ Add the chicken; cook, stirring occasionally, for 5 minutes or until lightly browned and thoroughly cooked. Transfer the chicken to a bowl and cover to keep warm.

▶ While the chicken is cooking, combine the orange juice, brown sugar, and ginger in a small bowl, stirring until the sugar is dissolved.

▶ Add the peaches and orange juice mixture to the sauté pan. Stir for 2 minutes or until the fruit is lightly cooked and the sauce is bubbly. Add the chicken; stir gently for 1 minute. Season with salt and pepper.

▶ Garnish the servings with walnuts.

Variations: For the fresh peaches, substitute 3 cups frozen peach wedges; thaw in advance and follow the same procedure, taking care not to overcook the fruit.

Alternatively, substitute one (15-ounce) can sliced peaches, pear slices, pineapple chunks, or apricots (or a mixture of fruits); drain, reserving ½ cup juice, which may be used in place of the orange juice. Omit the brown sugar and cook only until the sauce is bubbly and the fruit is warm.

SPICY CHICKEN AND RICE

Makes **4** servings

Have it your way: This entrée can be pleasantly spicy or seriously fiery simply by adjusting the amounts of chili powder, jalapeño chili, and black pepper.

1	tablespoon olive oil
12	ounces chicken tenders, cut into ½-inch strips
1	green bell pepper, finely chopped
½	cup finely chopped onion
1	tablespoon minced jalapeño chili, or to taste
1	teaspoon minced garlic
1	(14-ounce) can stewed tomatoes with Mexican seasonings, cut into smaller pieces using kitchen shears
1	tablespoon finely chopped fresh oregano or 1 teaspoon dried oregano
1½	teaspoons chili powder, or to taste
½	teaspoon ground cumin
½	teaspoon salt
½	teaspoon pepper
¼	teaspoon cayenne pepper
3	cups cooked rice

▶ Heat the oil in a large sauté pan over medium-high heat. Add the chicken; cook, stirring occasionally, for 2 minutes or until no longer pink on the outside. Stir in the bell pepper, onion, chili, and garlic. Cook, stirring occasionally, for 5 minutes or until the vegetables are tender and the chicken is thoroughly cooked.

▶ Reduce the heat to medium. Stir in the remaining ingredients, except the rice. Heat, stirring occasionally, for 5 minutes or until heated through.

BRAISED CHICKEN WITH BUTTERNUT SQUASH

Makes **4** servings

Beta-carotene-rich butternut squash has a smooth surface, making it quick and easy to peel. Remove the stem and even the bottom. Slice the squash in half horizontally and scoop out the seeds. Place each half, bottom down, on a cutting board. Cut down from the top to remove strips of the peel. Then cut the squash into ½-inch slices, line them up on the cutting board, and chop into ½-inch cubes. In addition to the chicken and vegetables, I like to add a mound of basmati rice to the bowl before ladling in the chicken broth.

3	tablespoons all-purpose flour
¼	teaspoon salt, or to taste
¼	teaspoon pepper, or to taste
16	ounces chicken tenders
2	tablespoons olive oil
1	(14-ounce) can reduced-sodium chicken broth
1	butternut squash, peeled and cut into ½-inch cubes (about 4 cups)
½	red bell pepper, coarsely chopped
1	tablespoon coarsely chopped fresh rosemary or 1 teaspoon dried rosemary, crushed
2	tablespoons unsalted butter
	Salt and pepper to taste

❿ Combine the flour, salt, and pepper in a large zip-top plastic bag. Add the chicken and shake to lightly coat.

❿ Heat the oil in a large sauté pan over medium-high heat. Use tongs to transfer the chicken to the pan. (Discard the bag and excess flour mixture.) Cook, turning occasionally, for 4 minutes or until lightly browned but not thoroughly cooked.

❿ Pour the chicken broth into the pan. Stir in the squash, bell pepper, and rosemary. When the liquid comes to a boil, reduce the heat to medium. Cover and cook for 8 minutes or until the squash is tender and the chicken is thoroughly cooked. Add the butter and stir as it melts. Season with salt and pepper.

❿ To serve, spoon the chicken and vegetables into shallow bowls. Use a ladle to add the chicken broth.

TIP

When mincing fresh herbs with twiglike stems, such as rosemary and thyme, use only the leaves and tender tips. To efficiently remove fresh rosemary leaves, run two fingers along the length of the stem.

To enhance the flavor and reduce the splintery texture of dried rosemary, crush the leaves between your fingers just before adding to the recipe. Rosemary has a bold taste, especially in dried form. Use it sparingly.

AUTUMN CHICKEN AND PEARS

Makes **4** servings

Pears, when they're at their prime, join cranberries in the perfect dish to welcome autumn. Serve the aromatic mixture over fluffy couscous, and add a topping of chopped pecans to make the meal memorable.

For the chicken:

4   boneless, skinless chicken breasts (about 4 ounces each)

3   tablespoons all-purpose flour

     Dash of salt and pepper

2   tablespoons olive oil, divided

To complete the recipe:

2   pears, cored and cut into ¼-inch wedges

3   green onions, finely chopped

½   teaspoon minced garlic

¾   cup apple juice

¼   cup dried cranberries

1   tablespoon finely chopped fresh thyme

     Toasted chopped pecans for garnish

▶ Place the chicken breasts between 2 sheets of plastic wrap or place in a plastic bag; flatten to an even ½-inch thickness.

▶ Combine the flour, salt, and pepper in a flat-bottomed shallow bowl. Press both sides of the chicken breasts into the mixture to lightly coat.

▶ Heat 1 tablespoon oil in a large sauté pan over medium-high heat. Add the chicken breasts; cook for 2 minutes per side or until lightly browned but not thoroughly cooked. Using tongs, transfer the chicken to a plate and cover to keep warm.

▶ Heat the remaining 1 tablespoon oil in the sauté pan. Add the pears, green onions, and garlic. Cook, stirring for 2 minutes or until the pears are slightly tender.

▶ Reduce the heat to medium. Stir in the remaining ingredients, except the pecans, and return the chicken

to the pan. Cover and cook for 8 minutes or until the chicken is thoroughly cooked.

▶ Garnish the servings with pecans.

TURKEY PATTIES WITH PAPAYA-PINEAPPLE SALSA
Makes **4** servings

Ketchup and mustard, step aside. No need for buns either. A fruity salsa is a cool and refreshing topping for these healthful patties. Cook them in a skillet or outdoors on the grill.

1   egg

16   ounces lean ground turkey

¼   cup finely chopped red onion

2   tablespoons dried bread crumbs

2   tablespoons sweet-and-sour sauce

½   teaspoon lemon pepper

1   tablespoon canola oil

1½   cups Papaya-Pineapple Salsa (page 275)

▶ To make the patties, lightly beat the egg in a medium bowl. Stir in the remaining ingredients, except the oil and salsa. Divide the mixture into 4 equal portions and form into patties about 4 inches in diameter and ½ inch thick.

▶ Heat the oil in a large skillet over medium-high heat. Cook the patties for 5 minutes per side or until thoroughly cooked.

▶ To serve, mound the salsa on the cooked patties.

CHICKEN WITH BLACK BEAN– TOMATO SAUCE

Makes **4** servings

This braised chicken is zesty, colorful, and, above all, easy to prepare. It's hearty on its own, but even better served over rice.

For the chicken:

3	tablespoons all-purpose flour
1/8	teaspoon salt
1/8	teaspoon pepper
16	ounces chicken tenders
1	tablespoon olive oil

For the sauce:

1	tablespoon olive oil
1	green bell pepper, coarsely chopped
1/3	cup coarsely chopped onion
1	(15-ounce) can black beans, drained and rinsed
1	(14-ounce) can stewed tomatoes with Mexican flavors (jalapeños, garlic, and cumin)
1	(4-ounce) can chopped green chilies, drained
1/2	teaspoon pepper, or to taste
1/4	cup finely chopped fresh cilantro
2	tablespoons fresh lime juice
	Salt to taste

⊙ Combine the flour, salt, and pepper in a large zip-top plastic bag. Add the chicken and shake to lightly coat.

⊙ Heat the oil in a large sauté pan over medium-high heat. Use tongs to transfer the chicken to the pan. (Discard the bag and excess flour mixture.) Cook, stirring occasionally, for 4 minutes or until lightly browned but not thoroughly cooked.

⊙ Using tongs, transfer the chicken to a plate and cover to keep warm.

⊙ To prepare the sauce, heat the oil in the same sauté pan over medium-high heat. Add the bell pepper and onion; cook, stirring occasionally, for 4 minutes or until crisp-tender. Stir in the beans, tomatoes, chilies, and pepper. Use a wooden spoon to break up the tomatoes.

⊙ Reduce the heat to medium and stir in the chicken. Cover and cook for 8 minutes or until the chicken is thoroughly cooked. Stir in the cilantro and lime juice. Season with salt.

TIP

Just how hot a chili is depends on the amount of a substance called capsaicin (kap-SAY-ih-sihn), found mainly in the veins near the seeds. Unaffected by high temperatures, capsaicin retains its potency despite cooking time, so removing the membranes and seeds before using chilies is the only way to reduce the heat. Small chilies have more membranes and seeds than large ones, so generally they are hotter.

To avoid irritation from the caustic oils in chilies, do not touch your eyes, nose, or lips while handling them. Many cooks wear disposable plastic gloves when working with chilies. Afterwards, wash your hands, knife, and cutting board in hot, soapy water.

CHICKEN WITH GRAPES IN WHITE ZINFANDEL SAUCE

Makes **4** servings

Enjoy every bit of this luscious sauce by serving the chicken over couscous or rice. This is 15-Minute chicken at its best. The dish is elegant, stylish, and ideal for entertaining, especially when served with a fruity, dry blush wine.

For the chicken:

2	tablespoons all-purpose flour
¼	teaspoon paprika
¼	teaspoon salt
⅛	teaspoon pepper
16	ounces boneless, skinless chicken breasts
1	tablespoon unsalted butter

For the sauce:

1	tablespoon cold water
1	tablespoon cornstarch
¾	cup white Zinfandel wine
¾	cup reduced-sodium chicken broth
¼	teaspoon pepper, or to taste
1½	teaspoons finely chopped fresh rosemary or ¼ teaspoon dried rosemary, crushed
1	tablespoon unsalted butter
¼	cup finely chopped shallot

To complete the recipe:

1½	cups halved seedless red gsrapes (about 7 ounces)
	Sprigs of fresh rosemary for garnish

◗ Combine the flour, paprika, salt, and pepper in a flat-bottomed shallow bowl. Press both sides of the chicken breasts into the mixture to lightly coat.

◗ Heat the butter in a large sauté pan over medium-high heat. Add the chicken and cook for 5 minutes per side or until thoroughly cooked.

◗ Meanwhile, to prepare the sauce, stir together the water and cornstarch in a medium bowl until smooth. Stir in the wine, chicken broth, and pepper. Set aside.

◗ Melt the butter in a small saucepan over medium heat. Add the shallot; cook, stirring for 1 minute or until transparent but not browned. Stir the chicken broth mixture and pour it into the saucepan. Bring to a boil, stirring constantly, over medium-high heat. Reduce the heat to low; simmer, stirring frequently, for 2 minutes or until the sauce is thickened and glossy.

◗ Pour the sauce over the chicken and stir, scraping the bottom of the pan around the chicken. Reduce the heat to low. Add the grapes and stir gently for 1 minute or until warm.

◗ To serve, spoon the grapes and sauce over the chicken. Garnish with rosemary sprigs.

─── TIP ───

White Zinfandel is not a white wine, but rather what is often called a "blush wine" in the United States and a "rosé" or "blanc de noir" in France. It's made from Zinfandel, a red-wine grape, but the skins and stems are quickly removed from the juice once the grapes are pressed, a process that eliminates the transfer of color from the grape's dark skin, keeping the wine pale. Most white Zinfandels are light bodied and slightly sweet.

ASIAN CHICKEN STRIPS WITH LEMON-SESAME SAUCE

Makes **4** servings

This lemon-sesame sauce boasts a citrus flavor kicked up with a hint of sesame oil—an interesting complement to the lightly browned chicken strips. Serve this with buttered couscous or Chinese wheat-flour noodles. Steamed vegetables, such as asparagus or broccoli florets, are a nice addition to the meal, but my favorite is to top off the feast with portobello mushroom strips sautéed with fresh ginger and garlic.

For the sauce:

¼   cup soy sauce

1   teaspoon lemon zest

¼   cup fresh lemon juice

1½   tablespoons dark (Asian) sesame oil

1   teaspoon minced garlic

1   teaspoon sugar

To complete the recipe:

¼   cup all-purpose flour

½   teaspoon pepper

16   ounces boneless, skinless chicken breasts, cut into 2 x ½-inch strips

1   tablespoon canola oil

4   cups salad spinach

1   (11-ounce) can Mandarin orange segments, drained

    Black sesame seeds for garnish

▶ Combine all the sauce ingredients in a small bowl and stir to dissolve the sugar.

▶ Combine the flour and pepper into a large zip-top plastic bag. Add the chicken and shake to lightly coat.

▶ Heat the oil in a large skillet over medium-high heat. Add the chicken strips in a single layer. (Discard the bag and excess flour mixture.) Cook the chicken for 4 minutes, turning once, or until crisp, golden brown, and thoroughly cooked.

▶ While the chicken is cooking, line the plates with spinach. Place the warm chicken strips on the greens. Surround with the orange segments. Drizzle each serving with about 2 tablespoons sauce and garnish with sesame seeds. Serve the remaining sauce in a container on the side.

BRAISED CHICKEN WITH PAPAYA

Makes **4** servings

This tropical chicken dish is one of the simplest of all to prepare. And who can resist sweet, juicy papaya? It's also one of my favorites, especially when paired with basmati rice or couscous.

For the chicken:

3   tablespoons all-purpose flour

¼   teaspoon salt

¼   teaspoon pepper

16   ounces chicken tenders

2   tablespoons olive oil

To complete the recipe:

1   (14-ounce) can reduced-sodium chicken broth

1   papaya, cut into ½-inch slices

¼   cup coarsely chopped fresh cilantro

    Salt and pepper to taste

    Freshly ground pepper and sprigs of fresh cilantro for garnish

- Combine the flour, salt, and pepper in a large zip-top plastic bag. Add the chicken and shake to lightly coat.

- Heat the oil in a large sauté pan over medium-high heat. Use tongs to transfer the chicken to the pan. (Discard the bag and excess flour mixture.) Cook, turning occasionally, for 4 minutes or until lightly browned but not thoroughly cooked.

- Reduce the heat to medium and pour the chicken broth over the chicken. Place the papaya slices atop the chicken. Cover and cook for 8 minutes or until the chicken is thoroughly cooked. Stir in the cilantro and season with salt and pepper.

- To serve, arrange the chicken strips and papaya slices in shallow bowls. Drizzle with the chicken broth, sprinkle with pepper, and garnish with cilantro sprigs.

CHICKEN WITH PORT WINE CHERRY SAUCE

Makes **4** servings

When you need a dish that is exceptionally elegant yet quick, this is it. The rich, fruity combination of the cherries and the port is an ideal match. Add a sprinkle of goat cheese for a perfect counterpoint to the sauce. To complete the plate, serve with mashed sweet potatoes and also a bright green vegetable—steamed asparagus, green beans, or sugar snap peas.

For the chicken:

1	teaspoon paprika
1	teaspoon dried tarragon
½	teaspoon salt
¼	teaspoon pepper

4	boneless, skinless chicken breasts
1	tablespoon olive oil

For the sauce:

½	cup port or other sweet wine
½	cup reduced-sodium chicken broth
⅓	cup dried cherries
1	tablespoon cold water
1	teaspoon cornstarch
1	tablespoon unsalted butter
¼	teaspoon salt, or to taste

To complete the recipe:

¼	cup crumbled chèvre cheese
	Finely chopped fresh flat-leaf parsley for garnish

- Combine the paprika, tarragon, salt, and pepper in a small bowl. Rub over all surfaces of the chicken.

- Heat the oil in a large skillet over medium-high heat. Add the chicken; cook for 5 minutes per side or until thoroughly cooked. Transfer to a plate and cover to keep warm.

- While the chicken is cooking, combine the wine, chicken broth, and dried cherries in a small saucepan. Bring to a boil over high heat; continue boiling for 3 minutes or until the mixture is reduced by half. Reduce the heat to medium.

- Stir together the water and cornstarch in a small bowl. Stir into the wine mixture. Cook, stirring constantly, for 2 minutes or until the sauce thickens and becomes glossy. Add the butter and salt; stir until the butter is melted.

- To serve, spoon the sauce over the chicken and sprinkle with chèvre cheese and parsley.

TURKEY AND MUSHROOMS IN MADEIRA WINE SAUCE

Makes **4** servings

As the wine heats, the alcohol burns off, leaving its distinct flavor. Serve this aromatic turkey dish with a green vegetable, such as broccoli, peas, or green beans. To add to the visual appeal and to make the meal complete, lightly brown polenta slices as the turkey cooks. Or serve the turkey and sauce over mashed potatoes.

2	tablespoons olive oil, divided
16	ounces turkey cutlets, cut into ½-inch strips
½	teaspoon salt, or to taste
¼	teaspoon pepper, or to taste
1	tablespoon finely chopped fresh tarragon or 1 teaspoon dried tarragon
2	carrots, cut into ¼-inch slices
8	ounces fresh shiitake mushrooms, stems discarded, caps cut into ¼-inch slices
1	cup reduced-sodium chicken broth
⅓	cup Madeira wine
1	teaspoon cornstarch
¼	cup finely chopped fresh flat-leaf parsley

◑ Heat 1 tablespoon oil in a large skillet over medium-high heat. Add the turkey; sprinkle with the salt and pepper. Cook, stirring frequently, for 7 minutes or until lightly browned and thoroughly cooked. Stir in the tarragon.

◑ While the turkey is cooking, heat the remaining 1 tablespoon oil in a large skillet over medium-high heat. Add the carrots; cook, stirring frequently, for 3 minutes. Add the mushrooms; continue to cook, stirring frequently, for 3 more minutes or until the mushrooms are softened and the carrots are tender.

◑ Stir together the chicken broth, wine, and cornstarch in a medium bowl until smooth.

◑ Add the carrots and mushrooms and the chicken broth mixture to the turkey strips. Cook, stirring frequently, over medium heat for 2 minutes or until the sauce is slightly thickened. Stir in the parsley.

> ——— • TIP • ———
>
> Wines, such as Madeira and Port, are fortified when the winemaker adds brandy or a neutral spirit in order to boost alcohol content and stop fermentation.

Baked and Broiled Dishes

MEXICAN TORTILLA PIZZAS

Makes **4** servings

Combining pizza and Mexican food—two all-time favorites—in this quick-to-prepare recipe guarantees a call for seconds.

4	(7-inch) flour tortillas
	Olive oil for brushing
2	cups rotisserie chicken in ½-inch chunks, skin removed

1¼	cups taco sauce
½	cup oil-packed julienned sun-dried tomatoes, drained
1	teaspoon dried oregano
½	cup finely shredded Mexican cheese blend

● Position the oven rack about 5 inches from the heating element and preheat the broiler.

● Brush both sides of the tortillas with oil. Place on a baking sheet and prick the tortillas several places with a fork. Broil for 1 minute per side or until lightly browned. Watch closely.

● Stir together the remaining ingredients, except the cheese, in a medium bowl. Spread over the tortillas and sprinkle with the cheese.

● Broil for 1 minute or just until the cheese melts.

CHICKEN SATAYS WITH SPICY PEANUT SAUCE

Makes **4** servings

These tasty kabobs with an Indonesian influence make an enticing entrée with rice on the side to complement the sweet-hot flavors. When time permits, I like to make the Spicy Peanut Sauce in advance, allowing the flavors to blend a day or so. Also, the chicken can be covered and refrigerated in the soy sauce mixture for up to 24 hours. The satays also make a great appetizer, and they're fun to pass around as a tasty cocktail snack.

| 2 | tablespoons soy sauce |
| 2 | tablespoons fresh lemon juice |

1	teaspoon finely chopped fresh ginger
1	teaspoon honey
16	ounces chicken tenders
	Orange slices and sprigs of fresh cilantro for garnish
½	cup Spicy Peanut Sauce (page 265)
	Special equipment: 8 (6-inch) bamboo skewers

● Stir together the soy sauce, lemon juice, ginger, and honey in a medium bowl. Add the chicken and stir to coat evenly. (If you plan to marinate the chicken for longer than a few minutes, use a covered glass, ceramic, stainless steel, or plastic container. Cover and refrigerate the chicken, and stir occasionally. Chilled chicken will take a minute or so longer under the broiler to thoroughly cook.)

● When ready to cook, position the oven rack about 5 inches from the heating element and preheat the broiler.

● Lightly coat a baking sheet or broiler pan with cooking oil spray. Thread the chicken onto the bamboo skewers and place on the prepared pan. Discard the remaining marinade. Broil, turning once, for 8 minutes or until the chicken is lightly charred and cooked through but still moist inside. (Test the center pieces for doneness, since they take the longest to cook.)

● Serve the warm skewered chicken on plates garnished with orange slices and cilantro sprigs with a bowl of the peanut sauce on the side for dipping.

Tomato-Soy
Chicken Kabobs

TOMATO-SOY CHICKEN KABOBS

Makes **4** servings

Here's a summertime entrée just begging for the grill—but you can recreate this warm-weather classic indoors when the snow is flying, too. With chicken and vegetables broiled together, these kabobs make a colorful meal, needing only the addition of rice, a green salad, and hearty bread. Follow the ingredient list or thread other vegetables onto the skewers, such as mushrooms, cherry tomatoes, and red onion wedges. For even cooking, the chunks of chicken should be uniform in size.

For the basting sauce:

¼	cup soy sauce
1	tablespoon honey
1	tablespoon tomato paste
1	teaspoon minced garlic
¼	teaspoon pepper, or to taste

For the chicken and vegetables:

12	ounces boneless, skinless chicken breasts, cut into 28 or 32 (1-inch) pieces
8	(1-inch) cubes fresh pineapple
1	red or orange bell pepper, cut into 1-inch chunks
1	small zucchini, cut into ¼-inch slices
	Special equipment: 4 (12-inch) skewers

◗ Whisk together the basting sauce ingredients in a medium bowl.

◗ Position the oven rack about 5 inches from the heating element and preheat the broiler.

◗ Lightly coat a baking sheet or broiler pan with nonstick cooking spray. Thread 7 or 8 pieces of chicken onto each skewer, alternating with the pineapple, bell pepper, and zucchini. Place the skewers on the prepared pan and baste with the sauce. Set aside the remaining sauce.

◗ Broil for 4 minutes; turn and baste with the marinade. Broil for 4 more minutes or until the chicken is thoroughly cooked. (Test the center pieces for doneness, since they take the longest to cook.) Discard any remaining marinade.

— TIP —

To prevent them from burning and darkening under the broiler, soak bamboo or wooden skewers in water for 30 minutes. Drain the skewers just before threading the food onto them, and cook immediately while they remain moist.

HOISIN-GLAZED CHICKEN WITH BELL PEPPER–CABBAGE SLAW

Makes **4** servings

Here hoisin sauce does double duty, adding lots of flavor while serving as a basting sauce for the chicken and also as a dressing for the slaw.

4	boneless, skinless chicken breasts
⅓	cup hoisin sauce
1	tablespoon soy sauce
1	tablespoon white rice vinegar
1	teaspoon Asian fish sauce
3	cups finely shredded green cabbage
1	red bell pepper, cut into thin strips
2	green onions, cut into matchstick strips
½	cup coarsely chopped fresh cilantro

● Position the oven rack about 5 inches from the heating element and preheat the broiler.

● Place the chicken breasts between sheets of plastic wrap and flatten to an even ½-inch thickness. Place on a lightly oiled broiler pan.

● Stir together the hoisin sauce, soy sauce, vinegar, and fish sauce in a small bowl.

● Transfer 2 tablespoons of the hoisin sauce mixture to a separate small bowl. Use a basting brush to spread the sauce on the tops of the chicken breasts.

● Combine the remaining ingredients in a medium bowl. Add the remaining hoisin sauce mixture and stir to combine.

● Broil the chicken for 3 minutes. Turn, brush the tops with the remaining hoisin sauce mixture, and broil for 3 more minutes or until thoroughly cooked.

● Serve the chicken topped with mounds of the slaw.

CHICKEN AND CHEESE ENCHILADAS

Makes **4** servings

No need to spend an hour making enchiladas. Rotisserie chicken, your favorite bottled salsa, and a Mexican cheese blend turn this once-laborious favorite into a speedy casserole.

For the sauce:

1	tablespoon olive oil
1	cup coarsely chopped onion
½	red bell pepper, coarsely chopped
1	cup tomato salsa

For the enchiladas:

2	cups shredded rotisserie chicken, skin removed
1	cup shredded Mexican cheese blend, divided
¼	cup finely chopped fresh cilantro
½	teaspoon ground cumin
8	(6-inch) corn tortillas
	Sour cream for garnish

○ Position the oven rack about 5 inches from the heating element and preheat the broiler.

○ Heat the oil a medium skillet over medium-high heat. Add the onion and bell pepper; cook, stirring occasionally, for 4 minutes or until tender. Stir in the salsa.

○ While the sauce is cooking, combine the chicken, ¾ cup cheese, cilantro, and cumin in a medium bowl.

○ Place the tortillas on a plate and cover with a moist paper towel. Microwave on HIGH for 1 minute or until softened and warm. Spoon ¼ cup of the chicken mixture down the center of each tortilla and roll.

○ Place the tortillas in a row, seam-side down, in a 9-inch square baking dish. Pour the sauce in a strip over the tortillas and sprinkle with the remaining ¼ cup cheese.

○ Broil for 3 minutes or until the cheese melts.

○ Garnish the servings with sour cream.

HONEY-MUSTARD CHICKEN WITH PAPAYA-PINEAPPLE SALSA

Makes **4** servings

This tangy chicken with its fruity salsa accompaniment is a natural for summer dinners on the patio. So if you have an outdoor grill, consider grilling rather than broiling the chicken.

⅓	cup Dijon mustard
3	tablespoons honey
2	tablespoons ketchup
½	teaspoon minced garlic
½	teaspoon Tabasco sauce
16	ounces boneless, skinless chicken breasts
1½	cups Papaya-Pineapple Salsa (page 275)

○ Position the oven rack about 5 inches from the heating element and preheat the broiler.

○ Stir together the mustard, honey, ketchup, garlic, and Tabasco sauce in a medium bowl.

○ Place the chicken breasts between two sheets of plastic wrap and press to an even ¾-inch thickness. Place on a lightly oiled broiler pan.

○ Use a basting brush to spread the mustard mixture on the tops of the chicken breasts. Broil for 3 minutes. Turn, brush the tops with the mustard mixture, and broil for 3 more minutes or until thoroughly cooked.

○ Serve the chicken with the salsa on the side.

Seafood

ISPEND A portion of each year teaching and lecturing on cruise ships that take me to some of the world's most splendid ports, as well as some small seaside cities. Whenever possible, I love to visit the local fish market, especially early in the morning as the fishermen are unloading their catch. It's always a lively and colorful scene. And I also stop to eat in the nearby seafood restaurants, which inspire my recipes.

In these markets, I've learned that to retain freshness, seafood is often put on ice in the fishing boats immediately after being caught. It's either sold right away in the market or quickly frozen. If the frozen fish are promptly shipped, the loss of quality and flavor is minimal. In fact, it's less than if the fish were shipped fresh. Knowing this has broadened my options for using the world's best seafood in addition to locally fished walleye. If you live in a seaside area, by all means purchase freshly caught fish, but don't shy away from those that have been frozen if you live in landlocked areas like I do. I'm not talking about breaded and flavored fish that you find in the freezer section of the supermarket, which may have been frozen for months, but rather fish displayed on ice in a fish market or the fish department of your local supermarket.

I prefer using seafood soon after purchasing it rather than storing it in the freezer. If it is still frozen when you bring it home, thaw it placed on a dish in its packaging in your refrigerator rather than on the kitchen counter and use within a day.

The key is finding a reputable fishmonger. It's best to buy fish from a busy market where the high standards and quick turnover ensure freshness. Make sure that fillets have a bright look with uniform color and no gaps in the flesh. All seafood should have a clean scent.

For some recipes, I ask the fish man to remove the fish's skin for me, which he can quickly do with skill. To do it yourself, use your sharpest knife; you'll make the task easier if the fish is partially frozen.

Also, a wise fishmonger can help you make the best choices. The recipes in this chapter are flexible, so it's a good idea to buy whatever fish looks best at the market regardless of what is listed in the recipe ingredient list. Keep in mind the type you need, such as firm (tuna), fine textured (sole), or rich fleshed (salmon).

Fillets are the most convenient cut of fish for quick cooking. It's still a good idea to rub your fingers along the fillet before you begin to remove any of the annoying tiny bones that may remain. Fish steaks, like tuna, have no bones. Briefly place the fish under cool running water for a quick rinse. Be sure not to use warm or hot water, which would begin to cook the tender seafood.

Shellfish that must be cleaned before cooking take too long for 15-Minute recipes, but I do use canned crabmeat and clams in this book. They're precooked, so it's important to heat them only briefly so they don't end up with a rubbery texture.

Other shellfish, including scallops and shrimp, can be purchased uncooked but ready to use. For ease and speed, I select shrimp that are both peeled and deveined. For some presentations, I prefer that the tails are not removed. I've noted the size shrimp recommended for each recipe.

Sea scallops, which are larger than bay scallops, sometimes come with a small strip attached to one side of the muscle. For the most tender results, I usually remove these before cooking.

As in most chapters of this book, sautéing, pan frying, and steaming on the stovetop are the cooking methods used most frequently. Some fish are also cooked under the broiler. I don't use the microwave for the recipes in this chapter because it's difficult to control and avoid overcooking.

Seafood is always a good choice when you're in a hurry to get dinner on the table because it cooks so quickly. In fact, many people overcook it, which can result in a mushy rather than flaky texture for fish and in a rubbery rather than tender texture for shrimp and scallops.

The rule of thumb is to cook fish for 7 to 8 minutes per inch of thickness. I use a very thin-bladed knife and make a small cut near the center to pry apart the fish and judge the degree of doneness; all traces of translucence should be gone. Another test for doneness is that the fish springs back when lightly pressed with a finger.

Flaky fish can be tested with a fork. The exceptions are meaty fish like salmon and tuna. They need not be thoroughly cooked; here, personal preference prevails.

Shrimp are done just as soon as they turn pink, which takes only a few minutes. I call for cooked shrimp in several salads (in particular, tiny cooked salad shrimp), but I don't recommend them for hot dishes because, in the reheating process, they are likely to become rubbery.

Scallops are done as soon as they become opaque all the way through. Often I like them to have a browned exterior, achieved by searing the scallops on the outside while allowing the insides to remain moist and tender. It's important that scallops be dry for proper browning, so be sure to rinse them in cool water and then lightly pat them dry before cooking.

The recipes in this chapter require minimal effort for great, gourmet results, and many cuisines of the world are represented. You'll enjoy everything from a Brazilian seafood stew (Vatapa, page 114) to French Tuna Salade Niçoise (page 93) and Italian Linguine with Red Clam Sauce (page 124)—along with dishes from Greece to Spain, Vietnam and Thailand to India, and more, including some of my colorful, tropical favorites.

Crabmeat Martini Salad
with Gingered Plum Dressing

Salads

CRABMEAT MARTINI SALAD WITH GINGERED PLUM DRESSING

Makes **4** servings

This elegant salad deserves an equally elegant presentation. Make it in advance and refrigerate for several hours before serving. Then bring out your best martini glasses (large enough to accommodate greens and a heaping ¾ cup salad)—chill them in the refrigerator, too, before filling. Add artisan olive bread and a cheese plate. And presto! A light lunch served with style for your most discerning guests.

1	tablespoon canola oil
1	small zucchini, cut into ⅜-inch cubes
½	yellow bell pepper, finely chopped
½	green bell pepper, finely chopped
1½	teaspoons minced garlic
⅔	cup Gingered Plum Dressing (page 270)
1	(6-ounce) can lump crab, drained and broken into chunks
1	tomato, cut into ⅜-inch dice
2	green onions, finely chopped
	Salt to taste
2	cups finely shredded romaine lettuce
	Lime wedges for garnish

◗ Heat the oil in a large skillet over medium-high heat. Add the zucchini, bell peppers, and garlic. Cook, stirring constantly, for 2 minutes or until the vegetables are crisp tender. Transfer the vegetables to a large shallow bowl and stir occasionally as they cool.

◗ Pour the dressing into a medium bowl. Gently stir in the crab, tomato, green onions, and the cooled vegetables. Season with salt. If time permits, transfer the mixture to a refrigerator container; cover and refrigerate for at least 2 hours or up to 8 hours before serving.

◗ To assemble the serving, put lettuce in the bottom of martini glasses and top with the crab mixture. Garnish with lime wedges.

TUNA AND CANNELLINI BEAN SALAD

Makes **4** servings

The Italians call this *tonno e fagioli*, and my friend Judy Witts Francini, who lives in Florence, creates it by cooking her beans from scratch for two to three hours with olive oil, garlic, and sage. For those of us in a hurry, canned cannellini beans will do just fine. But for this dish, I always use Italian tuna packed in olive oil.

3	tablespoons fresh lemon juice
2	tablespoons extra-virgin olive oil
¼	cup finely chopped fresh flat-leaf parsley
1	(15-ounce) can cannellini beans, drained and rinsed
1	cup thinly sliced red onion
1	(6-ounce) can Italian solid light tuna in olive oil, drained
	Salt and pepper to taste

◗ Whisk together the lemon juice and olive oil in a medium bowl. Stir in the parsley.

◗ Add the beans, onion, and tuna; stir until evenly combined. Season with salt and pepper.

RASPBERRY-SHRIMP SALAD

Makes **4** servings

This refreshing salad is perfect when you're expecting guests for lunch on a sweltering summer day. No need to turn on the stove—and no one needs to know you created the meal in mere minutes. Proudly present this colorful dish on pretty plates, accompanied by crusty rolls served with honey butter.

For the raspberry-walnut vinaigrette:

¼	cup raspberry vinegar
¼	cup walnut oil
1	tablespoon fresh lemon juice
1	teaspoon Dijon mustard
1	tablespoon finely chopped fresh flat-leaf parsley
1	teaspoon packed brown sugar
¼	teaspoon salt, or to taste
¼	teaspoon pepper, or to taste

For the salad:

16	asparagus spears, diagonally cut into 2-inch lengths
8	cups coarsely chopped romaine lettuce
8	ounces cooked, peeled, and deveined large (16 to 20 count) shrimp, halved vertically
4	green onions, coarsely chopped
2	cups raspberries
	Freshly ground pepper for garnish

○ Whisk together all the vinaigrette ingredients in a small bowl.

○ Put the asparagus in a medium microwave-proof dish; add ¼ cup water. Cover and microwave on HIGH for 3 minutes or until crisp-tender. (Or cook the asparagus over simmering water in a stovetop steamer.) Drain and rinse with cold water.

○ Toss together the asparagus, lettuce, shrimp, and green onions in a large bowl. Add the vinaigrette; toss again. Add the raspberries and gently toss until evenly combined.

○ Sprinkle the salads with pepper.

WARM SCALLOP AND AVOCADO SALAD

Makes **4** servings

This colorful salad takes its flavors from the popular Latin American appetizer called ceviche, a dish made with fish "cooked" in a marinade of lime juice, onions, tomatoes, and peppers, which quickly renders the flesh opaque. Here, the scallops are cooked conventionally. Accompany this main dish salad with rustic bread.

2	tablespoons olive oil
¼	cup finely chopped red onion
2	tablespoons finely chopped jalapeño chili
½	teaspoon minced garlic
12	ounces sea scallops
1	plum tomato, cut into ½-inch cubes
½	orange bell pepper, cut into ½-inch chunks
1	avocado, cut into ½-inch cubes
¼	cup coarsely chopped fresh cilantro
2	tablespoons fresh lime juice
¼	teaspoon salt, or to taste
1	head Boston lettuce, leaves separated

○ Heat the oil in a large skillet over medium heat. Add the onion, chili, and garlic; cook, stirring constantly, for 2 minutes. Add the scallops and continue stirring gently for 2 minutes per side or until just cooked.

▶ Remove from the heat and gently stir in the remaining ingredients, except the lettuce.

▶ Arrange the lettuce leaves on plates and top with the warm salad.

TIP

Haricots verts is French for "green string beans." It refers to the very slender green beans that are found in most supermarket produce departments.

TUNA SALADE NIÇOISE

Makes **4** servings

Whenever I'm in Nice, France, I choose this salad for lunch daily—I just can't get enough of it. There, it is served everywhere, from bistros to sidewalk cafés to elegant restaurants. My very favorite location is a café next to Cours Saleya, the famous outdoor market, where most of the salad ingredients are purchased fresh each morning. The salad is made with France's special tuna canned in olive oil, which offers great flavor. It's now available in many markets at home, but you can use the water-packed variety if you prefer.

The variations of the salad are infinite. Here is the version I usually prepare, but there's no need to follow the amounts exactly. Sometimes I add garbanzo beans and cucumber or other salad ingredients I have on hand. You really can't go wrong with this exceptional blend of flavors. Of course, accompany the salad with a crusty French baguette.

4	small red-skinned potatoes, halved
8	ounces haricot verts (thin French green beans), ends trimmed
8	cups mesclun (mixed baby greens)
2	(6-ounce) cans solid white tuna packed in olive oil or water, drained and broken into large chunks
4	plum tomatoes, cut into ¼-inch slices
½	yellow bell pepper, cut into ¼-inch strips
2	hard-cooked eggs, each cut into 8 wedges
½	cup Niçoise olives
1	(2-ounce) can flat anchovies, drained, optional
1½	cups Basic Vinaigrette (page 268)
	Freshly ground pepper for garnish

▶ Put the potatoes in a small saucepan and cover with water. Cover the pan and bring to a boil over high heat. Reduce the heat to medium and cook for 8 minutes or until tender. Drain well and rinse with cold water. Cut into ¼-inch slices.

▶ While the potatoes are cooking, put the haricots verts in a microwave-proof dish; add ¼ cup water. Cover and microwave on HIGH for 4 minutes or until crisp-tender. (Or cook the green beans over simmering water in a stovetop steamer.) Drain and rinse with cold water.

▶ To assemble the salads, spread the mesclun on dinner plates. Top the greens with an artful arrangement of the remaining ingredients, except the vinaigrette. Drizzle each salad with about ¼ cup vinaigrette and garnish with pepper.

▶ Serve extra vinaigrette in a container on the side.

SHRIMP AND RED GRAPEFRUIT SALAD

Makes **4** servings

For this refreshing salad, rather than peeling the grapefruit by hand, it's best to slice away the peel on a cutting board with a sharp serrated knife. This method removes the bitter white pith and offers a more elegant look. I pick a large grapefruit (red because I love the color it adds to the salad) and use half for the vinaigrette and the other half for cutting into wedges. For speed, I purchase already-cooked shrimp that are chilled and ready to go.

For the red grapefruit vinaigrette:

¼	cup fresh grapefruit juice
3	tablespoons extra-virgin olive oil
1	tablespoon honey mustard
1	teaspoon minced garlic
	Salt and pepper to taste

For the salad:

½	cup (4 ounces) chèvre cheese
1	tablespoon honey
6	cups mesclun (mixed baby greens)
12	cooked, peeled, and deveined medium (26 to 30 count) shrimp
1	red grapefruit, peeled and cut into 12 wedges, each wedge halved horizontally
½	cup very thinly sliced fresh fennel
	Shelled salted pistachios for garnish

◉ Whisk together the vinaigrette ingredients in a small bowl.

◉ Stir the chèvre and honey together in another small bowl.

◉ To assemble the salads, toss the mesclun with the shrimp, grapefruit chunks, and fennel in a large bowl. Add the vinaigrette and toss again.

◉ Transfer the salad to 4 plates, dividing the shrimp evenly among servings. For each serving, form 2 tablespoons of the chèvre mixture into 3 balls. Arrange the chèvre on the salads and sprinkle with pistachios.

— TIP —

Hazelnut oil, most often imported from France, is fragrant and full flavored, tasting like the roasted nut. To prevent rancidity, store hazelnut oil in the refrigerator, where it will keep for up to three months.

TUNA AND GREEN BEAN SALAD WITH HAZELNUT VINAIGRETTE

Makes **4** servings

Hazelnut oil lends its distinctive aroma to this main dish salad. Serve the mixture atop arugula leaves to add the bonus of their peppery mustard flavor.

For the salad:

8	ounces green beans, trimmed and cut into 2-inch lengths (about 3 cups)

For the vinaigrette:

¼	cup hazelnut oil
3	tablespoons red wine vinegar
2	tablespoons extra-virgin olive oil

1   teaspoon Dijon mustard

Salt and pepper to taste

To complete the recipe:

½   red bell pepper, finely chopped

¼   cup finely chopped red onion

1   (6-ounce) can solid white albacore tuna packed in water, drained and broken into chunks

Sliced black olives for garnish

○ Put the beans into a medium microwave-proof dish; add ¼ cup water. Cover and microwave on HIGH for 5 minutes or until crisp-tender. (Or cook the beans over simmering water in a stovetop steamer.) Drain and rinse with cold water.

○ While the beans are cooking, whisk together the vinaigrette ingredients in a medium bowl. Stir in the green beans, bell pepper, and onion. Add the tuna and toss.

○ Garnish with olives.

SEARED TUNA SALAD WITH GINGERED PLUM VINAIGRETTE

Makes **4** servings

Sushi-grade fresh tuna, available in many supermarkets and fish shops, is a must for this recipe. Serve this mouthwatering dish to sushi lovers and those who like their tuna only lightly seared. Use jarred mango, a time-saver because it requires only quick slicing.

For the vinaigrette:

2   teaspoons orange zest

½   cup fresh orange juice

2   tablespoons white rice vinegar

2   tablespoons Chinese plum sauce

1   tablespoon canola oil

1   teaspoon finely chopped garlic

1   teaspoon finely chopped fresh ginger

1   teaspoon Dijon mustard

¼   teaspoon salt, or to taste

⅛   teaspoon pepper, or to taste

Pinch of red pepper flakes

For the salad:

8   cups mesclun (mixed baby greens)

1   cup mango in ½ x ½ x 2½-inch strips

½   cup thinly sliced red onion

16   ounces sushi-grade tuna

Salt and pepper to taste

2   tablespoons canola oil

Pickled ginger for garnish

○ Whisk together all the vinaigrette ingredients in a small bowl.

○ To make the salad, toss together the mesclun, mango, and onion in a large bowl. Add about half of the vinaigrette and toss. Divide evenly among 4 plates.

○ Lightly sprinkle the tuna with salt and pepper. Heat the oil in a large skillet over high heat. When water droplets sizzle in the pan, add the tuna. Quickly sear for 1 minute per side or until the outsides are well browned and the insides remain rare, or cook to desired doneness. Transfer the tuna to a cutting board and thinly slice.

○ Arrange the tuna on top of the salads and drizzle with the remaining vinaigrette. Garnish with small mounds of pickled ginger.

FIVE-SPICE SHRIMP WITH PLUM SAUCE

Makes **4** servings

The complex flavor of Chinese five-spice powder and the sweet-sour taste of plum sauce combine beautifully in this salad, which has long been one of my favorites. Rather than serving the vegetable-shrimp mixture in endive leaves, stir in the plum sauce and serve the mixture over Chinese wheat-flour noodles for a change of pace.

½	cup Chinese plum sauce
¼	cup water, or as needed
1	tablespoon canola oil
4	ribs bok choy, cut into ¼-inch cubes; green tops finely shredded
½	red bell pepper, finely chopped
½	orange bell pepper, finely chopped
3	green onions, finely chopped
8	ounces small (41 to 50 count) shrimp, peeled, deveined, and cut into ¼-inch slices
1	teaspoon minced garlic
1	teaspoon Chinese five-spice powder
	Salt and ground white pepper to taste
12	Belgian endive leaves
	Toasted pine nuts for garnish

◐ Spoon the plum sauce into a small bowl. Stir in water, as needed, to reach a maple-syrup consistency.

◐ Heat the oil in a large skillet over medium-high heat. Add the bok choy and greens, bell peppers, and green onions; cook, stirring occasionally, for 4 minutes or until crisp-tender. Add the shrimp, garlic, and five-spice powder; cook, stirring constantly, for 1 minute or until the shrimp turn pink. Season with salt and white pepper. Serve warm, at room temperature, or refrigerate to cool.

◐ To serve, spoon the vegetable-shrimp mixture into the endive leaves. Drizzle with plum sauce and sprinkle with pine nuts.

TIP

Chinese five-spice powder, sometimes called five-fragrance powder, is a sweet and pungent mixture of five ground spices including fennel, star anise, Szechuan peppercorns, cinnamon, and cloves. A licorice flavor predominates, thanks to the fennel seeds. Some brands also contain ginger and licorice root. The seasoning is available in the ethnic section of most supermarkets and in Asian markets.

Five-Spice Shrimp
with Plum Sauce

SPICY CELLOPHANE NOODLES WITH SCALLOPS

Makes **4** servings

My friend Nathan Fong, an award-winning Canadian food stylist, shared several of his favorite chilled noodle recipes with me. I've adapted this delicious salad for the 15-Minute cook.

For the noodles:

1	(4-ounce) package thin cellophane noodles

For the spicy soy dressing:

2	tablespoons soy sauce
2	tablespoons white rice vinegar
1	tablespoon dark (Asian) sesame oil
1	tablespoon canola oil
1	tablespoon chili paste with garlic, or to taste
1	tablespoon sugar
1	tablespoon minced fresh ginger
1	teaspoon Asian fish sauce, or to taste
	Salt and ground white pepper to taste

To complete the recipe:

16	ounces sea scallops
	Canola oil for brushing
½	red bell pepper, finely chopped
½	cup roasted and salted peanuts, coarsely chopped
1	green onion, finely chopped
¼	cup coarsely chopped fresh cilantro
	Sprigs of fresh cilantro for garnish

▶ Position the oven rack about 5 inches from the heating element and preheat the broiler.

▶ Cook the noodles according to package instructions.

▶ Meanwhile, whisk together the dressing ingredients in a small bowl.

▶ Rinse the scallops with cool water and pat dry. Place them on a broiler pan and lightly brush both sides with oil. Broil for 3 minutes, turning once, until thoroughly cooked. Transfer to a plate and let cool.

▶ Drain the noodles, rinse in cold water, and then drain again. Transfer to a large bowl. Use kitchen shears to randomly cut the noodles into shorter lengths for easier eating. Reserve 2 tablespoons of the dressing. Add the remaining dressing to the noodles and toss. Add the bell pepper, peanuts, green onion, and cilantro; toss again.

▶ To serve, arrange the scallops over the noodles. Drizzle the reserved dressing over the scallops and garnish with cilantro sprigs.

TIP

Asian fish sauce is a salty seasoning that flavors almost every savory dish in Thailand, Laos, Cambodia, and Vietnam. It's made essentially from anchovies and salt, but each country has a slightly different version. There is no substitute. Asian markets sell fish sauce by the quart, but supermarkets usually stock small bottles, which I prefer. Because the sauce is pungent and strong flavored, and the saltiness varies depending on the manufacturer, use it in moderation and then add more to taste. After using, tightly close the container and refrigerate.

SHRIMP LETTUCE WRAPS

Makes **4** servings

These wraps make a nice appetizer or first course
served solo, and they are a great accompaniment to
a soup, such as Gingered Carrot Soup (page 230).
They're also a good candidate for a light and tasty lunch
accompanied with a basket of pita chips.

1	teaspoon cold water
1	teaspoon cornstarch
12	ounces medium (26 to 30 count) shrimp, peeled, deveined, and cut into ¼-inch pieces (1¾ cups)
2	tablespoons Chinese hot oil
2	tablespoons canola oil
¼	cup finely chopped onion
½	cup frozen baby peas
4	green onions, finely chopped
1	tablespoon soy sauce
1	tablespoon water
1	teaspoon dark (Asian) sesame oil
1	teaspoon finely chopped fresh ginger
8	whole iceberg lettuce leaves

◗ Stir together the cold water and cornstarch in a
medium bowl until smooth. Add the shrimp and stir
until the mixture is evenly combined.

◗ Heat the Chinese hot oil in a large skillet over
medium-high heat. Add the shrimp; cook, stirring
constantly, for 1 minute or until they begin to turn pink.
Transfer to a medium bowl and cover to keep warm.

◗ Heat the canola oil in the skillet over medium-
high heat. Add the onion; cook, stirring occasionally,
for 2 minutes or until tender. Stir in the shrimp and

the remaining ingredients, except the lettuce. Stir for
30 seconds or until the shrimp turn pink and the peas
are warm. Remove from the heat.

◗ Spoon a scant ¼ cup of the shrimp mixture into
each lettuce leaf and roll.

CORN AND RICE SALAD WITH BABY SHRIMP

Makes **4** servings

The nicest thing about this substantial salad (next to
its appealing flavor, of course) is that it can be made
ahead—no last-minute kitchen time required.

1½	cups cooked brown basmati rice, at room temperature or chilled
1	cup yellow or white frozen corn kernels, thawed
2	plum tomatoes, cut into ½-inch cubes
½	cup cooked salad shrimp
¼	cup coarsely chopped fresh basil
½	cup Balsamic Vinaigrette (page 268)

◗ Stir together all the ingredients, except the
vinaigrette, in a medium bowl. Add the vinaigrette and
stir until evenly combined.

— TIP —

Shoepeg white corn is available frozen; it
has smaller kernels and is sweeter than
yellow corn.

POACHED SALMON AND GREEN BEAN SALAD WITH LEMON-CAPER SAUCE

Makes **4** servings

I prize this as the ultimate do-ahead dish when simple elegance is the order of the day. Prepare the ingredients early in the day and chill, and then assemble the salads just before your guests arrive. Most important is not to overcook the salmon or beans. Accompany the pretty salad with crusty rolls with Basil Pesto Butter (page 274) and chilled Sauvignon Blanc. (Asparagus can be substituted for the green beans. Also steam some fingerling potatoes if you'd like.)

For the salmon:

2	cups dry white wine
2	cups water
2	tablespoons sherry vinegar
1	teaspoon salt
½	teaspoon pepper
4	(6-ounce) salmon fillets

To complete the recipe:

12	ounces green beans, ends trimmed
8	cups mesclun (mixed baby greens)
2	tomatoes, thinly sliced
¾	cup Lemon-Caper Sauce (page 265)
	Freshly ground pepper for garnish

● Combine the wine, water, vinegar, salt, and pepper in a medium sauté pan. Cover and bring to a boil over high heat; reduce the heat to low and simmer for 5 minutes. Add the salmon, skin side up, and cook for 5 minutes or until the desired doneness.

● Meanwhile, put the green beans in a medium microwave-proof dish; add ¼ cup water. Cover and microwave on HIGH for 7 minutes or until tender. (Or cook the asparagus over simmering water in a stovetop steamer.) Drain and rinse with cold water.

● When the salmon is done, transfer to a plate, skin side up. Use tongs to remove the skin. (Discard the poaching liquid.)

● Spread the greens on salad plates. Artfully arrange the salmon (fillet side up), green beans, and tomatoes.

● Drizzle the sauce in a line across the ingredients and garnish with pepper.

CAESAR-STUFFED TOMATOES

Makes **4** servings

Caesar salad gets a colorful new lease on life when it steps in as a luscious topping for fresh tomatoes.

½	cup Lemon Caesar Dressing (page 269)
6	cups coarsely shredded romaine lettuce
4	large (3-inch) round tomatoes
1	cup Garlic Croutons (page 280)

● Add the dressing to the lettuce in a large bowl and toss until evenly combined.

● Slice each tomato into 8 wedges, cutting to, but not through, the bottom to keep the wedges attached. Drain and pat the tomatoes dry if they are very juicy.

○ Place the tomatoes on salad plates and spread the wedges apart. Mound each tomato with 1 cup of the lettuce mixture and top with croutons.

CRESTE DI GALLO WITH SMOKED SALMON IN GREEN PEPPERCORN SAUCE

Makes **4** servings

Its unique and ornate shape makes creste di gallo, or cock's crest, one of my favorite pastas for salads. Because it is not always available in supermarkets, I always buy a bag or two when I find it at an Italian market. But other more commonly available short-cut pastas can be substituted, such as penne rigate or farfalle (bow ties).

The pleasant pungency of green peppercorns complements any kind of fish, from canned albacore tuna to smoked salmon. Serve this dish at room temperature, along with crusty breadsticks.

For the pasta:

8   ounces creste di gallo

For the sauce:

¼   cup red wine vinegar

2   tablespoons hazelnut oil

1   tablespoon extra-virgin olive oil

1   tablespoon fresh lemon juice

1   tablespoon minced shallot

1   teaspoon green peppercorns in brine, drained and rinsed

1   teaspoon Dijon mustard

    Salt and pepper to taste

To complete the dish:

6   ounces smoked salmon, cut into ½-inch squares (remove and discard skin, then cut fish)

4   green onions, diagonally cut into thin slices

½   cup sliced Niçoise olives

    Finely chopped fresh flat-leaf parsley for garnish

○ Cook the pasta according to package instructions.

○ Meanwhile, process all the sauce ingredients in a blender until smooth.

○ When the pasta is done, drain and rinse well in cold water, and then drain again.

○ Transfer the pasta to a large bowl. Add the salmon, green onions, and olives; toss gently. Add the sauce and toss again.

○ Garnish the servings with parsley.

TIP

Green peppercorns are unripe pepper berries that, instead of being dried, are preserved in brine. Rinse them and then crush or purée before using. They share the basic taste of dried pepper and also have their own sharp, almost acidic flavor.

Makes **4** servings

Cellophane noodles hungrily soak up flavors, making them perfect partners in this enticing marriage of spicy and nutty tastes. If you prefer, use bottled peanut sauce rather than preparing the peanut-ginger dressing. When time permits, I like to refrigerate the completed dish for several hours before mealtime. As I've experienced, Thailand is in one of the hottest parts of the world, and this light dish is perfect for a muggy day.

For the noodles:

4	ounces thin cellophane noodles

For the peanut-ginger dressing:

½	cup lightly salted, dry-roasted peanuts
1	piece fresh ginger, 2 inches long by 1 inch thick, peeled and cut into ½-inch chunks (or 2 tablespoons minced fresh ginger)
1	teaspoon minced red chili (seeds removed) or ½ teaspoon red pepper flakes, or to taste
¼	cup fresh lime juice
2	tablespoons soy sauce
2	tablespoons sugar

To complete the recipe:

1	cup cooked salad shrimp
½	red bell pepper, finely chopped
2	tablespoons finely chopped fresh cilantro, Thai basil, or sweet basil

---

TIPS

Fresh mature ginger should be firm with a smooth brown skin and no soft spots. To test for freshness, break off one of the knobs. If the ginger is fresh, it will break with a clean snap. Store at room temperature and use within a few days. Or to preserve ginger, wrap it tightly in aluminum foil or seal it in a small zip-top plastic bag and then freeze. When you need ginger, there's no need to thaw. Simply use a fine grater to grate off the amount needed. Rewrap and replace immediately in the freezer. Frozen ginger will keep for up to three months.

Jars of minced ginger are available in most produce departments; check the labels since some products also contain garlic and sweeteners.

Ground dried ginger is used primarily in baked goods and should not be substituted for fresh in cooked recipes.

Cellophane noodles, also called bean thread noodles, glass noodles, or sai fun, are made with the starch of mung beans, which we know best as bean sprouts, and water. These noodles are coiled before being packaged, are very brittle, and have a cellophanelike translucence. They will keep indefinitely when stored in an airtight container. After being softened, cellophane noodles become almost transparent. Because they are virtually flavorless and soak up other flavors, they are a natural medium for spicy dishes.

▶ Cook the noodles according to package instructions.

▶ Meanwhile, process all the dressing ingredients in a food processor or electric mincer until the ginger is finely chopped. (The peanuts should remain slightly chunky.)

▶ Drain the noodles and rinse well in cold water, and then drain again. Transfer to a large bowl. Use kitchen shears to randomly cut the noodles into shorter lengths for easier eating. Add the dressing and toss. Add the remaining ingredients; toss again.

GREEK PASTA SALAD

Makes **4** servings

This salad will keep for up to a day before serving. Because the pasta absorbs the dressing, it's best to toss the salad with just half the dressing; refrigerate the remainder separately and add just before serving. This salad makes inviting picnic fare presented in a large serving bowl and accompanied with Crispy Pita Triangles (page 280). For dessert, offer juicy orange slices sprinkled with shelled, salted pistachios. For vegetarians, omit the tuna.

For the pasta:
6   ounces corkscrew pasta (rotini)

For the dressing:
¼   cup extra-virgin olive oil
¼   cup fresh lemon juice
1   tablespoon finely chopped fresh oregano or 1 teaspoon dried oregano

¼   teaspoon pepper, or to taste
⅛   teaspoon salt, or to taste

To complete the recipe:
1   (6-ounce) can solid white tuna packed in olive oil or water, drained and broken into large chunks
1   cup grape tomatoes
½   medium cucumber, quartered lengthwise, seeded, and cut into ¼-inch slices
⅓   cup coarsely chopped red onion
1   (6-ounce) jar marinated quartered artichoke hearts, drained and coarsely chopped
1   (2-ounce) can sliced pitted ripe olives, drained
1   cup coarsely crumbled feta cheese or feta cheese with peppercorns
    Freshly ground pepper for garnish

▶ Cook the pasta according to package instructions.

▶ Meanwhile, whisk together the dressing ingredients in a large bowl. Stir in the tuna, tomatoes, cucumber, onion, artichokes, and olives.

▶ When the pasta is done, drain well. Rinse with cool water; drain again. Add to the salad mixture and toss.

▶ Garnish the servings with feta cheese and pepper.

TONNATO AND TOMATO SALAD

Makes **4** servings

Tonnato comes from the Italian *tonno* (tuna). The best-known preparation is cold thinly sliced roasted veal accompanied by a puréed tuna sauce. Here, the tuna mixture provides a creamy, protein-rich surprise beneath a fresh green salad with juicy ripe tomatoes.

For the tuna spread:

1	(6-ounce) can Italian solid light tuna in olive oil
1	(2-ounce) can flat anchovies, drained
¼	cup fresh lemon juice
2	tablespoons extra-virgin olive oil
2	tablespoons mayonnaise
2	garlic cloves or 1 teaspoon minced garlic
	Salt and pepper to taste

For the salad:

2	tablespoons fresh lemon juice
2	tablespoons extra-virgin olive oil
6	cups mesclun (mixed baby greens)
2	tomatoes, cut into ½-inch cubes
½	cup very thinly sliced red onion
2	tablespoons small (nonpareil) capers, drained and rinsed
	Salt and pepper to taste
	Shaved Parmesan cheese and freshly coarse-ground pepper for garnish

▶ Purée the tuna spread ingredients in a food processor or blender until smooth.

▶ To make the salad, whisk together the lemon juice and olive oil in a small bowl.

▶ Toss together the mesclun, tomatoes, onion, and capers in a large bowl. Add the lemon juice mixture and toss again. Season with salt and pepper.

▶ For each salad, spread the tuna mixture on a salad plate. Top with a mound of the dressed greens and vegetables. Garnish with Parmesan cheese and pepper.

SHRIMP AND MANGO COUSCOUS

Makes **4** servings

Couscous, an ideal pasta for speedy cooking, pairs nicely with baby shrimp and juicy mango—the most commonly consumed fruit in the world. You can enjoy this dish immediately or cover, refrigerate, and serve it later for a cool lunch on a sunny summer day.

1	cup water
1	cup couscous
1	tablespoon olive oil
1½	cups jarred mango in 1-inch chunks
½	red bell pepper, finely chopped
2	tablespoons finely chopped jalapeño chili, or to taste
1	teaspoon minced garlic
5	ounces (1 cup) cooked salad shrimp
	Salt to taste

▶ Heat the water until hot but not boiling in a small saucepan over medium-high heat. Remove the pan from the heat; stir in the couscous. Let stand, covered, for 5 minutes or until the liquid is absorbed.

▶ Meanwhile, heat the oil in a medium skillet over high heat. Add the mango, bell pepper, chili, and garlic. Cook, stirring occasionally, for 4 minutes or until the mango is softened but not mushy.

○ Fluff the couscous with a fork and stir into the sauté pan. Stir in the shrimp. Season with salt.

Soups

SALMON PESTO SOUP

Makes **4** servings (6½ cups)

Here's a perfect recipe using Basil Pesto that you can make in advance. This dish deserves a place of honor in elegant soup bowls atop a candlelit table. To speed up prep time, I usually ask the fishmonger to use his sharp knife and expert skills to remove the salmon skin.

2	tablespoons unsalted butter
1	tablespoon olive oil
2	finely chopped leeks
½	yellow bell pepper, finely chopped
2	(14-ounce) cans reduced-sodium chicken broth
1	(8-ounce) bottle clam juice
½	cup orzo
12	ounces salmon fillet, skin removed, cut into 1-inch squares
3	tablespoons Basil Pesto (page 274)
	Salt and pepper to taste
	Freshly shredded Parmesan cheese for garnish

○ Melt the butter with the oil in a Dutch oven over medium heat. Add the leeks and bell pepper;

cook, stirring occasionally, for 3 minutes or until crisp-tender.

○ Stir in the chicken broth and clam juice. Increase the heat to high. When the liquid comes to a boil, stir in the orzo. Reduce the heat to medium-high; cover and cook for 4 minutes. Add the salmon; continue to cook for 5 more minutes or until the salmon is cooked and the orzo and vegetables are tender.

○ Stir in the pesto. Season with salt and pepper.

○ Garnish each serving with Parmesan cheese.

TIP

Leeks, which look like giant green onions, are available year-round in most areas. Select those with crisp, bright green leaves and unblemished, thin, white portions; leeks smaller than 1½ inches in diameter will be the most tender and delicate tasting. Refrigerate them in a plastic bag for up to five days. Before using, trim the rootlets and leaf ends, slit the leeks from top to bottom, and wash thoroughly to remove the dirt and sand that is often trapped between the leaf layers. You can use both the white base and the tender portions of the green leaves. The leek's flavor is related to both garlic and onion, although the taste and aroma of leeks are milder.

Salmon Ramen

SALMON RAMEN

Makes **4** servings

When buying the salmon for this recipe, I ask the fishmonger to remove the skin from the fillets. As you eat the grilled salmon with its ginger-garlic topping, all the flavors blend. I insist on topping my bowl with a dash of togarashi (a powdered hot red Japanese chili found in Asian markets) to add a lively touch. This substantial and sensational bowl of soup needs no accompaniment.

1	(49-ounce) can reduced-sodium chicken broth
2	tablespoons soy sauce, or to taste, divided
	Dash of ground white pepper, or to taste
4	(3-ounce) salmon fillets, skin removed
4	cups coarsely shredded fresh spinach leaves
3	cups sliced mushrooms
1	cup sugar snap peas
9	ounces ramen noodles (discard flavoring packets) or thin Chinese wheat-flour noodles
1	teaspoon canola oil
2	tablespoons minced fresh ginger
2	teaspoons minced garlic

● Position the oven rack about 5 inches from the heating element and preheat the broiler.

● Pour the chicken broth into a Dutch oven; stir in 1 tablespoon soy sauce and the white pepper. Cover and bring to a boil over high heat.

● Place the salmon fillets on a lightly oiled broiler pan. Broil for 4 minutes or until the desired doneness.

● Meanwhile, when the chicken broth comes to a boil, reduce the heat to medium, and stir in the spinach, mushrooms, and peas; drop in the noodles. Cover and cook for 3 minutes or until the vegetables and noodles are tender. As the noodles cook, stir occasionally with a fork to separate. Remove from the heat.

● While the salmon and soup are cooking, heat the oil in a small nonstick skillet over medium-high heat. Add the ginger and garlic; stir constantly for 1 minute or until the mixture becomes aromatic. Remove from the heat and stir in the remaining 1 tablespoon soy sauce.

● To serve, use tongs to transfer a generous amount of noodles and vegetables to each soup bowl; use a ladle to add the broth. Place a piece of grilled salmon on the soup and top with the ginger-garlic mixture.

GINGER, COCONUT, AND LEMONGRASS SOUP

Makes **4** servings (5 cups)

While hiking through Fiji en route to a waterfall, I meandered down narrow paths lined with lemongrass as far as the eye could see. At home, it's less commonly available, but fresh lemongrass can be found in Asian markets and with the fresh herbs in some supermarkets, ready to contribute its unique lemon-lime flavor to many an Asian-influenced recipe.

1	tablespoon canola oil
½	cup finely chopped onion
1	tablespoon finely chopped fresh ginger
2	(14-ounce) cans reduced-sodium chicken broth
1	russet potato (about 10 ounces), peeled and cut into ½-inch cubes
1	stalk lemongrass, peeled, pounded, and cut into 3-inch lengths
2	tablespoons white miso
1	(14-ounce) can "lite" coconut milk
6	ounces halibut (or other firm white fish), cut into ¾-inch cubes
2	green onions, finely chopped
2	tablespoons soy sauce
	Finely chopped green onions for garnish

▶ Heat the oil in a Dutch oven over medium heat. Add the onion and ginger; cook, stirring occasionally, for 3 minutes or until the onion is tender.

▶ Stir in the chicken broth, potato, and lemongrass. Bring to a boil over high heat. Reduce the heat to medium; cover and cook for 5 minutes or until the potato is very tender. Remove the lemongrass and discard.

▶ Use an immersion blender to purée the mixture until smooth. Whisk the miso into the soup. Stir in the remaining ingredients, except the garnish. Stir occasionally and gently over medium heat for 4 minutes or until the fish is cooked. (Do not allow the soup to boil.)

▶ Garnish the servings with green onions.

MEDITERRANEAN SEAFOOD STEW

Makes **4** servings (6 cups)

All over the Mediterranean, fish soups are made from the day's catch, and each region has its own different and wonderful variation. One of my fondest culinary memories is the entire experience of savoring the saffron-tinged bouillabaisse, along with all the ritual surrounding its expert preparation and presentation, at the famous Restaurant Miramar overlooking the Marseilles harbor and fish market. Traditionally, fish heads are simmered in seasoned water to make fish stock, but for quicker preparation, I substitute canned chicken stock. Also, to speed things up, I always have the fishmonger remove the fish skin for this stew.

2	tablespoons olive oil
1	cup finely chopped onion
1	carrot, finely chopped
2	teaspoons minced garlic
¼	teaspoon saffron threads, crushed, or more to taste
1	tablespoon hot water
2	(14-ounce) cans reduced-sodium chicken broth
1	(14-ounce) can diced tomatoes
3	small red-skinned potatoes, cut into ½-inch cubes
⅛	teaspoon red pepper flakes, or to taste
	Salt and pepper to taste
8	ounces firm white fish (such as sea bass, mackerel, or monk fish), skin removed and discarded, flesh cut into 1-inch squares
8	ounces sea scallops
	Coarsely chopped fresh flat-leaf parsley for garnish

❍ Heat the oil in a Dutch oven over medium-high heat. Add the onion, carrot, and garlic; cook, stirring occasionally, for 4 minutes or until tender.

❍ Meanwhile, mix the saffron with the hot water. Set aside.

❍ Pour the chicken broth and tomatoes into the Dutch oven. When the liquid comes to a boil, stir in the potatoes, red pepper flakes, and the saffron mixture. Reduce the heat to medium; cover and cook for 3 minutes or until the potatoes are nearly tender. Season with salt and pepper.

❍ Stir in the fish; cook for 3 minutes. Stir in the scallops; continue to cook for 2 more minutes or until the potatoes are tender and the fish is thoroughly cooked.

❍ Garnish the servings with parsley.

—— TIP ——

Saffron, the yellow-orange stigma of a small purple crocus, is the world's most expensive spice. Each flower provides only three stigma, which must be handpicked: It takes 14,000 of these to equal 1 ounce of saffron. A little goes a long way, and there is no substitute for its exquisite flavor and earthy aroma. Be sure to purchase whole saffron threads. Powdered saffron loses its flavor more readily and can easily be adulterated with less expensive powders like turmeric. Heat releases the flavor, so pinch the threads between your fingers and then soak them in hot water before using. Store saffron in an airtight container in a cool, dark place for up to six months.

ASIAN SHRIMP AND MUSHROOM NOODLE SOUP

Makes **4** servings (6 cups)

Asian noodle soups have different proportions from Western noodle soups. In these one-dish meals, a plentiful amount of noodles is transferred to the bowls, and then the broth and other ingredients are ladled over them. And speaking of bowls, I recommend deep noodle bowls rather than shallow soup bowls in order to keep the soup warm. Serve with chopsticks for the noodles and shrimp, and porcelain spoons for the broth.

1	(32-ounce) aseptic box reduced-sodium chicken broth (or use two 14-ounce cans plus ¼ cup water)
1	tablespoon Asian fish sauce
1	tablespoon oyster sauce
1	tablespoon soy sauce
6	ounces thin Chinese wheat-flour noodles
8	ounces small (41 to 50 count) shrimp, peeled and deveined
7	ounces shiitake and oyster mushrooms (any combination of quantities), stems removed and discarded, caps cut into ¼-inch slices
1	tablespoon dark (Asian) sesame oil
¼	teaspoon ground white pepper, or to taste
½	teaspoon red pepper flakes, divided

▶ Pour the broth into a Dutch oven. Bring to a boil over high heat; stir in the fish, oyster, and soy sauces. Add the noodles. Use a fork to separate the noodles as they soften, cooking for 2 minutes less than package instructions indicate for doneness.

▶ Reduce the heat to medium. Stir in the shrimp, mushrooms, sesame oil, and pepper. Cook, stirring occasionally, for 1 minute or until the shrimp turn pink.

▶ Remove from the heat to prevent overcooking the shrimp. Serve immediately. Use tongs to divide the noodles, shrimp, and mushrooms among 4 bowls. Then ladle in the broth. Sprinkle each serving with ⅛ teaspoon red pepper flakes.

— TIP —

Oyster mushrooms are fluted mushrooms that vary in color from pale gray to dark brownish gray. Their seafoodlike flavor is robust and slightly peppery but becomes milder when cooked. Look for young mushrooms, 1½ inches or less in diameter. Remove the tough stems before cooking.

HOT AND SOUR SHRIMP AND NOODLE SOUP

Makes **4** servings

Hot chilies are steeped in vegetable oil to release their heat and flavor, and the resulting red chili oil is a staple of Chinese cooking. The oil is spicy hot, so add more only if you dare.

6	ounces thin Chinese wheat-flour noodles
2	(14-ounce) cans reduced-sodium chicken broth
2	tablespoons soy sauce

2	tablespoons distilled white vinegar
½	teaspoon chili oil, or to taste
4	ribs bok choy, cut into ½-inch slices, including greens
8	ounces medium (26 to 30 count) shrimp, peeled and deveined
4	ounces snow peas
2	green onions, finely chopped

⬤ Bring a medium pot of water to a boil over high heat. Cook the noodles according to package instructions.

⬤ Meanwhile, stir together the chicken broth, soy sauce, vinegar, and chili oil in a Dutch oven over high heat. When the liquid comes to a boil, reduce the heat to medium. Add the bok choy; cook for 2 minutes or until crisp-tender.

⬤ Stir in the remaining ingredients; cook for 1 minute or until the shrimp are just thoroughly cooked. Taste and adjust the seasoning.

⬤ When the noodles are done, drain well.

⬤ To serve, divide the noodles among 4 deep soup bowls. Spoon the vegetables and shrimp over the noodles. Top with ladles of hot broth.

ASIAN SCALLOP SOUP WITH BOK CHOY

Makes **4** servings

This flavorful, aromatic soup makes a light Asian meal or a great beginning to a feast. Noisily slurp the noodles if you wish, as Asian custom dictates.

1	tablespoon canola oil
1½	teaspoons minced garlic
8	ounces sea scallops, rinse with cool water, pat dry, and halve horizontally
4	cups reduced-sodium chicken broth
5	ounces thin Chinese wheat-flour noodles
6	ribs bok choy including green tops, diagonally cut into ¼-inch slices
3	green onions, coarsely chopped
2	teaspoons soy sauce, or to taste
1	teaspoon dark (Asian) sesame oil, or to taste
¼	teaspoon red pepper flakes, or to taste
¼	teaspoon ground white pepper, or to taste

⬤ Heat the oil in a Dutch oven over medium-high heat. Add the garlic; stir for 30 seconds. Add the scallops; cook for 2 minutes per side or until lightly browned and thoroughly cooked. Transfer to a plate and cover to keep warm.

⬤ Pour the chicken broth into the pan over medium-high heat. Stir, scraping the bottom of the pan, as the broth comes to a boil. Add the noodles; separate with a fork as they cook for 3 minutes or until tender. Use tongs to transfer the noodles to 4 deep soup bowls.

⬤ Stir the remaining ingredients into the broth; cover and cook for 2 minutes or until the bok choy is crisp-tender.

⬤ Use tongs to transfer the noodles to deep bowls. Ladle the broth and vegetables over the noodles. Top with the scallops.

TUNA CHOWDER

Makes **4** servings (6½ cups)

Serve your family this comfort dish as dinner in a bowl accompanied with their favorite artisan bread. It's a speedy chowder, but make certain that the cooked potatoes are very tender so that the soup will thicken properly when puréed.

1	tablespoon olive oil
1	cup coarsely shredded carrots
½	cup coarsely chopped yellow onion
1	(14-ounce) can reduced-sodium chicken broth
2	russet potatoes (about 10 ounces each), peeled and cut into ½-inch chunks
2	tablespoons finely chopped fresh oregano or 1 teaspoon dried oregano
2	cups milk
2	(6-ounce) cans solid white tuna packed in water, drained and broken into ½-inch chunks
¾	cup frozen baby peas
2	tablespoons finely chopped fresh basil
	Salt and pepper to taste
	Paprika for garnish

◗ Heat the oil in a Dutch oven over medium heat. Add the carrots and onion; cook, stirring occasionally, for 3 minutes or until tender.

◗ Stir in the chicken broth, potatoes, and oregano. Increase the heat to high and bring to a boil. Reduce the heat to low; cover and simmer for 7 minutes or until the potatoes are very tender.

◗ Use an immersion blender to purée the soup until smooth. Stir in the milk, tuna, peas, and basil.

Stir over medium heat until warm. Season with salt and pepper.

◗ Garnish the servings with paprika.

SHRIMP AND ORZO SOUP

Makes **4** servings (6 cups)

This tasty soup can be on the table in less than 15 minutes. You need only some good bread and a platter of fresh veggies to make the meal complete.

2	(14-ounce) cans diced tomatoes with green pepper and onion
2	cups reduced-sodium chicken broth
2	tablespoons tomato paste
2	teaspoons finely chopped fresh rosemary or ½ teaspoon dried rosemary, crushed
¼	cup orzo
8	ounces small (41 to 50 count) shrimp, peeled and deveined
½	cup lightly packed, coarsely shredded salad spinach
¼	teaspoon pepper, or to taste
	Salt to taste

◗ Combine the tomatoes, chicken broth, tomato paste, and rosemary in a Dutch oven. Bring to a boil over high heat. Stir in the orzo. Reduce the heat to medium; cover and cook for 8 minutes or until the orzo is nearly tender.

◗ Stir in the remaining ingredients. Cook, stirring occasionally, for 1 minute or until the orzo is tender and the shrimp turn pink.

◗ Ladle into shallow bowls, dividing the shrimp evenly among servings.

CLAM AND PASTA SOUP

Makes **4** servings (6½ cups)

This satisfying soup was inspired by a memorable meal at a sidewalk café on a tiny street in charming Casco Vello, the old town of Vigo, Spain. Near the port, the clams, of course, were fresh. But canned will do, and you can substitute other small pasta shapes in this soup, such as small shells or orzo.

2	tablespoons olive oil
1	cup finely chopped onion
1	teaspoon minced garlic
2	(14-ounce) cans reduced-sodium chicken broth
1	(14-ounce) can diced tomatoes with basil, parsley, and garlic
½	cup dry red wine
1	tablespoon sun-dried tomato paste
½	cup ready-cut spaghetti
1	(6-ounce) can chopped clams (not drained)
¼	cup finely chopped fresh basil
	Salt and pepper to taste
	Freshly grated Parmesan cheese for garnish

▶ Heat the oil in a Dutch oven over medium-high heat. Add the onion and garlic; cook, stirring occasionally for 4 minutes or until tender.

▶ Stir in the chicken broth, tomatoes, wine, and tomato paste. Increase the heat to high; when the liquid comes to a boil, reduce the heat to medium-high. Add the spaghetti; cover and cook for 6 minutes or until tender.

▶ Reduce the heat to low; stir in the clams (with juice), and the basil. Stir occasionally for 1 minute or until warm. (Do not let the mixture come to a boil, or the clams may become tough.) Season with salt and pepper.

▶ Garnish the servings with Parmesan cheese.

GREEK LEMON SOUP WITH SCALLOPS

Makes **4** servings (6 cups)

Serve this light and lively, lemony soup as a first course for dinner or with warm, crusty bread for lunch. My friend Sue Smieja likes to substitute shrimp for the scallops.

2	tablespoons olive oil
1	cup finely chopped onion
½	red bell pepper, finely chopped
1½	teaspoons minced garlic
3	(14-ounce) cans reduced-sodium chicken broth
1	(15-ounce) can diced tomatoes
6	cups (about 6 ounces) coarsely chopped salad spinach
½	cup orzo
8	ounces bay scallops
¼	cup fresh lemon juice
	Salt and pepper to taste

▶ Heat the oil in a Dutch oven over medium-high heat. Add the onion, bell pepper, and garlic; cook, stirring occasionally, for 4 minutes or until tender.

▶ Add the chicken broth and tomatoes. Increase the heat to high and bring to a boil. Stir in the spinach and orzo. Reduce the heat to low; cover and simmer, stirring occasionally, for 9 minutes or until the spinach is wilted and the orzo is tender. Stir in the scallops for the last 2 minutes of cooking time.

▶ Stir in the lemon juice and season with salt and pepper.

CREAMY FISH CHOWDER

Makes **4** servings (6 cups)

Serve this rich, creamy soup with a chewy sourdough loaf to chase away the chills of winter. For advance preparation, cover and refrigerate the partially made soup after the potatoes are cooked. Just before serving, reheat the soup and complete the recipe.

1	tablespoon unsalted butter
½	cup coarsely shredded carrot
½	cup finely chopped onion
1	cup reduced-sodium chicken broth
1	(8-ounce) bottle clam juice
2½	cups red-skinned potatoes in ½-inch cubes (12 ounces)
1	tablespoon finely chopped fresh thyme or 1 teaspoon dried thyme
12	ounces cod or other firm white fish fillets, cut into 1-inch pieces
1	(6-ounce) can minced or chopped clams (do not drain)
1	cup half-and-half
	Salt and pepper to taste
	Paprika and finely chopped fresh chives for garnish

● Melt the butter in a Dutch oven over medium-high heat. Add the carrot and onion; cook, stirring occasionally, for 2 minutes or until the carrots are crisp-tender.

● Stir in the chicken broth, clam juice, potatoes, and thyme. Increase the heat to high. When the liquid comes to a boil, reduce the heat to medium-low; cover and simmer for 5 minutes or until the potatoes are tender. Stir in the fish and clams (with juice); cook for 2 minutes. Add the half-and-half; stir gently for 2 minutes or until the fish flakes easily with a fork. Season with salt and pepper.

● Garnish with paprika and chives.

VATAPA

Makes **4** servings (6 cups)

This Brazilian seafood stew is from the West-African-influenced state of Brazil known as Bahia. During my days there, I became intrigued with the blend of diverse cultures that influence the local cuisine.

My friend Cindy Jurgensen, a cooking instructor and recipe tester, shared this dish with me. After a two-year stint living in the Pacific during their Peace Corps days, Cindy and her husband, Curt, learned to love foods with an international flair. Cindy suggests serving this stew in a shallow bowl over a mound of white rice to absorb some of the delicious coconut milk. She likes to accompany it with small bowls of chopped peanuts and lime wedges.

2	tablespoons canola oil
1	cup coarsely chopped onion
2	tablespoons finely chopped serrano chili
2	teaspoons minced garlic
1	(14-ounce) can "lite" coconut milk
1	(8-ounce) bottle clam juice
1	tomato, coarsely chopped
1	(2-inch) piece fresh ginger, peeled and very thinly sliced
¼	cup coarsely chopped fresh cilantro plus extra for garnish
8	ounces red snapper, cut into 2-inch pieces

8	ounces medium (26 to 30 count) shrimp, peeled and deveined
8	ounces bay scallops
2	tablespoons fresh lemon juice
	Salt and pepper to taste

○ Heat the oil in a Dutch oven over medium-high heat. Add the onion, chili, and garlic; cook, stirring occasionally, for 4 minutes or until the onion is softened. Stir in the coconut milk, clam juice, tomato, ginger, and cilantro. Bring to a boil and cook for 5 minutes.

○ Reduce the heat to medium. Stir in the snapper; cook for 2 minutes. Stir in the shrimp and scallops; continue to cook for 2 minutes or until the shrimp turn pink and the scallops and fish are cooked. Stir in the lemon juice and season with salt and pepper.

○ Garnish the servings with cilantro.

Sandwiches and Tortillas

WARM CRAB SALAD SANDWICHES
Makes **4** servings

Start with a can and several ingredients you're likely to have on hand, and in minutes you'll have gourmet sandwiches to delight your family or favorite guests. You can prepare the crab salad up to two days before needed and store it in a covered container in the refrigerator.

For the crab salad:
| 1 | (6-ounce) can lump crab, drained |
| ⅓ | cup cream cheese, softened |

½	teaspoon minced garlic
¼	teaspoon Worcestershire sauce
¼	teaspoon Tabasco sauce, or to taste
	Salt to taste

To complete the recipe:
4	slices white sandwich bread
4	tomato slices
4	thin slices Cheddar cheese
	Dash of paprika

○ Put the crab in a medium bowl and use a spoon to break it into chunks. Stir in the remaining salad ingredients.

○ Position the oven broiler rack 4 to 5 inches from the heat source and preheat the broiler. Arrange the bread in a single layer on a baking sheet. Toast the bread for 45 seconds per side or until lightly browned.

○ For each sandwich, spread a slice of toasted bread with about ¼ cup of the crab salad mixture. Top with a tomato slice and cheese. Sprinkle with paprika.

○ Broil for 2 minutes or until the cheese is melted and lightly browned. Serve warm with knives and forks.

—— TIP ——

Once opened, refrigerate Tabasco (hot pepper) sauce to retain its zesty flavor and red color.

SCRAMBLED EGGS AND SMOKED SALMON ON RYE

Makes **4** servings

Here, the quintessential breakfast, scrambled eggs and toast, is made rich and elegant for a quick family dinner or for a deluxe brunch to serve company.

8	eggs
2	ounces cream cheese, cut into small pieces
	Dash of salt and pepper, or to taste
4	slices rye bread
3	tablespoons unsalted butter, divided, plus extra for spreading
3½	ounces shiitake mushrooms, stems removed and discarded, caps cut into ¼-inch slices (1½ cups)
¼	cup finely chopped shallots
6	ounces smoked salmon, coarsely chopped
	Freshly ground pepper and finely chopped fresh chives for garnish

● Use a fork to lightly beat the eggs in a medium bowl. Stir in the cream cheese, salt, and pepper.

● Toast the bread in a toaster.

● Meanwhile, melt 2 tablespoons butter in a large nonstick skillet over medium-high heat. Add the mushrooms; cook, stirring constantly, for 4 minutes. Add the shallots; continue to cook, stirring constantly, for 1 minute or until tender. Remove from the heat and stir in the salmon. Transfer to a bowl and cover to keep warm.

● Reduce the heat to low. Melt the remaining 1 tablespoon butter in the same skillet. Add the egg mixture. Cook, stirring constantly, for 4 minutes or until the eggs are cooked but still moist.

● Remove from the heat and gently stir in the mushroom mixture.

● Lightly butter the toasted bread. To serve, spoon about ⅓ cup of the egg mixture over each slice of toast. Sprinkle with pepper and chives.

→ TIP →

Shallots, a member of the onion family, are small bulbous herbs with a mild onion-garlic flavor. Always use fresh—never dried—shallots. If fresh are unavailable, substitute some onion and garlic. Fresh shallots will keep for up to a month in the bottom bin of your refrigerator; use before they begin to sprout. When cooking, don't allow shallots to brown or they will taste bitter.

SHRIMP CAESAR CROSTINI

Makes **4** servings

The noble Caesar never looked so good. If you're in a time crunch, you can use bottled Caesar dressing, but making the lemony mixture from scratch takes only minutes using ingredients you are likely to have on hand. The flavorsome little toasts are proven company-pleasers. Serve for a light lunch or pass them as an appetizer or cocktail snack.

16	(½-inch-thick) slices French bread
	Olive oil for brushing
¼	cup freshly grated Parmesan cheese
2½	cups finely shredded romaine lettuce hearts (cut the leaves in half lengthwise, then shred)

½ cup Lemon Caesar Dressing (page 269)

8 ounces cooked salad shrimp

Paprika for garnish

○ Preheat the oven to 400°F.

○ Lightly brush oil on both sides of each bread slice. Arrange the slices in a single layer on a baking sheet. Bake for 5 minutes or until the edges of the tops of the slices just begin to turn golden brown. Remove the pan from the oven and turn the bread slices.

○ Sprinkle the slices with Parmesan cheese, and bake for 2 more minutes or until the cheese is melted.

○ Toss the lettuce and dressing in a medium bowl. Using tongs, mound the lettuce on the crostini. Top each toast with about 2 shrimp. Garnish with paprika.

SMOKED SALMON QUESADILLA

Makes **4** servings

There's a lot of flavor packed between the tortillas in this quesadilla, and just as appealing, it can be made in less than 10 minutes.

¼ cup chèvre cheese

¼ cup cream cheese

¼ cup sour cream

2 green onions, finely chopped

1 tablespoon snipped fresh dill

2 (10-inch) flour tortillas

4 ounces smoked salmon, thinly sliced

Olive oil for brushing

○ Stir together the chèvre cheese, cream cheese, sour cream, green onions, and dill in a small bowl. Evenly

spread the mixture over one tortilla to within ½ inch of the edge. Sprinkle with a layer of salmon. Place the other tortilla on top and press gently.

○ Heat a stovetop grill pan over high heat. Brush the top surface of the quesadilla with olive oil. Reduce the heat to medium-high; place the quesadilla, oiled-side down, on the pan. Grill for 2 minutes or until lightly browned. Brush the top with oil, flip the quesadilla, and grill for 2 more minutes or until lightly browned.

○ Cut the quesadilla into 4 wedges and serve warm.

SMOKED SALMON TOAST

Makes **4** servings

On their own, these open-faced sandwiches make a speedy lunch. Or after spreading the toasts with the salmon mixture, slice each diagonally into four triangles to serve as a soup accompaniment or an appetizer.

4 ounces smoked salmon, finely chopped

1 green onion, finely chopped

¼ cup finely chopped fresh flat-leaf parsley, divided

2 tablespoons small (nonpareil) capers, drained and rinsed

1 tablespoon mayonnaise

Dash of pepper, or to taste

4 slices pumpernickel bread, toasted

○ Stir together the salmon, green onion, 2 tablespoons parsley, capers, mayonnaise, and pepper.

○ Spread about ¼ cup of the mixture on each slice of toasted bread and sprinkle with the remaining 2 tablespoons parsley.

Pasta and Noodles

CIOPPINO WITH LINGUINE

Makes **4** servings

This spicy seafood stew reminds me of dining in beautiful Italian ports, where I savor not only traditional food but also the local wine and my surroundings. The Italians don't use cheese on fish, nor is cioppino served on pasta. Let's call this recipe "culinary license." The ingredient list is lengthy. The time required is not. The hearty topping can be prepared while the linguine cooks.

12	ounces linguine
1	tablespoon olive oil
½	green bell pepper, finely chopped
½	cup finely chopped onion
1½	teaspoons minced garlic
2	(14-ounce) cans tomatoes with Italian herbs
¼	cup coarsely chopped fresh basil or 1 teaspoon dried basil
1	tablespoon fresh thyme leaves or ½ teaspoon dried thyme
¼	teaspoon red pepper flakes, or to taste
12	ounces cod fillet (or other firm white fish such as sea bass, flounder, or grouper), cut into 1-inch squares
8	ounces medium (26 to 30 count) shrimp, peeled and deveined, tails on if desired
1	tablespoon lemon juice
	Salt and pepper to taste
	Freshly shredded Parmesan cheese for garnish

▶ Cook the linguine according to package instructions.

▶ Meanwhile, heat the oil in a large sauté pan over medium-high heat. Add the bell pepper, onion, and garlic; cook, stirring occasionally, for 2 minutes or until the onion is tender. Stir in the tomatoes, basil, thyme, and red pepper flakes. Cover and cook, stirring occasionally, for 3 minutes.

▶ Add the cod; cook for 2 minutes, stirring occasionally gently so the fish will not be broken into pieces. Stir in the shrimp; continue to cook for 3 minutes or until the cod and shrimp are thoroughly cooked. Stir in the parsley, lemon juice, salt, and pepper.

▶ When the linguine is done, drain well.

▶ Transfer the linguine to shallow bowls. Top with the fish stew and garnish with Parmesan cheese.

SALMON AND NOODLES WITH PESTO CREAM SAUCE

Makes **4** servings

Here's one of my favorite dishes to serve guests, especially paired with Chenin Blanc. Organize the recipe components in advance, and the preparation will require only simple, last-minute attention. I guarantee that your friends will be impressed with your ease and speed in presenting such a fine meal. If you'd like, add a dash of red pepper flakes to the sauce for an element of surprise. For vegetarians, omit the salmon and add toasted pine nuts as an extra topping for the noodles.

6	ounces (5 cups) wide egg noodles
4	(6-ounce) salmon fillets
	Olive oil for brushing
	Salt and pepper to taste

1	cup half-and-half
¼	cup Basil Pesto (page 274)
	Halved grape tomatoes, freshly shredded Parmesan cheese, freshly ground pepper, and sprigs of fresh basil for garnish

◗ Position the oven rack about 5 inches from the heating element and preheat the broiler.

◗ Cook the noodles according to package instructions.

◗ Lightly brush the salmon with oil. Place skin side down on a baking sheet or broiler pan. Broil for 4 minutes or until the desired doneness. Sprinkle with salt and pepper.

◗ While the salmon is cooking, combine the half-and-half and pesto in a small saucepan. Stir occasionally over medium-low heat until warmed through. (Do not allow the sauce to come to a boil.)

◗ When the noodles are done, drain well. Return to the pasta pan. Add the pesto sauce and stir until evenly combined. Season with salt and pepper.

◗ To serve, spread the noodles in 4 shallow bowls. Top each serving with a salmon fillet. Garnish with tomatoes, Parmesan cheese, pepper, and basil sprigs.

SHRIMP WITH TOMATOES AND WHITE WINE SAUCE

Makes **4** servings

Keep frozen shrimp on hand and you can count on this for a delicious standby to serve unexpected company. For a change of pace, rather than couscous, serve the shrimp and their wine-scented sauce over vermicelli.

¾	cup water
¾	cup couscous
2	tablespoons olive oil
4	green onions, thinly sliced
2	teaspoons minced garlic
16	ounces medium (26 to 30 count) shrimp, peeled and deveined
½	cup dry white wine
1	pint cherry tomatoes, halved (2 cups)
¼	teaspoon salt, or to taste
¼	teaspoon pepper, or to taste
½	cup coarsely chopped fresh basil for garnish

◗ Heat the water in a small saucepan over high heat until very hot but not boiling. Remove the pan from the heat. Stir in the couscous. Let stand, covered, for 5 minutes or until the liquid is completely absorbed.

◗ Meanwhile, heat the oil in a large sauté pan over medium-high heat. Add the green onions and garlic; cook, stirring occasionally, for 30 seconds. Add the shrimp; continue to cook, stirring constantly, for 1 minute. Add the wine; stir, scraping the bottom of the pan for 1 minute. Add the tomatoes, salt, and pepper. Continue to cook, stirring occasionally, for 1 minute or until the shrimp turn pink.

◗ Fluff the couscous with a fork. Serve the shrimp mixture over the couscous. Sprinkle with basil.

ROTINI WITH CREAMY CLAM SAUCE

Makes **4** servings

There's no cream in this sauce—it's just an illusion, thanks to the lush but low-cal ricotta cheese. Keep a can of minced clams in your pantry so you can count on this tasty pasta dish as a last-minute dinner. When I shop in Italian markets, I always pick up a package of long fusilli noodles for this recipe because I love the look of the skinny, 12-inch spirals. But for convenience, I usually use rotini, which is found in most supermarkets.

For the pasta:

12 ounces rotini pasta

For the sauce:

1   cup milk

½   cup ricotta cheese

2   (6-ounce) cans minced or chopped clams, drained; ½ cup clam juice reserved

1   tablespoon olive oil

1½   teaspoons minced garlic

¼   cup finely chopped fresh flat-leaf parsley

¼   cup finely chopped fresh basil

1   tablespoon fresh lemon juice

½   teaspoon salt, or to taste

½   teaspoon pepper, or to taste

½   cup freshly grated Parmesan cheese

To complete the recipe:

Freshly ground pepper, freshly grated Parmesan cheese, and halved grape tomatoes for garnish

○ Cook the pasta according to package instructions.

○ Meanwhile, stir together the milk, ricotta cheese, and clam juice in a medium bowl.

○ Heat the oil in a small saucepan over medium heat. Add the garlic and cook, stirring constantly, for ½ minute or until aromatic but not brown. Stir in the ricotta mixture and the clams. Heat until thoroughly warm. Stir in the parsley, basil, lemon juice, salt, and pepper; heat for 1 minute. Remove from the heat and cover to keep warm.

○ When the pasta is done, drain well. Return it to the pasta pan, and add the clam sauce and Parmesan cheese; stir gently over low heat for 1 minute or until warm.

○ Serve the pasta in shallow bowls and garnish with pepper, Parmesan cheese, and tomatoes.

ITALIAN TUNA PASTA

Makes **4** servings

I always used to bring home canned tuna when I traveled to Italy, where it is packed in olive oil that makes it especially flavorful. Fortunately, I can now find this tasty tuna in several Italian markets and even a few supermarkets near home, and I hope you can, too. This delicious sauce, introduced to me by my friend Judy Witts Francini, is great on any Italian pasta shape, including strands as well as short cuts.

12   ounces penne

1   (2-ounce) can anchovies with capers in olive oil

3   teaspoons minced garlic

1   (15-ounce) can diced tomatoes

1   (6-ounce) can Italian solid light tuna in olive oil

1   cup julienned fresh basil

½   cup sliced ripe olives

½   teaspoon red pepper flakes, or to taste

Freshly ground pepper for garnish

- Cook the penne according to package instructions.

- Meanwhile, heat a medium sauté pan over medium-high heat. Add the anchovies with oil and the garlic. Stir constantly for 1 minute or until the anchovies are melted.

- Remove from the heat and add the remaining ingredients, except the garnish. Stir only until combined, leaving the tuna in chunks.

- When the pasta is done, drain well, and return it to the pasta pan. Add the tuna mixture and toss gently.

- Garnish the servings with pepper.

TIP

"Julienne" means to cut food into very thin strips. For leaves like basil, it's best to use large leaves. Stack them and then cut into ⅛-inch strips.

GRILLED PESTO SHRIMP WITH ISRAELI COUSCOUS

Makes **4** servings

This lavish dish is a gourmet meal worthy of serving to your most discriminating guests. Add a Californian or South African Sauvignon Blanc, not too dry, to complete the celebration.

2	cups reduced-sodium chicken broth
3	tablespoons olive oil, divided
2	cups (one 9-ounce package) Israeli couscous
½	cup finely chopped onion
2	tablespoons fresh lemon juice
3	cups arugula leaves
	Salt and pepper to taste
12	jumbo (8 to 12 count) shrimp, peeled and deveined, tails left on
	Olive oil for brushing
½	cup Basil Pesto (page 274)

- Bring the chicken broth to a boil in a medium saucepan over high heat.

- Meanwhile, heat 1 tablespoon oil in a medium saucepan over medium-high heat. Add the couscous and onion; cook, stirring constantly, for 2 minutes or until the onion is tender. Stir in the boiling chicken broth, reduce the heat to low, cover, and cook for 10 minutes or until the couscous is tender but firm.

- While the couscous is cooking, whisk together the remaining 2 tablespoons oil and the lemon juice in a medium bowl. Add the arugula and toss until evenly combined. Season with salt and pepper.

- Heat a stovetop grill pan over high heat. Lightly brush both sides of the shrimp with oil. Reduce the heat to medium-high; cook for 3 minutes per side or until lightly browned and thoroughly cooked.

- When the shrimp are done, transfer to a medium bowl and toss with the pesto.

- To serve, spoon the couscous into the center of salad plates. Top with the dressed arugula and arrange 3 shrimp on each serving.

UDON NOODLES WITH SCALLOPS AND MANGO IN GINGER-CHILI SAUCE

Makes **4** servings

Udon are white Japanese noodles made with wheat flour, water, and sea salt. They are round or flat, and they can be wide or thin and delicate. For speedy cooking, purchase thin noodles for this recipe.

For the noodles:

12   ounces udon noodles

For the sauce:

2   tablespoons balsamic vinegar
2   tablespoons soy sauce
2   tablespoons dark (Asian) sesame oil
1   teaspoon chili paste with garlic, or to taste
1   teaspoon finely chopped fresh ginger
½   teaspoon sugar

To complete the recipe:

1   tablespoon canola oil
16   ounces sea scallops
     Salt and pepper to taste
2   cups jarred mango in 1-inch chunks
½   red bell pepper, finely chopped
4   green onions, diagonally cut into thin slices
     Black sesame seeds for garnish

○   Cook the noodles according to package instructions.

○   Meanwhile, combine the sauce ingredients in a small bowl; whisk until the sugar is dissolved.

○   Also while the noodles are cooking, heat the oil in a large sauté pan over medium heat. Add the scallops

and cook for 2 minutes per side or until just cooked. Sprinkle with salt and pepper. Stir in the mango, bell pepper, green onions, and sauce.

○   When the noodles are done, drain well.

○   To serve, transfer the noodles to shallow bowls and top with the scallop mixture. Garnish with sesame seeds.

CHINESE NOODLES WITH CILANTRO-CITRUS PESTO AND SCALLOPS

Makes **4** servings

Blending the distinctive flavors of cilantro and citrus juices is a marriage made in heaven. Go ahead and add more chili paste if you prefer spicy flavor. This recipe can be served warm or chilled. Or you can omit the scallops and serve it as a tasty side dish that's great with grilled chicken.

For the noodles:

8   ounces thin Chinese wheat-flour noodles

For the pesto:

1   cup fresh cilantro sprigs, tender stems included
¼   cup finely chopped shallots
2   tablespoons peanut oil, preferably roasted peanut oil
2   tablespoons fresh lime juice
2   tablespoons fresh orange juice
1   tablespoon finely chopped fresh ginger
1   teaspoon chili paste with garlic, or to taste
     Salt and pepper to taste

To complete the recipe:

1   tablespoon canola oil

12   ounces bay scallops

        Sprigs of fresh cilantro for garnish

○   Cook the noodles according to package instructions.

○   Meanwhile, process all the pesto ingredients in a food processor until nearly smooth.

○   Heat the oil in a small skillet over medium-high heat. Add the scallops; stir constantly for 1 minute or until thoroughly cooked. Remove from the heat.

○   When the noodles are done, drain well, and return to the pasta pan. Add the pesto and toss. Add the scallops and toss again.

○   Garnish the servings with cilantro sprigs.

SPAGHETTI WITH BLACK OLIVE–TOMATO PESTO AND SHRIMP

Makes **4** servings

This unusual pesto calls for ingredients you're likely to have on hand in your pantry. If there isn't time to stop at the market for fresh shrimp, instead add one (6-ounce) can of water-packed solid white albacore tuna (drained and flaked) when you toss the spaghetti with the pesto. You can also substitute linguine or other pasta strands.

For the pasta:

12   ounces spaghetti

For the pesto:

1   (4-ounce) can chopped black olives, drained

¼   cup reduced-sodium chicken broth

3   tablespoons tomato paste

2   tablespoons extra-virgin olive oil

2   tablespoons red wine vinegar

1   tablespoon minced fresh oregano or 1 teaspoon dried oregano

2   garlic cloves or 1 teaspoon minced garlic

½   teaspoon pepper, or to taste

¼   teaspoon salt, or to taste

To complete the recipe:

1   tablespoon olive oil

12   ounces medium (26 to 30 count) shrimp, peeled and deveined

1   teaspoon minced garlic

        Freshly ground pepper and coarsely crumbled feta cheese for garnish

○   Cook the spaghetti according to package instructions.

○   Meanwhile, process all the pesto ingredients in a food processor until nearly smooth.

○   To complete the recipe, heat the oil in a large skillet over medium-high heat. Add the shrimp and garlic; stir constantly for 2 minutes or until the shrimp turn pink. Remove from the heat.

○   When the spaghetti is done, drain well, and return to the pasta pan. Add the pesto and toss.

○   Top each serving of spaghetti with shrimp. Sprinkle with pepper and feta cheese.

LINGUINE WITH RED CLAM SAUCE

Makes **4** servings

This pasta recipe, satisfying in its simplicity, is a snap to make. Because clams, even those from cans, will toughen if overcooked, add them near the end of the cooking period and heat gently. Serve this comforting dish with a robust green salad and soft breadsticks.

12	ounces linguine
2	tablespoons olive oil
2	teaspoons minced garlic
1	(28-ounce) can whole tomatoes
¼	cup coarsely chopped fresh flat-leaf parsley
⅛	teaspoon red pepper flakes, or to taste
½	teaspoon salt, or to taste
⅛	teaspoon pepper, or to taste
2	(6-ounce) cans minced or chopped clams, drained; ½ cup clam juice reserved
	Freshly ground pepper and freshly shredded Parmesan cheese for garnish

◗ Cook the linguine according to package instructions.

◗ Meanwhile, heat the oil in a large sauté pan over medium heat. Add the garlic; cook, stirring constantly, for 30 seconds. Stir in the tomatoes, parsley, red pepper flakes, salt, pepper, and the reserved clam juice. Use kitchen shears to coarsely chop the tomatoes in the pan. Cook, stirring occasionally, for 6 minutes or until slightly thickened and reduced by about one-fourth.

◗ Reduce the heat to low. Add the clams and stir gently for 1 minute or until thoroughly heated.

◗ When the linguine is done, drain well. Return it to the pasta pan, add the clam sauce, and toss over medium heat for 1 minute or just until heated through.

◗ Serve the linguine in shallow bowls. Garnish with pepper and Parmesan cheese.

JAPANESE NOODLES WITH SCALLOPS

Makes **4** servings

This versatile noodle dish will become a favorite in your repertoire because it is equally as enticing served warm or cold. Consider serving the warm noodles as dinner for two, followed by chilled leftovers for a satisfying, no-fuss lunch the next day.

8	ounces soba (buckwheat) noodles
1	tablespoon canola oil
12	ounces bay scallops
1	cup green onions in matchstick strips
1	tablespoon finely chopped fresh ginger
2	tablespoons soy sauce
1	tablespoon dark (Asian) sesame oil
⅛	teaspoon red pepper flakes, or to taste
	Finely shredded carrots and black sesame seeds for garnish

◗ Cook the noodles according to package instructions.

◗ Meanwhile, heat the oil in a large sauté pan over medium-high heat. Add the scallops, green onions, and ginger; cook, stirring constantly, for 1 minute or until the scallops are just cooked. Remove from the heat. If any liquid has accumulated in the pan, drain and discard.

◗ To serve as a cold noodle salad, transfer the scallops to a large bowl to cool. When the noodles are done, rinse with cold water and drain well. Add to the scallops along with the soy sauce, sesame oil, and red pepper flakes; toss until the noodles are evenly coated.

○ To serve warm, when the noodles are done, drain well and add to the sauté pan. Add the soy sauce, sesame oil, and red pepper flakes; toss to combine.

○ Garnish the servings with carrots and sesame seeds.

┌─ TIP ─┐

Sesame seeds come in shades of brown, red, and black. Because they contain oil, all sesame seeds will become rancid at room temperature. Store them in an airtight container in the refrigerator for up to six months or in the freezer for up to a year.

SEARED SCALLOPS WITH LEMON PEPPER FETTUCCINE

Makes **4** servings

Lightly coating the scallops with flour gives them a nice crust and color. Be sure not to overcook these delicate morsels, which spoils their texture. The fresh and vibrant lemon flavor and pleasing presentation makes this a good dish for company. For added color, serve steamed asparagus on the side.

For the pasta:

12   ounces fettuccine

For the scallops:

¼   cup all-purpose flour
½   teaspoon salt
½   teaspoon pepper
16   ounces sea scallops
1   tablespoon unsalted butter
1   tablespoon olive oil

To complete the recipe:

2   teaspoons minced garlic
½   cup full-bodied white wine, such as Chardonnay
¼   cup fresh lemon juice
2   teaspoons grated lemon rind
¼   cup freshly grated Parmesan cheese
1   tablespoon unsalted butter
½   teaspoon coarsely ground pepper, or to taste
         Salt to taste
¼   cup finely chopped fresh flat-leaf parsley

○ Cook the fettuccine according to package instructions.

○ Meanwhile, prepare the scallops. Combine the flour, salt, and pepper in a large zip-top plastic bag. Rinse the scallops with cool water and pat dry. Add the scallops to the bag and shake to lightly coat.

○ Melt the butter with the oil in a large sauté pan over medium-high heat. Add the scallops; cook for 2 minutes per side or until lightly browned and slightly firm to the touch. (Discard the bag and excess flour mixture.) Transfer the scallops to a plate and cover to keep warm.

○ Add the garlic to the same pan over medium-high heat; stir constantly for 15 seconds. Add the wine, lemon juice, and lemon rind; stir occasionally until the liquid comes to a boil. Remove from the heat.

○ When the fettuccine is done, drain well, and return it to the pasta pan. Add the wine mixture, Parmesan cheese, butter, and pepper. Stir gently over low heat until the butter is melted. Season with pepper and salt.

○ Serve the fettuccine in shallow pasta bowls. Top with the scallops and sprinkle with parsley.

SHRIMP AND GEMELLI WITH SPICY TOMATO SAUCE

Makes **4** servings

This bold herb-and-garlic-flavored dish is one of my favorite standbys for entertaining; the flavors remind me of a memorable al fresco lunch on the sunny Greek island of Mykonos. This dish offers spiciness paired with the saltiness of olives and feta—a winning combination. Add more red pepper flakes if you want to kick up the heat.

For the pasta:

8	ounces (about 2 cups) gemelli pasta

For the sauce:

1	(14-ounce) can Italian-style stewed tomatoes
2	tablespoons extra-virgin olive oil
2	teaspoons minced garlic
1	teaspoon paprika
½	teaspoon pepper, or to taste
¼	teaspoon salt, or to taste
¼	teaspoon red pepper flakes, or to taste
2	teaspoons finely chopped fresh oregano or ¾ teaspoon dried oregano

To complete the recipe:

8	ounces medium (26 to 30 count) shrimp, peeled and deveined
½	cup coarsely chopped pitted kalamata olives
2	tablespoons fresh lemon juice
1	cup (4 ounces) coarsely crumbled feta cheese
	Finely chopped fresh flat-leaf parsley for garnish

❍ Cook the gemelli according to package instructions.

❍ Meanwhile, process the sauce ingredients (except the oregano) in a food processor until smooth. Pour into a medium saucepan and stir in the oregano.

❍ Bring the sauce to a boil over medium-high heat. Reduce the heat to low, cover, and simmer, stirring occasionally, for 3 minutes. Add the shrimp; cover and cook, stirring occasionally, for 2 minutes or until pink. Stir in the olives and lemon juice.

❍ When the pasta is done, drain well, and return to the pasta pan. Add the sauce and heat, stirring occasionally over medium heat, for 1 minute or until the sauce adheres to the pasta.

❍ Serve the gemelli in shallow pasta bowls. Top with feta cheese and garnish with parsley.

TIP

Paprika is a powder made by grinding aromatic sweet red pepper pods. The flavor can range from mild to pungent and hot, and the color from red-orange to deep red. Most paprika comes from Spain, South America, California, or Hungary; the Hungarian variety is considered by many to be the best. Hungarian paprika comes in three levels of hotness: mild (also called "sweet"), hot, and exceptionally hot. To preserve the color and flavor, store paprika in a cool, dark place for no longer than six months.

SAVORY SHRIMP
AND PINE NUT LO MEIN

Makes **4** servings

I generally serve this dish warm just after preparing it, but any leftovers are delicious the next day as a chilled pasta salad. For an out-of-the-ordinary twist that adds both intrigue and nutrition, garnish the servings with hijiki seaweed: Boil ¼ cup of dried hijiki while the dish is being prepared. If you have never tasted these sea vegetables, you are in for a pleasant surprise—and the shimmering black color accentuates the eye-catching appearance of this dish.

6	ounces lo mein noodles
¼	cup soy sauce
1	tablespoon dark (Asian) sesame oil
¼	teaspoon red pepper flakes, or to taste
1	tablespoon canola oil
3	cups sliced mushrooms
4	green onions, coarsely chopped
16	ounces medium (26 to 30 count) shrimp, peeled and deveined
¼	cup pine nuts
2	teaspoons minced garlic
2	teaspoons finely chopped fresh ginger

◐ Cook the noodles according to package instructions.

◐ While the noodles are cooking, stir together the soy sauce, sesame oil, and red pepper flakes in a small bowl.

◐ When the noodles are done, drain well. Return to the pasta pan and toss with 3 tablespoons of the soy sauce mixture. Cover to retain the heat if serving warm.

◐ Heat the oil in a large skillet over high heat. Add the mushrooms and green onions. Cook, stirring occasionally, for 4 minutes or until tender. Add the shrimp, pine nuts, garlic, and ginger; cook, stirring constantly, for 2 minutes or until the shrimp turn pink and the pine nuts are lightly browned. Remove from the heat. Stir in the remaining soy sauce mixture.

◐ To serve, transfer the noodles to bowls and top with the shrimp mixture.

TIPS

Hijiki (sometimes spelled "hiziki"), found in Asian markets and in some supermarkets, is a dried black seaweed or sea vegetable, with a salty, slight anise flavor and high calcium content. To reconstitute before adding to recipes, put the hijiki into a saucepan and cover with water. Bring the water to a boil over high heat. Reduce the heat to medium-high and simmer for 10 to 15 minutes or until softened; drain well. Covered and refrigerated, the moistened hijiki will keep for up to two days. Add to stir-fries, soups, and salads.

Chinese lo mein noodles are made with wheat flour and water, or wheat flour and eggs. The flat strands are ⅛ inch wide, sometimes a bit wider. As an exception to the general rule that the specified Asian noodles should be used in recipes, linguine and spaghettini make satisfactory substitutes in most recipes.

PAD THAI

Makes **4** servings

I learned to love Pad Thai, Thailand's most well-known dish, in Bangkok, where I sampled street vendors' aromatic fare and also enjoyed this dish in fine restaurants. At home, I like to serve Pad Thai as a meatless meal, but only for vegetarians who include fish sauce, oyster sauce, and eggs in their diets. For others, I sometimes add shredded rotisserie chicken or cooked baby shrimp. To make an impressive presentation, serve the mélange on a large, pretty platter.

8	ounces rice noodles
3	tablespoons Thai fish sauce
2	tablespoons fresh lime juice
2	tablespoons packed brown sugar
1	tablespoon white rice vinegar
1	tablespoon chili paste with garlic, or to taste
1	tablespoon oyster sauce
2	tablespoons canola oil, divided
3	eggs, lightly beaten
1	cup fresh bean sprouts
1	tablespoon minced garlic
4	green onions, thinly sliced
⅓	cup salted peanuts, coarsely chopped
	Lime wedges for garnish

◗ Cook the noodles according to package instructions.

◗ Meanwhile, combine the fish sauce, lime juice, brown sugar, vinegar, chili paste, and oyster sauce in a small bowl; stir until smooth.

◗ Heat 1 tablespoon oil in a large nonstick skillet over medium-high heat. Add the eggs and cook for 30 seconds. Turn with a spatula and cook for 30 seconds

more or just until set. Use a spatula to transfer the eggs to a plate. Cut into strips about 2 x ¼ inch.

◗ When the noodles are done, drain well. Heat the remaining 1 tablespoon oil in the same skillet over high heat. Add the noodles, bean sprouts, and garlic; stir for 2 minutes. Stir in the fish sauce mixture; cook for 1 minute or until heated through.

◗ Top the servings with the egg strips, green onions, and peanuts. Garnish with lime wedges.

┤ TIP ├

White rice vinegar, made from fermented rice, has a low acidity and is mild and sweet. It can be found in Asian markets and most supermarkets. Look for unseasoned rice vinegar, which is more versatile in recipes.

Stovetop Dishes

CORNMEAL-CRUSTED TILAPIA ON TOMATO RAGU

Makes **4** servings

This is a just-right dinner for a busy weeknight and also a perfect meal for easy entertaining. Serve the sauce and fish in shallow bowls and add a mound of rice to absorb every last drop of the luscious sauce. Fresh Corn Salsa (page 275) is a nice accompaniment, too.

½	cup yellow cornmeal
4	(6-ounce) tilapia fillets
4	tablespoons canola oil, divided
1	cup coarsely chopped fresh flat-leaf parsley
	Zest of 1 lemon
¼	cup fresh lemon juice
	Salt and pepper to taste
2	(14-ounce) cans diced tomatoes with basil, garlic, and oregano

○ Spread the cornmeal in a shallow bowl. Press both sides of the fillets in the cornmeal to lightly coat.

○ Heat 2 tablespoons oil in a large skillet over medium-high heat. Add 2 fillets. Cook for 3 minutes per side or until lightly browned and thoroughly cooked. Transfer to a paper towel-lined plate and cover to keep warm. Repeat with the remaining 2 tablespoons oil and fillets.

○ While the fish is cooking, stir together the parsley, lemon zest, and lemon juice in a small bowl. Season with salt and pepper. Set aside.

○ Pour the tomatoes into a medium saucepan. Warm, stirring occasionally, over medium heat.

○ To serve, spoon the tomatoes into shallow bowls. Top with the fillets and sprinkle with the parsley mixture.

SHRIMP COCONUT MILK CURRY

Makes **4** servings

This dish carries the sensuous kind of Asian flavors that people travel halfway around the world to savor.

With this easy and delicious recipe, it's all about enjoyment—no jet lag.

Although tails make the shrimp a bit messy to eat, I like them for their visual appeal. Serve this dish with basmati rice, which provides a cooling element. So go ahead and add more curry paste if you savor zesty flavors.

1	(14-ounce) can "lite" coconut milk
¾	cup reduced-sodium chicken broth
1	tablespoon red curry paste, or to taste
1	tablespoon Asian fish sauce
1	teaspoon sugar
½	teaspoon salt
16	ounces large (16 to 20 count) shrimp, peeled and deveined, tails left on
1	cup grape tomatoes, halved
1	cup fresh sugar snap peas
¼	cup coarsely chopped fresh cilantro
2	tablespoons fresh lime juice
	Lime wedges for garnish

○ Whisk together the coconut milk, chicken broth, and curry paste in a large sauté pan. Bring to a boil over medium-high heat. Reduce the heat to low; stir in the fish sauce, sugar, and salt. Cover and simmer for 3 minutes.

○ Add the shrimp, tomatoes, and sugar snap peas; bring to a boil, stirring occasionally. Reduce the heat to low and cook, stirring occasionally, for 5 minutes or until the shrimp turn pink. Stir in the cilantro.

○ Serve in shallow bowls. Sprinkle the servings with lime juice and garnish with lime wedges.

VIETNAMESE STEAMED TROUT
Makes **4** servings

My Vietnamese friend An Nguyen owns Rice Paper, a small, charming Minneapolis restaurant. Every dish An serves not only reflects memories of her home in Saigon but also is meticulously prepared. She explained to me that this healthful steaming method, which also can be used for walleye or other mild white fish fillets, is important in her cuisine because the Vietnamese savor the sweetness of the fish bone that permeates the meat. Serve the fish with a green vegetable and steamed rice. And pour the cooked soy sauce mixture into ramekins and add some chili paste to make a sauce for dipping. According to An, in her country any leftover sauce is never wasted—it is served later on rice.

Before preparing this recipe, plan your method of steaming; the recipe offers two alteratives.

2	(10 to 12-ounce) whole rainbow trout
½	teaspoon salt
4	green onions, cut in half crosswise and lengthwise
⅓	cup soy sauce
3	tablespoons white rice vinegar
3	tablespoons canola oil
2	tablespoons fresh ginger cut in fine strips
1	cup coarsely shredded carrots
	Chili paste with garlic to taste

◗ Use a sharp knife to make diagonal cuts about 1 inch apart on both sides of the fish. Rub with the salt.

◗ Spread the green onions on a deep (about 10-inch) platter and place the fish on top.

◗ Stir together the soy sauce, vinegar, and oil in a small bowl. Pour evenly over the fish.

◗ Spoon the ginger and then the carrots on top of the fish.

◗ If you have a steamer, place the platter in the hot steamer with 1 inch of water in the bottom.

◗ If you don't have a steamer, use a large pot filled with 1 inch of water. Insert two upside-down ramekins or a small bowl with its flat bottom up. (This bowl should be large enough to hold the platter steady, but not too big to prevent the steam from rising in the pot.) Bring the water to a boil over high heat, and then reduce the heat to medium. Put the platter of fish in the steamer or pot.

◗ Cover and steam for 10 minutes or until the fish is flaky and thoroughly cooked. Then carefully remove the platter from the steamer.

◗ Serve the whole fish fillets topped with the green onions, ginger, and carrots on a serving platter. Spoon the sauce into 4 small ramekins and stir in chili paste.

◗ Your guests can slice the fillets in half horizontally and lift out the bones, which will come out simply in one motion. Instruct them to use the sauce mixture for dipping.

TILAPIA WITH BLACK BEAN SAUCE

Makes **4** servings

Tilapia is found worldwide, especially in Asia, where it's become integral to the cuisines of many countries. The plump pinkish white fillets become snowy white when cooked, and the delicate flavor appeals to even the most hesitant fish eater. Unlike many white fish, it holds its shape while cooking and tolerates an extra minute of cooking time without either breaking or becoming tough. Serve this aromatic dish with basmati rice.

¼	cup Chinese black bean garlic sauce
1	cup reduced-sodium chicken broth
2	teaspoons cold water
2	teaspoons cornstarch
2	tablespoons canola oil
16	ounces tilapia fillets, cut into 2-inch strips
	Pepper to taste
1	red bell pepper, cut into ¼-inch slices
4	green onions, cut diagonally into 3-inch lengths

◐ Combine the bean sauce and chicken broth in a small saucepan; bring to a boil over medium-high heat. Reduce the heat to medium.

◐ Meanwhile, stir together the water and cornstarch in a small bowl until smooth. Add to the saucepan; stir constantly for 2 minutes or until thickened to a maple-syrup consistency. Remove from the heat and cover to keep warm.

◐ Heat the oil in a large sauté pan over medium-high heat. Add the tilapia and sprinkle with pepper. Cook, turning once, for 4 minutes. Add the bell pepper and green onions; stir gently for 1 minute or until the vegetables are crisp-tender and the fish is thoroughly cooked. Reduce the heat to medium; add the bean sauce and stir gently until evenly combined.

SALMON WITH STIR-FRIED SWEET PEPPERS AND MANGO SAUCE

Makes **4** servings

If your guests are devotees of enticing flavor with a bit of an edge, dress up salmon with this succulent sweet-hot sauce. Present it upon a bed of rice to create a tantalizing balance. The mango needs to be extremely ripe for this sauce to work, so I recommend using mango from a jar. The serrano chili is very, very hot—only a little is needed.

For the sauce:

1	cup coarsely chopped jarred mango
⅔	cup reduced-sodium chicken broth
2	teaspoons fresh lime juice
1½	teaspoons finely chopped fresh ginger
½	teaspoon finely chopped serrano chili, or to taste
¼	teaspoon salt, or to taste

For the fish and vegetables:

1	tablespoon dark (Asian) sesame oil, divided
4	(6-ounce) salmon fillets (skin removed by fishmonger if possible)
	Salt and pepper to taste
1	red bell pepper, cut into ¼-inch strips
1	green bell pepper, cut into ¼-inch strips
1	orange bell pepper, cut into ¼-inch strips

◐ Purée all the sauce ingredients in a blender until smooth. Pour into a small saucepan.

To cook the fish, heat 1½ teaspoons of the sesame oil in a large skillet over medium heat. Sprinkle all sides of the salmon with the salt and pepper. Cook the salmon, turning once, for 5 minutes or until the desired doneness. Transfer to a plate and cover to keep warm.

Add the remaining 1 ½ teaspoons sesame oil to the same skillet over medium-high heat. Add the bell peppers; cook, stirring frequently, for 3 minutes or until crisp-tender.

Meanwhile, cook the mango sauce over medium-high heat, stirring frequently, for 2 minutes or until heated through.

Top each salmon fillet with vegetables and mango sauce.

SZECHUAN SHRIMP WITH CHILI SAUCE

Makes **4** servings

The ingredient list for this dish may appear daunting, but most items are Asian pantry staples, so little chopping is needed. Begin by cooking a pot of basmati rice, which is the perfect antidote to the spicy flavors. I like to present this dazzling dish on a large platter garnished with cilantro, along with thin slices of crisp Asian pears. Remind guests not to eat the hot chilies—or remove them before serving.

For the sauce:

¼	cup hoisin sauce
1	tablespoon dry sherry
2	teaspoons soy sauce
2	teaspoons Asian fish sauce
1	teaspoon Chinese chili paste with garlic, or to taste
1	teaspoon dark (Asian) sesame oil
½	teaspoon chili oil
½	teaspoon sugar

To complete the recipe:

2	tablespoons canola oil
16	ounces medium (26 to 30 count) shrimp, peeled and deveined
8	green onions, diagonally cut into 2-inch lengths
4	whole dried serrano chilies
2	tablespoons finely chopped fresh ginger
1	tablespoon minced garlic
	Finely chopped fresh cilantro for garnish

Stir together the sauce ingredients in a small bowl.

Heat the oil in a large sauté pan over medium-high heat. Add the remaining ingredients, except the garnish; cook, stirring frequently, for 1 minute or until the shrimp begin to turn pink. Add the sauce mixture; cook, stirring constantly, for 1 minute or until the shrimp are thoroughly cooked and the sauce is slightly thickened.

Transfer to a platter and garnish with cilantro.

TIP

Chili oil, a mainstay of Chinese cooking, is made with hot chilies that have been steeped in vegetable oil to release their heat, flavor, and red color. Refrigerate after opening to retain the oil's potency and color.

SHRIMP AND PINEAPPLE CURRY

Makes **4** servings

Red curry paste is a powerhouse of complex, spicy flavor; because it packs a punch, not much is needed. Like many curries, this dish contains a generous amount of broth, making it almost souplike. Ladle the shrimp, pineapple, and broth into shallow bowls over mounds of rice.

1	(14-ounce) can "lite" coconut milk, divided
¾	cup reduced-sodium chicken broth
2	teaspoons red curry paste, or to taste
1	tablespoon Asian fish sauce
1	tablespoon packed brown sugar
1	(8-ounce) can pineapple chunks, drained
½	red bell pepper, finely chopped
16	ounces medium (26 to 30 count) shrimp, peeled and deveined
½	cup coarsely chopped fresh Thai basil or sweet basil

○ Whisk together ½ cup coconut milk, the chicken broth, and curry paste in a large sauté pan over high heat. Cook, stirring frequently, until slightly thickened and reduced by about half.

○ Stir in the remaining coconut milk, fish sauce, brown sugar, pineapple, and bell pepper. When the liquid comes to a boil, add the shrimp. Cook, stirring occasionally, for 2 minutes or until the shrimp turn pink. Remove from the heat and stir in the basil.

○ To serve, ladle the shrimp, pineapple, and broth into shallow bowls.

— TIP —

Here's an easy method for determining when a sauce is reduced by half. Dip the handle of a wooden spoon or a wooden chopstick into the sauce before you begin reducing it. When the sauce appears to have lessened in quantity, dip it into the sauce again. You can see by comparing the two marks how much the volume has reduced

---

SHRIMP WITH CHIPOTLE CHILIES

Makes **4** servings

Chipotle chilies are dried, smoked jalapeño chilies with a smoky, sweet, and almost chocolaty flavor. They're a perfect 15-Minute ingredient when purchased canned in adobo sauce, which is packed with the lively flavors of ground chilies, herbs, and vinegar. The result is a smoky, spicy, satisfying shrimp dish that's great served with basmati rice.

1	(14-ounce) can diced tomatoes
2	chipotle chilies in adobo sauce (from a 7-ounce can), seeds removed; 1 tablespoon sauce reserved
1	tablespoon olive oil
1½	teaspoons minced garlic
16	ounces medium (26 to 30 count) shrimp, peeled and deveined
¼	cup coarsely chopped fresh cilantro Salt to taste

- Purée the tomatoes with the chilies and sauce in a blender or food processor until smooth.

- Heat the oil in a large sauté pan over medium-high heat. Add the garlic; stir constantly for 30 seconds or until aromatic. Add the tomato mixture; stir occasionally until it begins to bubble.

- Reduce the heat to medium. Add the shrimp; cook, stirring and turning occasionally for 2 minutes or until pink. Stir in the cilantro and salt.

HALIBUT WITH PINEAPPLE-CILANTRO SAUCE

Makes **4** servings

This fruity, flavorful recipe is a winner for company or every day. Serve it with rice to absorb every bit of the tasty, light sauce, and include steamed peapods for crunch. Children enjoy the dish because they're fond of pineapple, and poaching the fish in orange juice—another favorite fruit flavor—removes any trace of fishiness. If you'd like, add a little finely chopped fresh ginger to the juice when cooking the fish.

For the fish:

3	cups fresh orange juice
4	(6-ounce) halibut or haddock fillets

For the sauce:

1	(20-ounce) can pineapple chunks (do not drain)
½	cup finely chopped red bell pepper
¼	cup sugar
½	jalapeño chili, seeded and finely chopped, or more to taste
1	teaspoon finely chopped garlic
½	teaspoon salt
¼	teaspoon pepper
1	tablespoon cold water
1	tablespoon cornstarch
3	tablespoons fresh lime juice
2	tablespoons finely chopped fresh cilantro

- Pour the orange juice into a large sauté pan and bring to a boil over high heat. Reduce the heat to medium and add the fish; cover and simmer for 6 minutes or until it flakes when tested with a fork. Transfer to a plate and cover to keep warm.

- While the fish is cooking, combine the pineapple and its juice, bell pepper, sugar, chili, garlic, salt, and pepper in a medium saucepan. Bring to a boil over high heat. Reduce the heat to medium; cook, stirring occasionally, for 5 minutes.

- Stir together the water and cornstarch in a small bowl until smooth. Add to the pineapple mixture. Stir for 2 minutes or until thickened and clear. Stir in the lime juice and cilantro.

- Serve the sauce over the halibut.

TIP

For an attractive, simple garnish, make green onion curls. Slice the green part very thinly lengthwise and drop into ice water. Curls will form in 10 to 15 minutes.

SEA SCALLOPS IN CHUTNEY, APPLE, AND PEAR SAUCE

Makes **4** servings

This party-perfect dish sings with the sweet-sharp flavor of fruit and spicy chutney. Serve it with basmati rice and steamed asparagus or julienned carrots to add color to the plate.

20	ounces sea scallops
2	tablespoons olive oil, divided
2	firm pears (such as Bosc or Anjou), peeled, halved lengthwise, and cut into ¼-inch slices
1	apple (such as Braeburn), peeled, halved lengthwise, and cut into ¼-inch slices
1	cup half-and-half
½	cup mango chutney
2	teaspoons grated orange peel
⅓	cup golden raisins
	Salt and pepper to taste
	Coarsely chopped fresh chives for garnish

○ Rinse the scallops with cool water and pat dry.

○ Heat 1 tablespoon oil in a large skillet over medium heat. Add the scallops; cook for 2 minutes per side or until lightly browned and slightly firm to the touch. Remove from the heat and cover to keep warm.

○ Heat the remaining 1 tablespoon oil in a large sauté pan over medium-high heat. Add the pear and apple slices; cook, stirring occasionally, for 3 minutes or until they begin to cook.

○ Meanwhile, stir together the half-and-half, chutney, and orange peel in a small bowl.

○ Reduce the heat to low; stir in the chutney mixture and raisins. Cover and cook, stirring occasionally, for 3 minutes or until the fruit is tender. Stir in the scallops and season with salt and pepper.

○ Garnish the servings with chives.

CURRIED SHRIMP WITH TROPICAL FRUITS

Makes **4** servings

One of my favorite South American experiences was visiting the famous Manaus banana market in Brazil, a warehouse for banana trading, where I had never seen so many bananas. In the South Pacific, I learned that the Cavendish, which is the most common banana in U.S. markets, is offered as free pig food in Fiji, where workers still carry heavy "hands" of bananas on their heads from the field to the market. There they are paid by the weight of their efforts, which brings to mind the true lyrics, "Hey, Mr. Tally Man, tally me bananas."

I've tasted dozens of varieties of bananas in markets around the world. Among my favorites are dwarf or finger bananas, which are common in tropical and subtropical climates, and are now available in our markets. Try them and experience their sweet flavor and creamy texture.

When I enjoy this dish served over basmati rice, I am reminded of dinners in beautiful, warm places.

For the sauce:

2	teaspoons lime zest
½	cup fresh lime juice
2	teaspoons sugar
2	teaspoons curry powder
	Dash of ground cloves

For the fruit:

2   firm, ripe bananas, halved horizontally, and cut into ½-inch strips

1   papaya, halved vertically and horizontally, and cut into ½-inch strips

For the shrimp:

1   tablespoon canola oil

16   ounces small (41 to 50 count) shrimp, peeled and deveined

2   green onions, coarsely chopped

1   teaspoon minced garlic

      Salt to taste

2   tablespoons finely chopped fresh cilantro

      Hot cooked rice

      Sprigs of fresh cilantro for garnish

▶ Stir together the sauce ingredients in a small bowl. Set aside.

▶ To prepare the fruit, pour half of the sauce (¼ cup) into a medium skillet. Bring to a boil over medium-high heat. Add the bananas and papaya. Reduce the heat to medium-low and cook, stirring gently two or three times, for 2 minutes or until the fruit is heated through. Remove from the heat and cover to keep warm.

▶ While the fruit is cooking, prepare the shrimp. Heat the oil in a large skillet over medium-high heat. Add the shrimp, green onions, and garlic; stir for 30 seconds or until the shrimp just begin to turn pink but are not thoroughly cooked. Add the remaining sauce; stir for 1 minute or until the shrimp are thoroughly cooked. Stir in the cilantro and season with salt.

▶ To serve, spoon the fruit over the rice; top with the shrimp. Garnish with cilantro sprigs.

SHRIMP CREOLE

Makes **4** servings

Creole cooking reflects the French and Spanish heritage of New Orleans. It relies not only on herbs (dried for the traditional seasoning mixture) but also on the culinary "holy trinity" of green peppers, onions, and celery. Serve this tasty shrimp and vegetable mixture in shallow bowls over fluffy rice.

1   tablespoon olive oil

1   cup finely chopped onion

½   cup finely chopped celery

½   green bell pepper, finely chopped

1½   teaspoons minced garlic

2   (14-ounce) cans stewed tomatoes

1   teaspoon dried basil

¼   teaspoon dried thyme

¼   teaspoon dried oregano

⅛   teaspoon cayenne pepper, or to taste

16   ounces medium (26 to 30 count) shrimp, peeled and deveined

      Salt and pepper to taste

▶ Heat the oil in a large sauté pan over medium-high heat. Add the onion, celery, bell pepper, and garlic; cook, stirring occasionally, for 3 minutes or until crisp-tender.

▶ Stir in the remaining ingredients, except the shrimp, salt, and pepper. Increase the heat to high; when the liquid comes to a boil, cover and reduce the heat to low; simmer for 4 minutes. Stir in the shrimp; simmer, stirring frequently, for 2 minutes or until the shrimp turn pink. Season with salt and pepper.

SCALLOPS WITH LEMON-HERB SAUCE

Makes **4** servings

If you're looking for an elegant dinner to serve company, here's the answer. I measure out all the ingredients in advance and have the dinner plates handy so that the meal is ready in a flash at the last minute. Serve the shellfish and their rich, lemony sauce over basmati rice, and accompany with steamed asparagus and soft, buttery rolls.

20	ounces sea scallops
2	tablespoons canola oil
¼	teaspoon paprika
2	tablespoons fresh lemon juice
½	cup heavy cream
4	tablespoons unsalted butter, cut into ½-inch chunks
2	tablespoons finely chopped fresh chives
2	tablespoons finely chopped fresh flat-leaf parsley
1	tablespoon small (nonpareil) capers, drained and rinsed
	Salt and pepper to taste
	Sprigs of fresh flat-leaf parsley for garnish

◗ Rinse the scallops with cool water and pat dry.

◗ Heat the oil in a large skillet over medium-high heat until a drop of water sizzles. Lightly sprinkle the scallops with paprika. Sear them for 2 minutes per side or until lightly browned and slightly firm to the touch. Transfer to a plate and cover to keep warm.

◗ Add the lemon juice to the same skillet over medium heat; stir, scraping the bottom of the pan for 30 seconds. Pour in the cream and stir until well blended. Add the butter and whisk as it melts. Stir in the chives, parsley, capers, salt, and pepper.

◗ To serve, transfer the scallops to plates and drizzle each serving with about 3 tablespoons sauce. Garnish with parsley sprigs.

—— **TIP** ——

If you want your sea scallops to lightly brown, the best technique is to rinse them with cool water and then pat dry for proper browning. Sear them quickly so the outsides become golden while the insides remain moist and tender.

TILAPIA IN MANGO-TOMATO BROTH

Makes **4** servings

My travels to the South Pacific inspired this tropical dish. Mango is one of my favorite fruits, which is delicious not only eaten fresh, but also succulent when lightly cooked. Add scoops of rice to the bowls if you like.

2	tablespoons all-purpose flour
	Dash of salt and pepper
4	(6-ounce) tilapia fillets
1	tablespoon canola oil

1	tablespoon unsalted butter
½	cup finely chopped red onion
1	teaspoon minced garlic
1	(14-ounce) can reduced-sodium chicken broth
1½	cups jarred mango in ½-inch cubes
2	plum tomatoes, cut into ½-inch cubes
1	jalapeño chili, seeded and finely chopped
1	teaspoon ground turmeric
	Coarsely chopped fresh cilantro for garnish

● Stir together the flour, salt, and pepper in a flat-bottomed shallow bowl. Gently press both sides of the fish fillets into the mixture to lightly coat.

● Heat the oil in a large skillet over medium-high heat. Cook the fish for 3 minutes per side or until lightly browned and thoroughly cooked. (It may be necessary to cook just 2 fillets at a time.) Transfer to a plate and cover to keep warm.

● While the fish is cooking, melt the butter in a large sauté pan over medium heat. Add the onion and garlic; cook, stirring occasionally, for 3 minutes. Stir in the remaining ingredients, except the garnish. Increase the heat to high; when the liquid comes to a boil, reduce the heat to low. Cover and simmer for 3 minutes or until the mango and tomatoes are slightly softened but not mushy. Season with salt and pepper to taste.

● To serve, transfer the fish to shallow bowls. Top with the mango-tomato broth and sprinkle with cilantro. Serve with spoons and forks.

POACHED ORANGE ROUGHY WITH TOMATOES AND PEAS
Makes **4** servings

Serve this colorful, aromatic dish with fluffy couscous, which you can prepare while the fish cooks. It makes an easy family meal, and there's no chopping required. To complete the Mediterranean theme, add a salad of sliced oranges topped with toasted whole almonds.

1	tablespoon olive oil
1	teaspoon minced garlic
1	(14-ounce) can diced tomatoes with basil, garlic, and oregano
2	cups frozen baby peas
1	cup coarsely shredded carrots
	Salt and pepper to taste
4	(4-ounce) orange roughy fillets
	Finely chopped fresh flat-leaf parsley for garnish

● Heat the oil in a large sauté pan over medium-high heat; add the garlic and stir for 30 seconds. Stir in the tomatoes, peas, and carrots. Cover and cook for 6 minutes or until the carrots are tender. Season with salt and pepper.

● Add the fish to the pan, arranging it in a single layer. Reduce the heat to medium; cover and simmer for 5 minutes or until it flakes easily when tested with a fork.

● To serve, use a spatula to transfer the fish fillets to plates. Spoon the sauce over the fish and garnish with parsley.

Sole Amandine with Strawberry-Kiwi Salsa

SOLE AMANDINE WITH STRAWBERRY-KIWI SALSA

Makes **4** servings

Here, fresh strawberries and kiwi are combined with some unlikely ingredients to create a fish topping that's vibrant in both taste and color. Serve this dish with couscous, which makes a good sidekick to absorb the intriguing flavors. For the perfect beverage, I choose a fruity white wine, such as a Riesling or Chenin Blanc. I love this recipe because I'm especially fond of kiwis after seeing fields of them in New Zealand. I found it charming that the same farmers also raise sheep, who seek shelter from the hot sun under the canopy of kiwi branches.

For the salsa:

1	teaspoon lime zest
2	tablespoons fresh lime juice
1	tablespoon white rice vinegar
1	tablespoon olive oil
2	teaspoons sugar
1	teaspoon Dijon mustard
2	cups coarsely chopped strawberries
2	kiwi, peeled and coarsely chopped
2	green onions, coarsely chopped
1	tablespoon dried currants
1	tablespoon finely chopped cilantro

For the fish:

2	tablespoons olive oil, divided
½	cup sliced almonds
2	(7-ounce) sole or tilapia fillets

● To make the salsa, whisk together the lime zest, lime juice, vinegar, oil, sugar, and mustard in a medium bowl. Stir in the remaining ingredients. Set aside at room temperature.

● To prepare the fish, heat 1 tablespoon oil in a large skillet over medium heat. Add the almonds; stir constantly for 2 minutes or until lightly browned. Transfer to a plate.

● Heat the remaining 1 tablespoon oil in the same skillet over medium-high heat. Add the sole fillets; cook for 2 minutes per side (3 minutes per side for tilapia) or until the fish is lightly browned and flakes easily when tested with a fork.

● To serve, use a spatula to transfer the fish to plates. Top with the salsa and almonds.

SPANISH GARLIC SHRIMP WITH SHERRY

Makes **4** servings

Serve these succulent shrimp piping hot as a light entrée or at room temperature as part of an array of tapas, with lots of crusty bread for dipping in the delectable juices. For traditional Spanish flavoring, in place of the paprika use pimentón, a smoked and dried pepper powder that I discovered in Barcelona at Mercat La Boqueria, a large and lively market on Las Ramblas. Here at home it's available as "smoked paprika" in most spice shops. To preserve their color and flavor, all pepper powders should be stored in a cool, dark place for no longer than six months.

2	tablespoons olive oil
½	cup coarsely chopped onion
6	garlic cloves, thinly sliced
12	ounces medium (26 to 30 count) shrimp, peeled and deveined
½	teaspoon paprika or Spanish pimentón
¼	teaspoon ground cumin
⅓	cup dry sherry
1	tablespoon fresh lemon juice
¼	teaspoon red pepper flakes, or to taste
	Salt to taste
	Finely chopped fresh flat-leaf parsley for garnish

▶ Heat the oil in a large sauté pan over medium heat. Add the onion and garlic; cook, stirring constantly, for 15 seconds.

▶ Add the shrimp, paprika, and cumin; cook, stirring constantly, for 1 minute. Stir in the sherry, lemon juice, red pepper flakes, and salt. Continue to stir for 1 minute or until the shrimp turn pink.

▶ Transfer the shrimp and all juices to a serving dish or shallow bowls and garnish with parsley.

TIP

Red pepper flakes, also called crushed red pepper, are the seeds and flakes of fiery hot peppers. A small amount goes a long way. Refrigerate in a tightly covered container to preserve the color and flavor.

SALMON, POTATOES, AND ARTICHOKES IN TOMATO BROTH

Makes **4** servings

This meal is as beautiful as it is wholesome and satisfying in a homey way. It's perfect for serving to company when you want to be with your guests rather than spending lots of time in the kitchen. There's no need for side dishes, other than a salad and rustic artisan bread.

1	(14-ounce) can reduced-sodium chicken broth
2	tablespoons tomato paste
6	ounces fresh shiitake mushrooms, remove and discard stems, cut caps into ¼-inch strips (2 cups)
4	small red-skinned potatoes, cut into ¼-inch slices
2	plum tomatoes, cut into ½-inch cubes
2	tablespoons finely chopped fresh thyme
½	teaspoon salt, or to taste
¼	teaspoon pepper, or to taste

½	cup (½ of a 14-ounce can) quartered artichoke hearts packed in water, drained
4	(4-ounce) salmon fillets
	Olive oil for brushing
2	cups fresh watercress sprigs

○ Stir together the chicken broth and tomato paste in a large sauté pan over high heat. When the liquid comes to a boil, reduce the heat to low. Stir in the mushrooms, potatoes, tomatoes, thyme, salt, and pepper. Cover and cook, stirring occasionally, for 8 minutes or until the potatoes and mushrooms are tender. Stir in the artichoke hearts. Remove from the heat and cover to keep warm.

○ While the vegetables are cooking, heat a stovetop grill pan over high heat. Lightly brush both sides of the salmon fillets with oil. Reduce the heat to medium-high; cook, turning once, for 4 minutes or until lightly browned and the desired doneness.

○ To serve, place the fish in shallow bowls. Ladle about ½ cup of the tomato broth mixture over each serving and surround the fish with the potatoes, tomatoes, mushrooms, and artichokes. Garnish each serving with ½ cup watercress sprigs.

SCALLOPS AND ASPARAGUS WITH RED BELL PEPPER SAUCE

Makes **4** servings

Vibrant colors paired with the artful arrangement of scallops and asparagus make this an easy dish that's fit for guests. You can prepare it in minutes, just before your company is seated. Add a basket of bread served with Basil Pesto Butter (page 274), a green salad tossed with Balsamic Vinaigrette (page 268), and a side dish of rice, if you'd like, and your gourmet meal is complete.

¾	cup Roasted Red Bell Pepper Sauce made with fresh basil (page 267)
2	tablespoons olive oil, divided
16	ounces asparagus, cut into 2-inch diagonal slices
12	(about 12 ounces) large sea scallops
	Dash of salt and pepper
	Sprigs of fresh basil for garnish

○ If the sauce was prepared in advance and refrigerated, pour into a small saucepan and stir occasionally over low heat until warmed through. If freshly prepared, the sauce can be served at room temperature.

○ Heat 1 tablespoon oil in a large skillet over medium-high heat. Add the asparagus, and cook, stirring occasionally, for 5 minutes or until just tender. Transfer to a plate with a slotted spoon and cover to keep warm.

○ Rinse the scallops in cool water, pat dry, and sprinkle with salt and pepper. Heat the remaining 1 tablespoon oil in the same skillet over medium-high heat. Add the scallops; cook for 2 minutes per side or until lightly browned and just cooked through.

○ Divide the sauce among 4 dinner plates. Artistically arrange the scallops and asparagus over the sauce. Garnish with basil sprigs.

TERIYAKI TUNA WITH SPINACH

Makes **4** servings

For simplicity, cook this delicious tuna on your stovetop grill pan. But for a striking presentation, cook it on your outdoor grill. My friend Cindy Jurgensen cuts the tuna into 1-inch cubes and threads them onto bamboo skewers, alternating the tuna with the white parts of green onions cut into 1½-inch lengths. Baste with the Teriyaki Vinaigrette and grill about 6 inches from medium heat for 6 minutes, turning frequently to ensure even cooking. After grilling, serve the skewers atop the spinach and tomato slices on dinner plates.

⅔	cup Teriyaki Vinaigrette (page 271)
4	(6-ounce) tuna steaks
2	(6-ounce) bags salad spinach
2	large tomatoes, cut into ½-inch slices
	Toasted sesame seeds for garnish

○ Pour ¼ cup vinaigrette into a small container. Baste the tuna by brushing 1 side of each tuna steak with the vinaigrette. Set aside the remaining vinaigrette.

○ Heat a stovetop grill pan over high heat. Reduce the heat to medium-high; place the tuna steaks on the pan, basted side down, and cook for 2 minutes. Brush the tops of the tuna steaks with the remaining vinaigrette; turn and cook for 2 more minutes or until the desired doneness. (Most people prefer fresh tuna that is still pink in the center.)

○ While the tuna cooks, pour 2 tablespoons water into a large nonstick sauté pan; add the spinach. Cover and cook over high heat for 3 minutes or until the spinach is wilted but still bright green. Remove from the heat.

○ When the tuna is done, cut into ½-inch slices.

○ To serve, spread cooked spinach on the center of the plates. Arrange tomato slices to one side of the spinach and 1 sliced tuna steak over the spinach for each serving. Drizzle with the remaining vinaigrette. Sprinkle with sesame seeds.

TIP

Vegetable leaves, such as lettuce and spinach, and large-leafed herbs, such as basil, can be cut into shreds—sometimes called a chiffonade, which comes from a French word that describes something that has been torn into ribbons or shreds. To make chiffonade cuts, stack several leaves on a cutting board, roll them up lengthwise, and then slice crosswise into thin strips.

Teriyaki Tuna with Spinach

SOUTHWEST TOMATOES AND BEANS WITH CATFISH

Makes **4** servings

This wholesome dish is great served with cornbread, which you can purchase at your nearby bakery. If you have time to make your own, try adding jalapeños or shredded Jack cheese (or both) to embellish the Southwestern theme.

2	tablespoons olive oil, divided
1	red bell pepper, cut into ¼-inch strips
1½	teaspoons minced garlic
1	(15-ounce) can black beans, drained and rinsed
1	(14-ounce) can diced tomatoes with green pepper and onion
¼	cup water
2	tablespoons tomato paste
1	tablespoon finely chopped fresh oregano or 1 teaspoon dried oregano
½	teaspoon ancho chili powder, or to taste
½	teaspoon ground cumin, or to taste
¼	teaspoon cayenne pepper, or to taste
4	(4-ounce) catfish fillets
	Salt and pepper to taste
	Sprigs of fresh cilantro for garnish

⊙ Heat 1 tablespoon oil in a large sauté pan over medium-high heat. Add the bell pepper and garlic; cook, stirring occasionally, for 3 minutes or until tender. Stir in the remaining ingredients, except the fish, salt, pepper, and garnish; cook, stirring occasionally, for 4 minutes or until the mixture slightly thickens. Remove from the heat and cover to keep warm.

⊙ While the vegetables are cooking, heat the remaining 1 tablespoon oil in a large skillet over medium-high heat. Add the fish and sprinkle with salt and pepper; cook for 5 minutes, turning once, or until the fish is lightly browned and flakes easily when tested with a fork.

⊙ To serve, spoon the tomato-bean mixture into shallow bowls. Top each serving with a catfish fillet and garnish with cilantro sprigs.

CREAMY DILL CRAB CAKES

Makes **4** servings

These indulgent crab cakes offer the ultimate in textural enticement: creamy on the inside and crunchy on the outside. Serve with Roasted Red Bell Pepper Sauce (page 267) or your favorite tartar sauce. Check the fish counter for containers of fresh or pasteurized crabmeat, or purchase good-quality crabmeat in cans.

16	ounces fresh or pasteurized crabmeat, picked over
2	cups fresh white bread crumbs, divided
2	green onions, finely chopped
2	tablespoons finely chopped red bell pepper
1	tablespoon snipped fresh dill or 1 teaspoon dried dill
1½	teaspoons Old Bay seasoning
½	teaspoon salt, or to taste
¼	teaspoon pepper, or to taste
⅓	cup mayonnaise
1	egg, lightly beaten
2	tablespoons unsalted butter
2	tablespoons olive oil

○ Gently toss the crabmeat, ½ cup bread crumbs, green onions, bell pepper, dill, Old Bay seasoning, salt, and pepper in a large bowl. Add the mayonnaise and gently combine using a rubber spatula. Gently stir in the egg.

○ Divide the crab mixture into eight equal portions, about ⅓ cup each. Using your fingers, gently form the mixture into 1-inch-thick patties. Pour the remaining 1 ½ cups bread crumbs into a shallow dish. Lightly press the crab cakes into the crumbs to coat both sides.

○ Melt the butter with the oil in a large skillet over medium heat. Cook the crab cakes for 3 minutes per side or until golden brown.

TIP

Lump crabmeat is the highest quality crabmeat. Backfin costs a little less and may contain smaller pieces of meat mixed with the lumps. Claw meat is the least expensive grade and contains few if any lumps.

SALMON PATTIES WITH CUCUMBER-DILL SAUCE

Makes **4** servings

This is an updated, unpretentious version of an old classic. The cool quality of the cucumber-dill sauce nicely complements the spiciness of the salmon patties. For a light, fresh lunch, serve the patties on beds of chopped spinach accompanied by Fresh Corn Salsa (page 275) or a salad from the deli with bowls of fruity sorbet for dessert.

For the patties:

1	(15-ounce) can red sockeye salmon, drained
¼	cup dried bread crumbs
2	tablespoons finely chopped fresh flat-leaf parsley
2	tablespoons finely chopped shallot
½	teaspoon chili powder
⅛	teaspoon cayenne pepper
⅛	teaspoon salt
⅛	teaspoon pepper
2	eggs, lightly beaten
1	tablespoon canola oil

For the sauce:

½	cup peeled, seeded, and finely diced cucumber
¼	cup finely chopped red bell pepper
¼	cup sour cream
2	teaspoons fresh lemon juice
2	teaspoons snipped fresh dill
1	teaspoon minced garlic
	Salt and pepper to taste

○ Stir together all the patty ingredients, except the eggs and oil, in a medium bowl. Add the eggs and stir until evenly combined. Form the mixture into 8 patties about 2½ inches in diameter.

○ Heat the oil in a large skillet over medium-high heat. Cook the patties, turning once, for 3 minutes or until lightly browned and hot in the middle.

○ Meanwhile, stir together the sauce ingredients in a small bowl.

○ For each serving, arrange 2 patties on a plate. Top with about 2 tablespoons of the sauce.

Sautéed Scallops
with Mango Salsa

SAUTÉED SCALLOPS WITH MANGO SALSA

Makes **4** servings

I became friends with Bret Bannon at Cooks of Crocus Hill in Minneapolis, where we both offer cooking classes. I've adapted this recipe from Bret's Poached Scallops with Mango Salsa, which he serves in filo shells as a pretty appetizer. Here, the dish is served in larger portions as a beautiful main course. Bret recommends using dry-pack scallops and also removing the tough muscle before cooking. He suggests making the salsa early in the day to allow the flavors to blend. I agree. This makes a delicious and elegant combination.

For the salsa:

½	teaspoon lime zest
2	tablespoons fresh lime juice
1	tablespoon extra-virgin olive oil
1	teaspoon finely chopped fresh ginger
⅛	teaspoon cayenne pepper
2	cups jarred mango in ¼-inch cubes
¼	cup finely chopped shallots
2	tablespoons finely chopped fresh mint
	Salt and coarsely ground pepper to taste

For the scallops:

16	ounces sea scallops
1	tablespoon olive oil
1	teaspoon minced garlic
	Dash of salt and pepper
¼	cup fresh lemon juice
	Sprigs of fresh mint for garnish

▶ To make the salsa, stir together the lime zest, lime juice, oil, ginger, and cayenne pepper in a medium bowl. Add the remaining ingredients and stir until evenly combined.

▶ Prepare the scallops just before serving. Rinse them in cool water and pat dry. Heat the oil in a large skillet over medium-high heat. Stir in the garlic and then add the scallops in a single layer. Cook, turning as the scallops brown, for 2 minutes per side. Use a slotted spatula to remove the scallops before they are completely cooked and transfer to a bowl. Sprinkle lightly with salt and pepper.

▶ Pour the lemon juice into the liquid remaining in the pan; stir for 1 minute. Return the scallops to the skillet and stir to coat.

▶ To serve, arrange the scallops on plates and spoon the salsa on the side. Garnish with mint sprigs.

INDIAN-SPICED SALMON WITH PAPAYA-PINEAPPLE SALSA

Makes **4** servings

Garam is Hindi for "warm" or "hot," and the Indian blend of spices called garam masala creates an internal warmth when you eat this dish. The combination of crusty salmon and fruity salsa is the perfect marriage of spicy and sweet, and I thank my creative friend Karen Schmit for sharing her aromatic and flavorful recipe.

For the spice mixture:

1	teaspoon ground cumin
1	teaspoon paprika
1	teaspoon garam masala or curry powder
1	teaspoon ground cinnamon
½	teaspoon salt
½	teaspoon pepper

To complete the recipe:

4	(6-ounce) salmon fillets
1	tablespoon canola oil
	Sprigs of fresh cilantro for garnish
1½	cups Papaya-Pineapple Salsa (page 275)

❍ Stir together the spice mixture in a shallow, flat-bottomed bowl. Gently press the nonskin side of the salmon fillets into the mixture to lightly coat.

❍ Heat the oil in a large skillet over medium-high heat. Place the fillets skin-side down in the pan. Cook, turning once, for 4 minutes or until the desired doneness. (The spice-coated side will become brown and crusty.)

❍ Serve the salmon garnished with cilantro sprigs and accompanied by the fruit salsa.

CARIBBEAN SOLE WITH PLANTAINS AND PAPAYA-PINEAPPLE SALSA

Makes **4** servings

Plantains are simply a must in this dish, so choosing the right ones is important. At the market, look for those that are more brown than yellow, for they will be the sweetest and most tender. To peel, cut off both ends; then make three or four cuts down the length of the plantain peel, being careful not to cut into the flesh of the fruit. Then carefully remove the sections of the peel.

3	tablespoons unsalted butter, divided
2	plantains, halved horizontally, each half cut into ¼-inch-thick strips
	Pepper to taste
4	(4-ounce) sole fillets
	Salt to taste
1½	cups Papaya-Pineapple Salsa (page 275)
	Sprigs of fresh cilantro for garnish

❍ Melt 2 tablespoons butter in a large skillet over medium heat. Add the plantains, sprinkle with salt, and cook for 3 minutes per side or until lightly brown and tender. Transfer to a plate, cover, and set aside.

❍ To cook the sole, melt the remaining 1 tablespoon butter in the same skillet over medium-high heat. Place the sole in the pan, sprinkle with salt and pepper, and cook for 2 minutes per side or until it flakes easily when tested with a fork.

❍ For each serving, place 4 to 5 plantain strips on a dinner plate. Place one sole fillet over the strips and top with a heaping ⅓ cup of the salsa. Garnish with a cilantro sprig.

Baked and Broiled Dishes

BAKED FLOUNDER FLORENTINE WITH MUSTARD-DILL SAUCE

Makes **4** servings

Here's a quick and easy dish for the end of a busy day when you are hungry for a filling meal. If you have a few extra minutes, at the same time as the fish bakes, you can roast vegetables to provide a colorful companion dish. Toss sliced carrots, Brussels sprouts, or asparagus with a little olive oil, salt, and pepper. Bake for 10 minutes or until tender. Also prepare couscous.

For the fish:

4	(4-ounce) flounder fillets (or other white fish fillets such as cod, walleye, or orange roughy)
4	cups finely chopped salad spinach
2	eggs
¼	cup Italian-flavored dried bread crumbs
½	teaspoon ground nutmeg
⅛	teaspoon salt, or to taste
⅛	teaspoon pepper, or to taste
2	tomatoes, cut into ¼-inch slices
2	tablespoons freshly grated Parmesan cheese

For the sauce:

½	cup sour cream
1	tablespoon Dijon mustard
1	tablespoon snipped fresh dill or 1 teaspoon dried dill
1	teaspoon Tabasco sauce, to taste
	Ground white pepper, to taste

▶ Preheat the oven to 500°F.

▶ Lightly spray a baking sheet with nonstick cooking spray. Place the fish fillets on the prepared pan.

▶ Stir together the spinach, eggs, bread crumbs, nutmeg, salt, and pepper. Spread over the fish. Top each fillet with a row of 3 overlapping tomato slices. Sprinkle with the Parmesan cheese. Bake for 8 minutes or until the fish flakes easily when tested with a fork.

▶ Meanwhile, stir together the sauce ingredients in a small bowl. Spoon into a small serving bowl.

▶ To serve, transfer the fish with the tomato topping to plates, and serve the sauce on the side.

— TIP —

Dill, a sharply aromatic herb with a mild lemony taste, is commonly used to complement the flavors of fish and cucumbers. When chopping fresh dill, I like to use kitchen shears to cut the feathery dill tips, which is the flavorful part of the plant. Dried dill is unacceptable. Dill seeds, which have more concentrated flavor, are also used in some recipes (but none of the recipes in this book).

BROILED SALMON
WITH CHERRY SAUCE

Makes **4** servings

This recipe proves that sometimes less is indeed more. Although this simple dish calls for just a few ingredients, it always makes a big hit with guests. As the fish cooks, I like to prepare buttered couscous and haricots verts to serve as accompaniments.

For the fish:

4	(6-ounce) salmon fillets
	Olive oil for brushing
	Salt and pepper to taste

For the sauce:

1	(12-ounce) package frozen pitted red cherries
½	cup fresh orange juice
1	teaspoon cold water
1	teaspoon cornstarch
1	tablespoon raspberry vinegar
1	teaspoon extra-virgin olive oil

❍ Position the oven rack about 5 inches from the heating element and preheat the broiler.

❍ Lightly brush the salmon with oil. Place, skin-side down, on a baking sheet or broiler pan. Broil for 4 minutes or until the desired doneness. Sprinkle with salt and pepper.

❍ While the salmon is cooking, combine the cherries and orange juice in a small saucepan over high heat. Cook, stirring occasionally, for 3 minutes, and then reduce the heat to medium. Stir together the water and cornstarch in a small bowl until smooth. Add to the saucepan and stir for 2 minutes or until thickened to a maple-syrup consistency. Stir in the vinegar and oil. Remove the pan from the heat.

❍ To serve, transfer the salmon fillets to plates and top with the sauce.

TIP

To prevent lumping, mix cornstarch with a small amount of cold liquid to form a thin, smooth paste, and then stir it into a warm liquid near the end of the cooking time. Cook, stirring constantly, until the mixture is thickened. It's important to cook for at least 1½ minutes to remove the "cornstarchy" flavor. Cooking the thickened mixture too long or stirring too vigorously may cause the sauce to become thin.

Cornstarch gives a clear, glossy quality to a soup or sauce, while flour-thickening results in a cloudy appearance.

Broiled Salmon
with Cherry Sauce

GREEK SNAPPER WITH FETA CHEESE

Makes **4** servings

Served with buttered orzo, steamed broccoli, crusty bread—and a dry to slightly off-dry German or California Riesling—Greek Snapper with Feta Cheese becomes an elegant dinner menu perfect for serving to your most discriminating guests. You, as the host, can enjoy the dinner party, too. The fish and cooked sauce with feta cheese topping may be assembled in the baking dish and refrigerated for several hours. If chilled, add about 5 minutes to the baking time.

1	tablespoon olive oil
¼	cup finely chopped shallots
1	(14-ounce) can diced tomatoes with basil, garlic, and oregano
1	tablespoon finely chopped fresh oregano or 1 teaspoon dried oregano
½	teaspoon salt, or to taste
¼	teaspoon pepper, or to taste
4	(6-ounce) red snapper or tilapia fillets
½	cup coarsely crumbled peppercorn-feta or plain feta cheese
¼	cup coarsely chopped fresh flat-leaf parsley
3	tablespoons small (nonpareil) capers, drained and rinsed

❍ Preheat the oven to 450°F.

❍ Heat the oil in a medium sauté pan over medium heat. Add the shallots; cook, stirring occasionally, for 1 minute or until tender but not brown. Stir in the tomatoes, oregano, salt, and pepper. Increase the heat to medium-high and bring to a boil, stirring occasionally.

❍ Meanwhile, spray a 13 x 9-inch baking dish with olive oil cooking spray. Place the fish in the dish, skin-side down. Pour the tomato sauce mixture over and around the fish. Cover and bake for 8 minutes or until the fish flakes easily when tested with a fork.

❍ While the fish is cooking, toss together the feta cheese, parsley, and capers in a small bowl.

❍ To serve, use a spatula to transfer the fish and tomato sauce to plates and top with the feta cheese mixture.

BAKED SALMON WITH ROASTED GARLIC TOMATO SAUCE

Makes **4** servings

The magic of this recipe is in the blending of flavors when goat cheese melts into the tomato sauce. It's a great hearty dish for special-occasion entertaining. Try accompanying the salmon with the sturdy flavors of lemon-buttered orzo, lots of crusty bread, and a Caesar salad. And nothing pairs better with tomatoes and roasted garlic than Classic Italian Sangiovese (Chianti Classico).

1	(14-ounce) can diced tomatoes with roasted garlic
1	tablespoon finely chopped fresh rosemary or 1 teaspoon dried rosemary, crushed
¼	teaspoon red pepper flakes
¼	teaspoon salt
4	(6-ounce) salmon fillets
1	(4-ounce) package chèvre cheese, cut into 8 slices
	Pepper to taste
	Sprigs of fresh rosemary for garnish

- Preheat the oven to 500°F.

- Stir together the tomatoes, rosemary, red pepper flakes, and salt in a small bowl.

- Lightly coat a 13 x 9-inch baking pan with olive oil cooking spray. Place the salmon fillets in the dish, skin-side down. Pour the tomato sauce mixture over and around the fish. Top each fillet with 2 slices of the goat cheese. Sprinkle with pepper.

- Cover the pan with aluminum foil and bake for 10 minutes or until the salmon is the desired doneness.

- To serve, use a spatula to transfer the salmon with goat cheese to 4 dinner plates. Spoon the tomatoes and sauce around the fish. Garnish with rosemary sprigs.

BROILED SALMON AND TOMATOES WITH ROASTED BELL PEPPER VINAIGRETTE

Makes **4** servings

The buttery richness of salmon, an especially good source of healthful omega-3 oils, is balanced nicely with the acidity of the vinaigrette. You'll need only thick slices of crusty bread to make this simple, healthful meal complete.

For the vinaigrette:

¼	cup extra-virgin olive oil
¼	cup white wine vinegar
¼	cup jarred roasted red bell peppers, drained and finely chopped
1	tablespoon finely chopped fresh oregano or 1 teaspoon dried oregano
2	tablespoons minced shallot
1	teaspoon minced garlic
	Salt and pepper to taste

For the salmon:

4	(6-ounce) salmon fillets

For the tomatoes:

2	tomatoes, each cut into 4 slices
¼	cup dried bread crumbs
¼	cup freshly shredded Parmesan cheese
1	tablespoon plus 1 teaspoon extra-virgin olive oil
	Pepper to taste

- Position the oven rack about 5 inches from the heating element and preheat the broiler.

- Stir together the vinaigrette ingredients in a small bowl.

- Lightly coat a 13 x 9-inch baking pan with cooking spray. Place the salmon fillets, skin-side down, in the pan. Spoon ¼ cup of the vinaigrette over the salmon. Broil for 4 minutes or until the desired doneness. Remove from the oven and cover to keep warm.

- While the fish is cooking, place the tomatoes in a single layer on a baking sheet. Stir together the remaining tomato ingredients in a small bowl. Spread a layer of this mixture over the tomatoes and sprinkle with pepper. Broil for 30 seconds or until the tomatoes are softened and the bread crumbs are lightly browned.

- For each serving, place 1 salmon fillet and 2 tomato slices on a dinner plate. Spoon 2 tablespoons of the remaining vinaigrette over the salmon.

CREOLE SHRIMP WITH ASIAGO-TOPPED POLENTA

Makes **4** servings

This dish offers fusion flavors at their best. It melds the sunny flavors of Italy with the slightly spicy kick of Louisiana's cooking, which gives oomph to these shellfish served atop polenta—store-bought for ease—enriched with Asiago cheese. Accompany with a green salad tossed with creamy dressing.

1	(16-ounce) package cooked polenta, cut into 12 (½-inch) slices
½	cup finely shredded Asiago cheese
2	tablespoons unsalted butter
¾	cup finely chopped celery
½	green bell pepper, finely chopped
1	tablespoon finely chopped fresh thyme or 1 teaspoon dried thyme
2	teaspoons minced garlic
2	(10-ounce) cans diced tomatoes with green chilies
16	ounces medium (26 to 30 count) shrimp, peeled and deveined
	Salt to taste
2	green onions, thinly sliced

● Preheat the oven to 350°F. Lightly coat a large baking sheet with olive oil cooking spray. (Or line the baking sheet with foil.)

● Place the polenta slices on the baking sheet. Top each with some of the Asiago cheese. Bake for 12 minutes or until the cheese is slightly melted and the polenta is heated through. Cover to keep warm.

● While the polenta is baking, melt the butter in a large sauté pan over medium-high heat. Add the celery, bell pepper, thyme, and garlic. Cook, stirring frequently, for 3 minutes or until the celery and green pepper are softened. Stir in the tomatoes. When the liquid comes to a boil, reduce the heat to low and simmer for 3 minutes. Stir in the shrimp; cook for 2 minutes or until pink. Season with salt.

● To serve, place the polenta slices in shallow bowls; top with the shrimp mixture. Sprinkle with green onions.

COD WITH TOMATO-OLIVE SAUCE

Makes **4** servings

Combining your favorite salsa with olives and capers adds a Mediterranean flair to this mild and flaky fish. Best of all, the result is great flavor with little effort. I like to bake the fish in an attractive dish that can be brought to the table accompanied by bowls of rice or buttered new potatoes, along with sautéed zucchini or green beans tossed with extra-virgin olive oil.

4	(6-ounce, 1-inch-thick) cod fillets, skin removed
1	teaspoon dried oregano
¼	teaspoon pepper
1	cup chunky tomato salsa
⅓	cup pimiento-stuffed green olives, coarsely chopped
1	tablespoon small (nonpareil) capers, drained and rinsed
¼	cup coarsely chopped fresh cilantro

● Preheat the oven to 450°F.

● Lightly coat a 13 x 9-inch baking dish with olive oil cooking spray. Arrange the cod in a single layer in the dish; sprinkle with oregano and pepper.

◗ Stir together the salsa, olives, and capers in a medium bowl; spoon over the fish.

◗ Cover the baking dish with foil. Bake for 8 minutes or until the fish flakes when tested with a fork. Sprinkle with cilantro.

MAHI-MAHI WITH TOMATILLO SAUCE
Makes **4** servings

Tomatillos offer the flavors of lemons, apples, and herbs. This delicious combination pairs nicely with spinach noodles for a dish that reminds me of happy times in sunny Mexico.

For the fish:

4	(6-ounce) skinless mahi-mahi fillets (or grouper or red snapper fillets), about ¾ inch thick
	Olive oil for brushing
	Salt and pepper to taste

For the sauce:

8	ounces tomatillos, quartered
4	green onions, cut into 1-inch lengths
½	cup fresh cilantro sprigs
¼	cup fresh flat-leaf parsley sprigs
1	jalapeño chili, or more to taste, seeded and coarsely chopped
2	tablespoons fresh lemon juice
3	garlic cloves or 1½ teaspoons minced garlic
¼	cup water
¼	cup tequila
¼	cup olive oil
1	tablespoon finely chopped fresh oregano
2	teaspoons ground cumin
	Salt and pepper to taste

To complete the recipe:

Sliced black olives for garnish

◗ Position the oven rack about 5 inches from the heating element and preheat the broiler.

◗ Coat a broiler pan with nonstick cooking spray. Place the fish on the broiler pan and brush the tops with olive oil. Season with salt and pepper. Broil for 5 minutes or until the fish flakes when tested with a fork. Remove from the oven and cover to keep warm.

◗ While the fish is broiling, process all the sauce ingredients, except the salt and pepper, in a blender until smooth (though it will still have a "pulpy" texture). Transfer the mixture to a medium saucepan. Bring to a boil over high heat; reduce the heat to medium-high and cook, stirring frequently, for 2 minutes or until slightly thickened. Season with salt and pepper.

◗ To serve, transfer the fish to dinner plates, top with the tomatillo sauce, and garnish with sliced olives.

TIP

Tomatillos resemble small green tomatoes in size and shape, but they also have a thin parchmentlike covering, which should be removed before cooking. You'll find tomatillos in Latin American markets and in some supermarkets. Choose firm fruit with tight-fitting husks, and store in the refrigerator for up to a month. Canned tomatillos can be substituted in most recipes; drain before using.

Beef
and Pork

COOKING MEAT in 15 minutes goes well beyond a steak on the grill or under the broiler. You don't need to settle for a plain, unadorned piece of beef just because your time is limited.

In many countries, meat is primarily used as a flavoring, not the main event. So in this chapter, you will find it in smaller quantities in many recipes, combined with a variety of other ingredients, to which meat adds protein and also the hearty flavor that people love.

To save time, most supermarkets sell beef in ready-to-cook strips. This may be round steak, flank steak, top round, sirloin, or tenderloin, any of which work well for stir-fries. Keep in mind that the butcher will slice any cut you wish into strips just the right size for your recipe. His skills and sharp knife accomplish the task quickly. If you choose to do this yourself, you'll find that it's easier to make clean cuts if the beef is partially frozen. Flank steak is a good choice because it is thin. Also, it's best to slice against the grain (on a diagonal) to break down any tough fibers.

Ground beef comes with many different labels in the supermarket. The main difference is the amount of fat in the ground meat, which ranges from 73 percent lean (ground beef) to 80 percent lean (ground chuck) to 85 percent lean (ground sirloin) to 90 percent lean (ground round). They are all equally tender, but regular ground beef, because it has more fat, is likely to be more juicy than ground round. And the higher fat content also means that regular ground beef will cook down more than ground round. Most people choose the leaner ground beefs, which I usually prefer when the meat is to be combined with other ingredients, as in Scrambled Eggs and Beef Burritos (page 175). (If necessary after cooking, drain the excess fat before adding the other ingredients.) But ground chuck makes the best choice for juicy hamburgers, as in Chipotle Burgers (page 178).

It's advisable to keep fresh uncooked meat in the original wrapping placed on a dish in the refrigerator for up to two days. Or it should be wrapped in plastic-backed freezer paper, sealed with freezer tape, and stored in the freezer for up to three months. Frozen meat should be placed in a dish and defrosted in the refrigerator in its freezer wrapping.

Beef from a reputable butcher, which has been properly stored, does not need to be cooked all the way through, a benefit when it comes to quick cooking. Today there is less concern than in past years regarding the safety of pork, but it's still recommended that it be cooked thoroughly. Yet overcooking results in gray, dry meat.

Other meats used in this chapter include pancetta, which is the Italian equivalent of bacon. It is cured with salt and spices but not smoked, and is chewier, leaner, and saltier than the familiar bacon. The Italians often use it for seasoning. Here, too, a small amount is all it takes to impart its unique flavor to Pancetta-Pea Soup (page 171) and Ragu Bolognese (page 184).

Prosciutto, an Italian delicacy, is a nonsmoked ham

that has been seasoned, salt-cured, and air-dried. It has a firm, dense texture and is usually sold in very thin slices that are ready to eat without cooking, as in the Fava Bean Salad with Prosciutto and Pecorino (page 166). It's often used as a flavoring in cooked dishes but should be added toward the end because prolonged heat will toughen it.

There are thousands of different types of sausages, some already cooked, others not. Here, I've used some that I have grown to love in markets and restaurants during my travels. You'll find kielbasa, a smoked Polish sausage usually made of pork; andouille sausage, used in the Sausage Jambalaya (page 194) because it is a specialty of Cajun cooking; and chorizo, a highly sea-soned, coarsely ground pork sausage flavored with gar-lic, chili powder, and other spices, and widely used in both Mexican and Spanish dishes, such as the Spanish Chorizo Frittata (page 204).

In some of the most-quick-to-prepare recipes, I've called upon deli favorites—pepperoni, salami, corned beef, and ham. You'll also find that Chinese barbecued pork, found in most Asian markets, adds character to rice noodles.

For an elegant entertaining dish, keep in mind Filet Mignon with Sherried Mushrooms (page 203), which is hard to beat when serving discriminating guests who also appreciate fine red wine.

Grilled Steak and Vegetable Salad
with Fresh Herb Vinaigrette

GRILLED STEAK AND VEGETABLE SALAD WITH FRESH HERB VINAIGRETTE

Makes **4** servings

All the colorful vegetables and sliced strips of steak make a feast for the eyes, as well as the palate. The salad perfumes each bite with the fresh, summery aromas of fresh herbs. Toss the ingredients together quickly just before serving because refrigeration seems to dull the herbs' vibrant flavors and the olive oil becomes congealed.

For the meat:

16	ounces beef flank steak
	Olive oil for brushing

For the vinaigrette:

1/3	cup red wine vinegar
3	tablespoons extra-virgin olive oil
2	tablespoons fresh lemon juice
3	tablespoons finely chopped fresh thyme
3	tablespoons finely chopped fresh oregano
3	tablespoons finely chopped fresh basil
2	tablespoons sugar
1	teaspoon minced garlic
1/2	teaspoon salt, or to taste
1/4	teaspoon pepper, or to taste

For the vegetables:

1	medium red onion, cut into 1/2-inch wedges
3	plum tomatoes, cut into 1/2-inch wedges
1	green bell pepper, cut into 1/4-inch strips
1	cup frozen corn kernels, thawed

▶ Heat a stovetop grill pan over high heat. Lightly brush both sides of the steak with oil. Reduce the heat to medium-high; cook for 6 minutes per side for medium-rare doneness. (Or cook the steak on an outdoor grill for cooking over medium-hot charcoal or moderate heat for gas.) Slice the steak diagonally across the grain into 1/4-inch slices.

▶ While the steak is cooking, whisk together all the vinaigrette ingredients in a small bowl.

▶ Combine the steak and vegetables in a large bowl. Add the vinaigrette and toss. Serve immediately while warm.

TIP

To store fresh herbs: Trim the stem ends, wrap them with a moist paper towel, put in sealed plastic bags, and refrigerate. Or place the bunch, stems down, in a glass of water and cover with a plastic bag, securing the bag to the glass with a rubber band; change the water every two days. The herbs will last for about a week (it's best to use them in a few days). Just before using, wash fresh herbs in cool water and dry with paper towels or in a salad spinner.

SOBA NOODLE AND STEAK SALAD

Makes **4** servings

Fusion cooking at its best: Americans love their steak just as Asians love their soba noodles. Especially when deeply flavored with a teriyaki-hoisin vinaigrette, this dish combines the best of both worlds on a salad plate.

For the meat:

16	ounces boneless beef sirloin steak (½ to ¾ inches thick)
	Canola oil for brushing

For the salad:

8	ounces soba (buckwheat) noodles
1	tablespoon canola oil
1	(4-ounce) package shiitake mushrooms, caps sliced, stems removed and discarded
½	cup coarsely chopped red onion
1	(9-ounce) package salad spinach, coarsely shredded
¼	cup water
⅔	cup Teriyaki Vinaigrette (page 271), divided

● Heat a stovetop grill pan over high heat. Brush both sides of the steak with oil. Reduce the heat to medium-high; cook for 5 minutes per side or until the desired doneness. (Or cook the steak on an outdoor grill: Position the grill rack 4 to 5 inches from the heat, and cook on medium-hot.)

● Meanwhile, cook the noodles according to package instructions.

● Heat the oil in a large sauté pan over medium-high heat. Add the mushrooms and onion; cook, stirring occasionally, for 3 minutes or until nearly tender.

Reduce the heat to medium-low. Add the spinach and water; cover and cook for 3 minutes or until the spinach is wilted. Remove the pan from the heat.

● When ready to serve, place the steak on a cutting board and cut across the grain into ¼-inch slices.

● When the noodles are done, drain well. Stir them into the spinach and mushrooms in the sauté pan. Add ⅓ cup vinaigrette and toss.

● To serve, transfer the noodle mixture to 4 shallow bowls. Top with the steak slices and drizzle with the remaining ⅓ cup vinaigrette.

MEXICAN BEEF AND BEAN SALAD WITH MESQUITE TOMATO DRESSING

Makes **4** servings

Here's a sturdy salad that can be made early in the day for dinner on a busy weekend. Serve a basket of corn muffins from your favorite bakery, and your easygoing meal is complete. To offer as a side dish or for vegetarians, simply leave out the beef. The oranges and smoky-flavored dressing are the secrets to its surprising and satisfying flavors.

For the salad:

1	tablespoon canola oil
8	ounces boneless beef sirloin, thinly sliced

For the dressing:

3	tablespoons ketchup
3	tablespoons canola oil
2	tablespoons red wine vinegar

1   tablespoon minced fresh oregano or
       ½ teaspoon dried oregano

½   teaspoon Worcestershire sauce

¼   teaspoon mesquite liquid smoke, or to taste
       Salt and pepper to taste

To complete the salad:

1   (15-ounce) can pinto beans, drained and
       rinsed

1   large orange, coarsely chopped

1   avocado, coarsely chopped

½   cup thinly sliced red onion

½   cup coarsely chopped fresh cilantro

● Heat the oil in a medium skillet over medium-high heat. Add the beef; cook, stirring occasionally, for 3 minutes or until thoroughly cooked. Transfer to a plate and set aside to cool slightly.

● Whisk together the dressing ingredients in a large bowl. Add the cooked beef and the remaining salad ingredients; toss gently.

BLT SALAD

Makes **4** servings

This salad changes the proportions of the classic sandwich, pumping up the volume of the vegetables while offering just enough bacon and bread to add their flavor and crunch.

For the meat:

4   strips bacon

For the dressing:

¼   cup mayonnaise

2   tablespoons fresh lemon juice

½   teaspoon Dijon mustard

½   teaspoon honey

2   teaspoons finely chopped fresh thyme or
       ½ teaspoon dried thyme

To complete the recipe:

2   teaspoons olive oil

4   slices whole-wheat bread, cut into 1-inch
       squares

½   teaspoon minced garlic

5   cups torn romaine lettuce

1   cup grape tomatoes

1   small red onion, thinly sliced

● Cook the bacon in a small nonstick skillet over medium heat, turning as needed, for 5 minutes or until crisp. (Or place the bacon on a triple layer of paper towels on a microwave-safe plate, and cover with a double layer of towels. Microwave on HIGH for 2 minutes. Continue to microwave for 1-minute intervals until done.) Transfer to a paper-towel-lined plate. Crumble when cool.

● While the bacon is cooking, whisk together the dressing ingredients in a small bowl.

● Pour off the fat remaining in the skillet and add the oil. Return the pan to medium-high heat. Add the bread; stir for 5 minutes or until lightly browned. Add the garlic; stir for 1 more minute or until the bread is crispy. Transfer to a plate. (The bread will continue to become crisper as it cools.)

● Toss the lettuce, tomatoes, onion, and bread cubes in a large salad bowl. Add the dressing and toss again. Sprinkle with bacon.

FAVA BEAN SALAD WITH PROSCIUTTO AND PECORINO

Makes **4** servings

Beans and ham, a classic combination in Spain, inspired this recipe. I love the addition of manchego cheese, which is made from sheep's milk and has a slightly nutty flavor. Or try mahon, a Spanish cow's milk cheese with a buttery taste. Rather than Spanish ham, I've substituted prosciutto, the more readily available Italian version of air-cured ham. These ingredients are a good match for the peppery flavor of arugula.

For the dressing:

3	tablespoons extra-virgin olive oil
1	teaspoon lemon zest
2	tablespoons fresh lemon juice
2	tablespoons finely chopped fresh flat-leaf parsley
½	teaspoon minced garlic
	Salt and pepper to taste

For the salad:

1	(19-ounce) can fava beans, drained and rinsed
½	red bell pepper, finely chopped
2	tablespoons finely chopped red onion
2	cups arugula leaves
4	very thin slices (2 ounces) prosciutto
8	very thin slices manchego cheese

▶ Whisk together the dressing ingredients in a medium bowl. Stir in the beans, bell pepper, and onion.

▶ To assemble each salad, arrange a layer of arugula leaves on a plate. Add a mound of the bean mixture. Top with 1 slice of prosciutto and 2 shaved slices of cheese.

─── TIP ───

Use a sharp vegetable peeler to shave very thin slices of firm cheeses.

Fava Bean Salad with
Prosciutto and Pecorino

Taco Salad
with Lime Vinaigrette

TACO SALAD
WITH LIME VINAIGRETTE

Makes **4** servings

Here's a lighter, fresher version of the ever-popular taco salad. For the best flavor, be sure to use good-quality extra-virgin olive oil for the vinaigrette.

For the meat:

16	ounces extra-lean ground beef
½	cup coarsely chopped yellow onion

For the vinaigrette:

3	tablespoons extra-virgin olive oil
2	tablespoons fresh lime juice
1	teaspoon minced garlic
¼	teaspoon ground cumin
	Salt and pepper to taste

To complete the recipe:

½	cup taco sauce
	Salt and pepper to taste
2	romaine hearts, coarsely shredded
1	large tomato, cut into ½-inch cubes
2	cups coarsely crumbled yellow corn tortilla chips
½	cup finely shredded sharp Cheddar cheese
½	cup coarsely chopped fresh cilantro

○ Cook the ground beef and onion in a large sauté pan over medium-high heat, occasionally breaking the beef into small chunks as it cooks, for 5 minutes or until the beef is lightly browned.

○ Meanwhile, whisk together the vinaigrette ingredients in a small bowl.

○ Stir the taco sauce into the beef. Reduce the heat to low and simmer, stirring occasionally, for 2 minutes. Season with salt and pepper. Remove from the heat and cover to keep warm.

○ Toss the romaine and tomato with the vinaigrette in a large bowl. Divide among 4 salad bowls. Top with the warm meat mixture, tortilla chips, cheese, and cilantro.

⊢ TIP ⊣

To squeeze more juice from citrus fruits, first bring them to room temperature or microwave chilled fruit (first pierce the fruit skin with a fork or knife) for 30 seconds on HIGH. Then roll the fruit on the kitchen counter, pressing hard with the palm of your hand, to break the inner membranes.

WARM POTATO SALAD WITH BACON

Makes **4** servings

Small fingerling potatoes cook quickly, making them perfect for a 15-Minute recipe. This warm salad, hearty with bits of bacon and robustly seasoned with mustard and garlic, will beckon your family to the table as the irresistible aroma drifts their way.

For the vinaigrette:

¼	cup extra-virgin olive oil
¼	cup red wine vinegar
1	teaspoon Dijon mustard
1	teaspoon minced garlic
½	teaspoon pepper, or to taste
¼	teaspoon salt, or to taste

For the salad:

16	ounces small (3-inch) fingerling potatoes, cut into thirds
8	strips bacon
6	cups mesclun (mixed baby greens)
2	cups Garlic Croutons (page 280)

▶ Fill a medium saucepan with salted water. Bring to a boil over high heat.

▶ Meanwhile, whisk together all the vinaigrette ingredients in a large bowl.

▶ When the pan of water comes to a boil, add the potatoes, reduce the heat to medium, and simmer for 10 minutes or until the potatoes are tender.

▶ While the potatoes are cooking, cook the bacon in a large nonstick skillet over medium heat, turning as needed, for 12 minutes or until crisp. (Or place the bacon,

4 strips at a time, on a triple layer of paper towels on a microwave-safe plate, and cover with a double layer of towels. Microwave on HIGH for 2 minutes. Continue to microwave for 1-minute intervals until done.) Transfer to a paper-towel-lined plate. Tear into 1-inch pieces when cool.

▶ When the potatoes are done, drain well. Add the warm potatoes and the bacon to the vinaigrette and toss. Add the greens and croutons; toss again. Serve warm.

THAI BEEF SALAD

Makes **4** servings

There's no need to turn on the stove, and this satisfying, colorful salad can be on the table in minutes. Because of the distinctive flavors, I like to serve it in deep, Asian-style bowls with chopsticks rather than forks.

For the dressing:

	Zest of 1 lime
¼	cup fresh lime juice
3	tablespoons dark (Asian) sesame oil
2	tablespoons Thai fish sauce (nam pla)
1	tablespoon canola oil
	Salt and pepper to taste

For the salad:

8	ounces thinly sliced deli roast beef, cut into ½-inch strips
4	cups finely sliced romaine lettuce
2	carrots, finely shredded
4	green onions, thinly sliced

▶ Whisk together the dressing ingredients in a small bowl.

▶ Toss together the salad ingredients in a large bowl. Add the dressing and toss again.

Soups

PANCETTA-PEA SOUP

Makes **4** servings (8 cups)

The Italians use risotto in making this soup, but for the 15-Minute cook, it's a perfect destination for leftover cooked white rice. If you don't have fresh mint, substitute fresh flat-leaf parsley.

1	tablespoon unsalted butter
1	tablespoon olive oil
4	ounces pancetta, cut into ½-inch pieces
4	green onions, finely chopped
1	(49-ounce) can reduced-sodium chicken broth
2½	cups frozen baby peas
2	cups cooked white rice
3	tablespoons finely chopped fresh mint
⅛	teaspoon salt, or to taste
⅛	teaspoon pepper, or to taste
	Freshly grated Parmesan cheese for garnish

❍ Melt the butter with the oil in a Dutch oven over medium-high heat. Add the pancetta and green onions; cook, stirring constantly, for 4 minutes or until the pancetta is cooked but not browned.

❍ Stir in the chicken broth, peas, and rice. Increase the heat to high and cook for 3 minutes or until the peas are thawed and the soup is heated through. Remove the pan from the heat; stir in the mint and season with salt and pepper.

❍ Garnish the servings with Parmesan cheese.

KIELBASA AND POTATO SOUP

Makes **4** servings (8½ cups)

This homey soup is comfort in a bowl, particularly welcome on a chilly winter day. Kielbasa is a smoked Polish sausage usually made of pork. For this soup, be sure to buy it precooked.

1	(49-ounce) can reduced-sodium chicken broth
2	pounds red-skinned potatoes, cut into ¾-inch cubes (3 cups)
1	bay leaf
1	tablespoon unsalted butter
8	ounces precooked kielbasa sausage, cut into ¼-inch slices
¼	cup coarsely chopped yellow onion
1	bunch kale, stems removed and leaves coarsely chopped (about 4 cups)
	Salt and pepper to taste

❍ Bring the chicken broth, potatoes, and bay leaf to a boil in a Dutch oven over high heat. Reduce the heat to low; cover and simmer for 5 minutes or until the potatoes are tender.

❍ Meanwhile, melt the butter in a medium skillet over medium-high heat. Add the sausage and onion; cook, stirring frequently, for 4 minutes or until lightly browned.

❍ Stir the sausage mixture and kale into the Dutch oven. Reduce the heat to medium; cover and simmer for 5 minutes or until the kale is tender. Remove and discard the bay leaf. Season with salt and pepper to taste.

VIETNAMESE BEEF SOUP

Makes **4** servings (4 cups)

They call it *pho,* and as you walk down the streets in Vietnam, its aroma urges you to find the source, which most often is just a "pavement" restaurant with low tables and tiny stools—or simply a sidewalk vendor with soup stock kept warm over a tiny flame and ingredients and serving utensils in baskets. This comfort food is a balanced meal in a bowl, and it costs you well under a dollar. It's cheap, filling, yet seductively delicious.

In Vietnam, a bowl of *pho* begins the day before you eat it. The process is a slow simmering of beef shinbones, oxtails, and scraps of meat; the herbs added to the pot may be a family secret. At the time you eat the soup, you personalize the flavors by adding a squeeze of lime, a dash of chilies or fish sauce, and a sprinkling of fresh cilantro or mint leaves. Then you pull the noodles up with your chopsticks and slurp them into your mouth.

This speedy version multiplies easily and is wonderful for an informal gathering. Supply everyone with a large soup bowl filled with noodles, broth, and meat. Show your guests how to add their choice of toppings and flavorings.

4	ounces thin rice noodles
3	(14-ounce) cans reduced-sodium beef broth
1	medium yellow onion, thinly sliced
2	(½-inch) slices peeled fresh ginger
1	tablespoon Asian fish sauce, or to taste
2	garlic cloves, peeled and halved
1	cinnamon stick
1	star anise
½	teaspoon whole cloves
4	leaves romaine lettuce, thinly sliced
1	cup fresh bean sprouts
3	green onions, diagonally cut into 1-inch slices
½	cup fresh cilantro leaves
2	small red chilies, very finely chopped
1	lime, cut into 8 wedges
8	ounces beef flank steak, very thinly sliced and cut into 3 x ½-inch strips

▶ Cook the noodles according to package instructions.

▶ Meanwhile, combine the beef broth, onion, ginger, fish sauce, garlic, cinnamon, anise, and cloves in a Dutch oven. Bring to a boil over high heat. Reduce the heat to low, cover, and simmer for 10 minutes.

▶ During this time, put the lettuce, bean sprouts, green onions, cilantro, chilies, and lime wedges into bowls for serving.

▶ Strain the broth through a sieve into a large bowl. (Discard the solids.) Return the broth to the Dutch oven and bring to a boil. Stir in the beef; the hot broth will cook the slices in less than 1 minute.

▶ Drain the noodles and use kitchen shears to randomly cut them into about 4-inch lengths.

▶ Use tongs to transfer the noodles and steak slices into deep bowls. Top with broth.

▶ Encourage your guests to mound their soup servings with generous amounts of lettuce, green onions, cilantro, a dash of chilies, and a squeeze of lime juice.

Vietnamese Beef Soup

SPICY SAUSAGE SOUP

Makes **4** servings

Look for cans of chipotle chilies in adobo sauce in the Mexican section of your supermarket. It's the peppers' distinctive smoky heat that makes this full-flavored soup a winner, and you may want to add two chilies for a bit more fire. Precooked sausage, which speeds up preparation time, is found in bags in both the freezer and refrigerated meat sections of most supermarkets.

1	tablespoon canola oil
1	green bell pepper, coarsely chopped
½	cup coarsely chopped onion
1½	teaspoons minced garlic
1	(14-ounce) can chicken broth
1	(15-ounce) can diced tomatoes with green chilies
1	(15-ounce) can black beans, drained and rinsed
2	precooked sausages, cut into ¼-inch slices
1	chipotle chili in adobo sauce (from a 7-ounce can), seeds removed, or to taste
1	tablespoon finely chopped fresh oregano or 1 teaspoon dried oregano
½	teaspoon ground cumin
¼	teaspoon salt, or to taste
¼	teaspoon pepper, or to taste

▶ Heat the oil in a Dutch oven or large pot over medium-high heat. Add the bell pepper, onion, and garlic; cook, stirring occasionally, for 5 minutes or until the peppers begin to soften.

▶ Stir in the remaining ingredients. Increase the heat to high. When the liquid comes to a boil, reduce the heat to low. Cover and simmer for 5 minutes.

HUNGARIAN BEEF PAPRIKA STEW

Makes **4** servings

This stew features the traditional flavors of Hungary, especially if you season the dish with sweet Hungarian paprika, which is available in most supermarkets. Hungarians are fond of dumplings, but for quick preparation, this dish is delicious served with wide egg noodles that cook while the stew simmers on the stove.

12	ounces wide egg noodles
1	tablespoon olive oil
1	large onion, coarsely chopped
1	green bell pepper, coarsely chopped
16	ounces lean ground beef
1	(14-ounce) can diced tomatoes
½	cup reduced-sodium beef broth
2	teaspoons sweet Hungarian paprika
½	teaspoon caraway seeds
½	teaspoon dried marjoram
½	teaspoon salt, or to taste
⅛	teaspoon pepper, or to taste
	Sour cream for garnish

▶ Cook the noodles according to package instructions.

▶ Meanwhile, heat the oil in a large sauté pan over medium-high heat. Add the onion and bell pepper; cook, stirring occasionally to break up the ground beef for 3 minutes. Add the ground beef; continue to cook, stirring occasionally, for 5 more minutes or until it is lightly browned and the vegetables are tender.

▶ Stir in the remaining ingredients. When the liquid comes to a boil, reduce the heat to low; simmer for 5 minutes to allow the flavors to blend.

When the noodles are done, drain well. Spoon the noodles into shallow bowls and top with the meat mixture. Stir gently to combine. Garnish with sour cream.

Sandwiches and Tortillas

SCRAMBLED EGGS AND BEEF BURRITOS

Makes **4** servings

This meaty burrito steps up to the plate as a one-dish meal for breakfast, lunch, or brunch. The orange-cilantro sauce offers a citrusy flavor dimension to complement the burrito's spicy filling.

For the meat:

16	ounces extra-lean ground beef
1	red bell pepper, finely chopped
1/2	cup finely chopped onion
2	teaspoons chipotle chili powder or ancho chili powder
1	teaspoon minced garlic
1	teaspoon ground cumin
1/2	teaspoon salt, or to taste

For the eggs and tortillas:

6	eggs
2	tablespoons cold water
1/4	teaspoon salt, or to taste
1	tablespoon olive oil
1/4	cup finely chopped fresh cilantro
4	(10-inch) spinach or tomato flour tortillas

For the cilantro cream:

1/2	cup sour cream
1	tablespoon fresh orange juice
1/2	teaspoon grated orange rind
1	tablespoon finely chopped cilantro

Combine all the meat ingredients in a large skillet over medium-high heat. Cook, stirring frequently, for 8 minutes or until the beef is thoroughly cooked and the vegetables are very tender.

Meanwhile, whisk together the eggs, water, and salt in a medium bowl just until blended. Heat the oil in a large nonstick skillet over medium heat. Add the egg mixture; cook, stirring frequently, for 2 minutes or until the eggs are scrambled and cooked, but still moist.

Add the eggs and cilantro to the beef mixture in the skillet; stir gently to combine.

Stack the tortillas between 2 paper towels. Microwave on HIGH for 1 minute or until moist and warm.

Meanwhile, stir together all the cilantro cream ingredients in a small bowl.

To assemble each burrito, spoon about 1 cup of the beef filling in a row across the center of a tortilla; spoon about 2 tablespoons of the cilantro cream over the beef filling. Fold the right and left sides of the tortilla over the filling. Fold the bottom edge up over the filling and roll up; slice diagonally in half.

ITALIAN PEPPERONI PANINI

Makes **4** servings

I always enjoy panini in Italy, where they sustain me through museum and sightseeing jaunts. I join the midday crowds of locals in Rome, where it is the fashion to stand at the counter of tiny espresso bars to lunch on these satisfying grilled sandwiches, which offer a fistful of Italian flavors. Now panini have overtaken America, just as they've done for ages on their native turf. The ingredients pair best with assertive bread that becomes toothsome and crusty after toasting. Accompany the sandwiches with pepperoncini.

4	Italian ciabatta rolls (about 4 x 4 inches)
½	cup Tapenade (page 277)
12	thin slices pepperoni
4	thin slices provolone cheese
8	thin tomato slices
	About 16 fresh basil leaves
	Olive oil for brushing

❍ Slice off the domed tops of the ciabatta, and cut each roll into 2 (½-inch-thick) slices. (Save the removed portions of the bread for snacking.)

❍ For one sandwich, spread the inside of each ciabatta roll with 1 tablespoon Tapenade. On the bottom slice, arrange 3 slices of pepperoni, 1 slice of cheese, and 2 tomato slices. Top with about 4 basil leaves. Close the sandwich, olive-spread-side down. Lightly brush both sides of the sandwich with oil.

❍ Toast the sandwiches in a preheated panini grill for 3 minutes or until the bread is golden brown and the cheese is melted.

❍ Or toast both sides of the sandwiches in a skillet or stovetop grill pan over medium heat. Place another heavy skillet, bottom down, on top of the sandwiches and press gently for even browning.

❍ Depending on the size of your panini grill or skillet, you may need to toast the sandwiches in two batches.

> ——— **TIP** ———
>
> Pepperoncini are thin chili peppers usually sold pickled. The slightly sweet flavor can range from medium to medium-hot. They make great sandwich accompaniments.

MUFFULETTA SANDWICHES

Makes **4** servings

This robust sandwich comes straight from New Orleans, where the muffuletta was invented and still reigns as the city's signature sandwich. The olive salad layer, which sets this apart from all other sandwiches, moistens the bread and offers an enticingly sharp and salty flavor. Traditionally, muffulettas are made with a loaf of crusty Italian bread that's hollowed out to accommodate the filling. For this sandwich, I've used a chewy ciabatta loaf, which you can find in most artisan bread shops.

For the olive salad:

½	cup pitted kalamata olives, coarsely chopped
½	cup pimiento-stuffed green olives, coarsely chopped

1/3	cup extra-virgin olive oil
2	tablespoons red wine vinegar
2	teaspoons minced garlic
1	teaspoon dried oregano

For the sandwich:

1	Italian ciabatta loaf (about 14 x 5 inches), cut in half lengthwise
2	tablespoons extra-virgin olive oil
8	ounces thinly sliced provolone cheese
4	ounces thinly sliced Genoa salami
4	ounces thinly sliced smoked ham
1/2	cup pickled mild banana pepper rings

● Combine all the olive salad ingredients in a medium bowl.

● Brush the outside bottom and top of the ciabatta loaf with oil. Place the bread, cut sides up, on a cutting board. Spread the olive salad over the bottom half of the bread; top with layers of half of the cheese slices and all of the salami, ham, and pepper rings. Top with the remaining cheese slices. Cover with the top of the ciabatta, cut-side down. Slice the assembled loaf into 4 equal sandwiches.

● Toast the sandwiches in a preheated panini grill for 3 minutes or until the bread is golden brown, the cheese is melted, and the sandwich is heated through.

● Or toast the sandwiches in a large skillet or stovetop grill pan over medium heat. Place another heavy skillet, bottom down, on top of the sandwiches and press gently for even browning.

● Depending on the size of your panini grill or skillet, you may need to toast the sandwiches in two batches.

PORK CARNITAS TACOS

Makes **4** servings

In Mexico, *carnitas* means "little meats"—and it's also the name of the traditional dish of small bits of pork fried in pork fat until well browned. Here, sautéed pork is combined with potatoes and mushrooms to make a complete meal in a taco. Use mild, medium, or hot salsa to suit your desire for heat.

3	tablespoons canola oil, divided
12	ounces boneless pork loin, cut into 1 x 1/4-inch strips
	Salt and pepper to taste
1	cup frozen hash browns (shredded potatoes)
1	cup coarsely chopped mushrooms
1/2	cup coarsely chopped onion
1	teaspoon minced garlic
1	cup chunky tomato salsa
8	taco shells
1/2	cup finely shredded Cheddar cheese

● Heat 1 tablespoon oil in a large skillet over medium-high heat. Add the pork; cook, stirring occasionally, for 3 minutes or until thoroughly cooked and nicely browned. Sprinkle lightly with salt and pepper.

● While the pork is cooking, heat the remaining 2 tablespoons oil in a large skillet over medium-high heat. Add the potatoes, mushrooms, onion, and garlic; cook, stirring occasionally, for 5 minutes or until tender. Stir in the pork and salsa; stir for 1 minute to warm.

● Spoon the mixture into the taco shells and top the filling with cheese.

CHIPOTLE BURGERS

Makes **4** servings

These beef patties are infused with potent seasoning and topped with layers of tasty condiments. Cook them indoors on a stovetop grill or outside on a gas or charcoal grill. You can use lean ground sirloin or ground round if you'd like, but 73 percent lean ground beef, with its additional fat, will make more juicy burgers.

16	ounces ground beef
½	cup finely chopped onion
2	chipotle chilies in adobo sauce (from a 7-ounce can), seeds removed, finely chopped; 1 tablespoon sauce reserved
½	teaspoon salt
4	hamburger buns, halved horizontally
½	cup tomato salsa plus extra for accompaniment
4	(⅜-inch) tomato slices
2	cups finely shredded romaine lettuce
½	cup Guacamole (page 272)

○ Prepare the outdoor grill for cooking over medium-hot charcoal or moderate heat for gas (if using).

○ Mix together the beef, onion, chilies with sauce, and salt in a medium bowl. Form into 4 (4 ½-inch, ¾-inch-thick) patties.

○ To cook on a stovetop grill pan, heat the pan over high heat. Reduce the heat to medium-high; cook the burgers for 7 minutes, turning once, for medium-rare. (For outdoor charcoal or gas grills, grill the burgers on a lightly oiled grill rack for 4 minutes, turning once for medium-rare.) Or cook longer, if desired.

○ Meanwhile, toast the buns.

○ To assemble each burger, spread 2 tablespoons salsa on the cut side of the bun bottom. Top with a cooked patty, tomato slice, and ½ cup lettuce. Spread the cut side of the bun top with 2 tablespoons guacamole. Close the buns, spread-side down.

CORNED BEEF ON RYE WITH SAUERKRAUT

Makes **4** servings

Here's a twist on the classic deli favorite. What's new? Easy homemade dressing, sautéed onions, and pepper Jack cheese. Serve the warm sandwiches with potato salad or coleslaw and dill pickles to carry out the deli theme.

For the dressing:

½	cup mayonnaise
1	tablespoon finely chopped fresh flat-leaf parsley
2	teaspoons ketchup
2	teaspoons finely chopped onion
¼	teaspoon Worcestershire sauce

For the sandwiches:

1	tablespoon canola oil
3	cups thinly sliced onion
1	(8-ounce) jar sauerkraut, drained
8	slices pumpernickel bread
8	ounces shaved deli corned beef
4	thick slices pepper Jack cheese
2	tablespoons unsalted butter

○ Stir together the dressing ingredients in a small bowl.

● Heat the oil in a large skillet over medium-high heat. Add the onion and cook, stirring occasionally, for 5 minutes or until tender. Add the sauerkraut and stir until warm.

● For each sandwich, spread the dressing on two slices of bread. Over the dressing on one slice, layer one-fourth of the beef, cheese, and sauerkraut mixture. Top with another slice of bread, spread-side down.

● Lightly spread the outside of the sandwiches with butter. Toast in a preheated panini grill for 3 minutes or until the bread is golden brown and the cheese is melted.

● Or toast the sandwiches in a skillet or stovetop grill pan over medium heat. Place another heavy skillet, bottom down, on top of the sandwiches and press gently for even browning.

● Depending on the size of your panini grill or skillet, you may need to toast the sandwiches in two batches.

● Slice the sandwiches diagonally and serve warm.

CROQUE MONSIEUR

Makes **4** servings

A classic croque monsieur, like those I've enjoyed in bistros throughout France, is basically a ham and cheese sandwich made with crustless, buttered bread and pan-fried in butter. This updated version makes a satisfying meal with family appeal. Serve extra honey mustard on the side and accompany the sandwiches with a salad of baby greens lightly dressed with a squeeze of lemon, extra-virgin olive oil, salt, and freshly ground pepper.

2	large eggs
¼	cup milk
	Dash of salt and pepper
8	(½-inch) slices artisan bread, such as Vienna or Italian (from an oblong loaf)
4	teaspoons honey mustard
1	large tomato, cut into 8 thin slices
4	ounces thinly sliced deli smoked turkey or ham
4	slices (4 ounces) aged Swiss cheese
2	tablespoons unsalted butter
2	tablespoons olive oil

● Whisk together the eggs, milk, salt, and pepper in a shallow bowl. Set aside.

● Spread one side of 4 bread slices with mustard. Top each with 2 tomato slices, 1 ounce turkey, and 1 slice cheese. Top with the remaining 4 bread slices.

● Melt the butter with the oil in a large skillet over medium heat. Dip both sides of each sandwich into the egg mixture. Place the sandwiches in the skillet, cheese-side down. Cook for about 2 minutes per side or until the bread is golden brown and the cheese is melted.

● Depending on the size of your skillet, you may need to cook the sandwiches in two batches.

● Slice the sandwiches in half and serve warm.

COBB SANDWICHES

Makes **4** servings

Here's the perfect adult sandwich for blue cheese lovers who also enjoy the peppery flavor of arugula. Pair the sandwiches with a marinated vegetable salad, such as cooked cut green beans, finely chopped red bell pepper, and shallots tossed with Balsamic Vinaigrette (page 268) for a satisfying weeknight supper.

12	strips bacon
½	cup mayonnaise
1	(4-ounce) package crumbled blue cheese
8	slices firm white bread
2	rotisserie chicken breasts, skin removed, thinly sliced
1	ripe avocado, peeled and thinly sliced
1	large tomato, cut into 4 slices
	Salt and pepper to taste
1	cup tightly packed arugula leaves

❍ Cook the bacon in a large nonstick skillet over medium heat, turning as needed, for 12 minutes or until crisp. (Or place the bacon, 4 strips at a time, on a triple layer of paper towels on a microwave-safe plate, and cover with a double layer of towels. Microwave on HIGH for 2 minutes. Continue to microwave for 1-minute intervals until done.) Transfer to a paper-towel-lined plate. Cover to keep warm.

❍ Combine the mayonnaise and blue cheese in a small bowl.

❍ Toast the bread.

❍ To assemble each sandwich, spread one-fourth of mayonnaise mixture on 2 slices of toast. Layer the mayonnaise-coated side of one slice with chicken, bacon, avocado, and tomato. Season with salt and pepper. Top with arugula leaves and cover with the other slice of toast, mayonnaise-coated side down. Cut in half to serve.

TIP

To cook bacon in the oven, preheat the oven to 400°F. Place the bacon on a rimmed baking sheet. Bake for 12 minutes or until the desired crispness.

GRILLED CUBANO SANDWICHES

Makes **4** servings

Cubanos, the classic sandwich of the Latin Caribbean, are made with Cuban bread (a soft, French-style loaf), but any soft rolls will do. I've been told that the recipe originated as a use for leftover roast pork, but deli meats also work nicely. And frankly, there's really no reason to measure the ingredients—just use what looks good to you. Add a handful of chips and some slaw from the deli and this sandwich will satisfy just about any appetite.

4	soft hoagie rolls or other sandwich rolls
	Unsalted butter for spreading
2	tablespoons mustard
6	ounces thinly sliced deli turkey
4	ounces thinly sliced deli ham
4	ounces thinly sliced Swiss cheese
8	dill pickle "planks"

- Cut the rolls in half lengthwise. Lightly spread butter on one cut side of the rolls and spread mustard on the other. Over the butter, layer the turkey, ham, cheese, and pickles. Close the sandwich, mustard-side down, and press.

- Toast the sandwiches in a preheated panini grill for 3 minutes or until the bread is golden and the cheese is melted.

- Or toast the sandwiches in a skillet or stovetop grill pan over medium heat. Place another heavy skillet, bottom down, on top of the sandwiches and press gently for even browning.

- Depending on the size of your panini grill or skillet, you may need to toast the sandwiches in two batches.

- Slice the sandwiches diagonally and serve warm.

BEEF FAJITAS
Makes **4** servings

Fajitas are traditionally prepared with grilled marinated meat. But cooking all the ingredients in a skillet speeds up the preparation and efficiently blends the flavors. Serve the fajitas with bowls of your favorite chunky tomato salsa and sour cream.

2	tablespoons olive oil, divided
12	ounces thinly sliced boneless beef top sirloin steak, cut into ½-inch strips
2	teaspoons ground cumin
1	teaspoon chili powder
1	red bell pepper, cut into ¼-inch strips
1	green bell pepper, cut into ¼-inch strips
1	red onion, thinly sliced (about 2 cups)
2	teaspoons minced garlic
3	tablespoons fresh lime juice
2	tablespoons Worcestershire sauce
	Salt and pepper to taste
8	(7-inch) flour tortillas
2	limes, cut into wedges
	Tomato salsa and sour cream for accompaniments

- Heat 1 tablespoon oil in a large skillet over medium-high heat. Add the beef, cumin, and chili powder; cook, stirring constantly, for 3 minutes or until thoroughly cooked. Transfer to a plate and cover to keep warm.

- Heat the remaining 1 tablespoon oil in the same skillet. Add the bell peppers, onion, and garlic. Cook, stirring occasionally, for 5 minutes or until tender. Stir in the cooked beef, lime juice, and Worcestershire sauce. Season with salt and pepper. Remove from the heat and cover to keep warm.

- While the beef mixture is cooking, stack the tortillas between two paper towels. Microwave on HIGH for 1 minute or until moist and warm.

- To serve, transfer the beef mixture to a serving bowl. Place the tortillas in a covered basket. Accompany with bowls of lime wedges, salsa, and sour cream. Spoon the beef mixture into the center third of the tortillas (add a squeeze of extra lime juice if desired) and fold the sides over the filling.

HAM AND CHEESE–STUFFED FRENCH TOAST

Makes **4** servings

Treat your family to a special weekend brunch or lunch. And be sure to serve the toast with pure maple syrup, which is far superior to maple-flavored pancake syrup. If you'd like, substitute croissants or challah for the cinnamon-raisin bread.

4	eggs
3	tablespoons milk
1	tablespoon sugar
8	slices cinnamon-raisin bread
½	cup cream cheese spread
16	thin slices deli honey-baked ham
1	tablespoon unsalted butter
	Pure maple syrup as needed

▶ Beat the eggs lightly in a 9-inch pie plate or flat-bottomed shallow bowl. Stir in the milk and sugar.

▶ For each serving, spread one side of a bread slice with 1 tablespoon cream cheese and top with 4 ham slices. (If the ham slices are large, tuck them to fit inside the bread.) Spread another slice with 1 tablespoon cream cheese, cover the sandwich spread-side down, and lightly press. Dip both sides of each sandwich into the egg mixture.

▶ Melt the butter in a large skillet over medium heat. Cook the sandwiches for 2 minutes per side or until golden brown.

▶ Slice diagonally and serve warm. Offer syrup for drizzling over the sandwiches.

MONTE CRISTO SANDWICHES

Makes **4** servings

When is a ham and cheese sandwich more than a ham and cheese sandwich? When it's a Monte Cristo. Traditionally, this is an old-fashioned ham, cheese, and turkey sandwich dipped in egg batter, fried in butter, and served with jelly and powdered sugar. Here's a healthier version the kids will love.

¼	cup strawberry jam
8	slices white bread
4	slices deli ham
4	slices deli turkey
4	slices Swiss cheese
8	teaspoons mustard, preferably honey mustard
3	eggs
3	tablespoons milk
1	tablespoon canola oil
	Additional strawberry jam, if desired

▶ Spread 1 tablespoon jam over each of 4 bread slices. Top with ham and turkey slices. Then add a layer of the cheese.

▶ Spread 2 teaspoons mustard on each of the remaining 4 bread slices. Close the sandwiches and press lightly.

▶ Lightly whisk the eggs and milk together in a medium shallow bowl. Dip the sandwiches in the egg mixture, turning carefully to evenly coat.

▶ Heat the oil in a large skillet over medium-high heat. Add the sandwiches and cook for 3 minutes per side or until the bread is lightly browned and the cheese is melted.

▶ Slice and serve the sandwiches warm with additional jam, if desired.

SPICED BEEF AND ONION PITAS WITH CHIMICHURRI SAUCE

Makes **4** servings

These pita sandwiches fuse ethnic ingredients in a nontraditional way. But when it comes to sandwiches, there are no rules. Just be sure to eat them with your hands!

½	teaspoon ground coriander
½	teaspoon ground cumin
½	teaspoon salt
¼	teaspoon pepper
12	ounces boneless beef sirloin for stir-fry, thinly sliced and cut into ½-inch strips
2	tablespoons olive oil, divided
2	cups yellow onions in thin lengthwise slivers
4	(6-inch) pita bread rounds
½	cup Chimichurri Sauce (page 267)

◐ Stir together the coriander, cumin, salt, and pepper in a medium bowl. Add the beef and toss until lightly coated with the spices.

◐ Heat 1 tablespoon oil in a large skillet over medium-high heat. Add the onions; cook, stirring occasionally, for 6 minutes or until well browned and very tender. Add the remaining 1 tablespoon oil and the beef; continue to cook, stirring occasionally, for 3 more minutes or until the beef is just cooked. Remove from the heat and cover to keep warm.

◐ While the beef is cooking, stack the pitas on a microwave-proof plate and cover with a paper towel. Microwave on HIGH for 1 minute or until warm.

◐ Halve each pita to form 2 pockets. Fill with the beef and onions. Drizzle each half with about 1 tablespoon sauce. Serve while warm.

PORK SAUSAGE SOFT TACOS

Makes **4** servings

Here's a great meal to serve weekend guests. Prepare all the ingredients in advance, and then set up a taco buffet with bowls of cooked crumbled sausage, colorful vegetable salsa, lettuce, cheese, and sour cream. Your guests will enjoy assembling tacos with just the right amount of their favorite fillings.

12	ounces bulk pork sausage
¾	cup taco sauce
8	(7-inch) flour tortillas
2	cups finely shredded head lettuce
1	cup finely shredded Mexican cheese blend
3	cups Vegetable Salsa (page 274)
1	cup sour cream plus extra for topping if desired

◐ Cook the sausage in a medium sauté pan over medium-high heat, stirring to crumble, for 5 minutes or until lightly browned. Drain well. Stir in the taco sauce.

◐ Stack the tortillas between 2 paper towels. Microwave on HIGH for 1 minute or until moist and warm. Put the tortillas in a basket or on a plate and cover to keep warm.

◐ To assemble each taco, spread lettuce down the center third of a tortilla. Top with the cheese, cooked sausage, salsa, and sour cream. Fold in the sides of the tortilla to overlap.

◐ Serve, while the sausage is warm, with small bowls of the remaining salsa and sour cream.

Note: To thaw frozen bulk sausage, transfer the sausage from the package to a microwave-proof bowl. Microwave on DEFROST for 1 minute. Break the sausage into pieces. Microwave for 1 minute more.

CHIPOTLE PORK TENDERLOIN SOFT TACOS

Makes **4** servings

Some like it hot? No problem. Simply increase the amount of chili powder to 1½ teaspoons. The heat is tamed by a cool drizzle of sour cream and the addition of sweet corn kernels to balance texture in these delicious tacos. Substitute chicken for the pork, if you prefer.

1	teaspoon chipotle chili powder
1	teaspoon ground cumin
1	teaspoon minced garlic
½	teaspoon salt, or to taste
16	ounces pork tenderloin, cut into 2 x ½ x ½-inch strips
1	tablespoon olive oil
1	cup frozen corn kernels
¾	cup thick and chunky tomato salsa
½	cup thinly sliced green onions
2	tablespoons finely chopped cilantro
8	(7-inch) flour tortillas
¼	cup sour cream

◗ Combine the chili powder, cumin, garlic, and salt in a large zip-top plastic bag. Add the pork strips and toss until lightly coated.

◗ Heat the oil in a large skillet over medium-high heat. Add the pork. (Discard the bag and excess flour mixture.) Cook the pork, stirring frequently, for 6 minutes or until thoroughly cooked. Add the corn and salsa; cook for 2 minutes until the corn is heated through. Stir in the green onions and cilantro.

◗ While the pork mixture is cooking, stack the tortillas between 2 paper towels. Microwave on HIGH for 1 minute or until moist and warm.

◗ To serve, spoon the pork mixture down the center of the warm tortillas and top with sour cream. Fold the sides of the tortillas to the center to overlap.

Pasta and Noodles

RAGU BOLOGNESE

Makes **4** servings

This sauce is delicious on short-cut pastas, such as penne, rotini, ziti, or farfalle. But to tell the truth, I like it best the way it's traditionally served in Bologna, Italy, where the sauce originated—and that's atop spaghetti. Add a mesclun salad with bottled Italian dressing and warm Italian bread, and your meal is complete.

8	ounces spaghetti
2	tablespoons olive oil, divided
½	cup finely chopped onion
1	carrot, finely chopped
1	rib celery, finely chopped
16	ounces lean ground pork
4	ounces thinly sliced pancetta, finely chopped
1	(14-ounce) can diced tomatoes with basil, garlic, and oregano
⅓	cup tomato paste
⅓	cup full-bodied red wine (such as Cabernet Sauvignon or Pinot Noir)
⅓	cup half-and-half
	Salt and pepper to taste
	Freshly grated Parmesan cheese for garnish

◗ Cook the spaghetti according to package instructions.

● Meanwhile, heat 1 tablespoon oil in a medium skillet over medium-high heat. Add the onion, carrot, and celery; cook, stirring occasionally, for 5 minutes or until tender.

● At the same time, heat the remaining 1 tablespoon oil in a large sauté pan over high heat. Add the pork and pancetta; cook, allowing the moisture to evaporate while breaking the pork into pieces for 5 minutes or until firm but not thoroughly cooked. Stir in the cooked vegetables, tomatoes, tomato paste, and wine. When the liquid comes to a boil, reduce the heat to low; cover and simmer, stirring occasionally, for 3 minutes.

● Add the half-and-half and stir until heated through. Season with salt and pepper.

● When the spaghetti is done, drain well.

● To serve, pour the sauce over the spaghetti and sprinkle with Parmesan cheese.

GINGERED FLANK STEAK AND VEGETABLES WITH RICE NOODLES

Makes **4** servings

Serve this colorful combination on a bed of shredded lettuce, and feel free to substitute or add other vegetables to the mix.

For the noodles:

2   ounces thin rice noodles

For the sauce:

¼   cup white rice vinegar
2   tablespoons soy sauce
2   tablespoons hoisin sauce

2   teaspoons dark (Asian) sesame oil
2   teaspoons finely chopped fresh ginger
2   teaspoons cornstarch
1   teaspoon sugar
1   teaspoon minced garlic
     Salt to taste

To complete the recipe:

2   tablespoons canola oil, divided
8   ounces beef flank steak, cut into ¼-inch slices, then cut into 3 x ½-inch strips
1   cup sugar snap peas
1   red bell pepper, cut into ¼-inch slices
     Salt and pepper to taste
     Coarsely chopped green onions for garnish

● Cook the noodles according to package instructions.

● Stir together the sauce ingredients in a small bowl.

● Heat 1 tablespoon oil in a large sauté pan over medium-high heat. Add the beef; cook, stirring occasionally, for 3 minutes or until lightly browned. Transfer to a plate and cover to keep warm.

● Heat the remaining 1 tablespoon oil in the sauté pan over medium-high heat; add the snap peas and bell pepper. Cook, stirring frequently, for 3 minutes or until crisp-tender. Reduce the heat to medium; add the steak and the sauce mixture. Stir constantly for 1 minute or until the sauce thickens.

● When the noodles are done, drain well. Use kitchen shears to randomly cut them into shorter lengths for easier mixing. Add to the sauté pan and stir until evenly combined. Season with salt and pepper.

● Garnish the servings with green onions.

PENNE WITH TOMATO-SAGE SAUSAGE SAUCE

Makes **4** servings

My friend Mary Brindley shared her favorite pasta. She uses "hot" sausage and also adds a generous pinch of red pepper flakes. Mary, who owns my favorite clothing store, not only has great taste when it comes to fashion but also when it comes to pasta.

8	ounces penne
12	ounces bulk pork sausage
½	cup minced shallots
1	teaspoon minced garlic
2	(14-ounce) cans diced tomatoes
1	teaspoon dried oregano
1	teaspoon dried sage
⅛	teaspoon red pepper flakes, or to taste
½	cup heavy cream
	Freshly shredded Parmesan cheese for garnish

● Cook the penne according to package instructions.

● Add the sausage, shallots, and garlic to a large sauté pan. Cook over medium heat, stirring to crumble the sausage, for 5 minutes or until lightly browned and thoroughly cooked.

● Stir in the tomatoes, oregano, sage, and red pepper flakes. When the liquid comes to a boil, cook, stirring occasionally, for 4 minutes.

● When the penne is done, drain well, and return to the pasta pan. Add the tomato sauce and cream. Stir over low heat for 1 minute or until warm.

● Garnish the servings with Parmesan cheese.

SPAGHETTI WITH TOMATO-PANCETTA SAUCE

Makes **4** servings

Pancetta, which originated in northern Italy, is thickly sliced smoked bacon that is dry-cured with salt and spices and aged to create a flavor and texture sweeter and more buttery than ordinary bacon. Here, pancetta adds its rich flavor to a traditional Italian tomato pasta sauce.

12	ounces spaghetti
1	cup thinly sliced red onion
4	ounces sliced pancetta, coarsely chopped
2	(14-ounce) cans diced tomatoes
⅛	teaspoon red pepper flakes, or to taste
⅛	teaspoon pepper, or to taste
	Freshly shredded Parmesan cheese for garnish

● Cook the spaghetti according to package instructions.

● Meanwhile, heat a large sauté pan over medium-high heat. Add the onion and pancetta; cook, stirring occasionally, for 5 minutes or until the onion is tender and the pancetta begins to brown. Stir in the tomatoes, red pepper flakes, and pepper. When the liquid begins to boil, reduce the heat to low. Simmer, uncovered, for 5 minutes, allowing the sauce to thicken slightly.

● When the spaghetti is done, drain well.

● Return the spaghetti to the pasta pan. Add the sauce and toss.

● Garnish the servings with Parmesan cheese.

SUMMER SQUASH AND PROSCIUTTO PASTA WITH ROSEMARY VINAIGRETTE

Makes **4** servings

Here's a tasty place for all that zucchini multiplying in the garden. This dish, bursting with flavor, is great served warm, or allow it to chill to do duty later the same day as a do-ahead salad. Rather than sprinkling Parmesan on the chilled salad, I like to stir in about 4 ounces of fresh mozzarella cut into ½-inch cubes.

For the salad:

8	ounces (2½ cups) rotini
1	tablespoon olive oil
1	yellow summer squash, cut into 2-inch matchstick strips
1	small zucchini, cut into 2-inch matchstick strips
½	cup finely chopped red onion

For the vinaigrette:

¼	cup oil-packed, julienned, sun-dried tomatoes, drained
¼	cup extra-virgin olive oil
3	tablespoons red wine vinegar
1	teaspoon Dijon mustard
2	teaspoons finely chopped fresh rosemary or ½ teaspoon dried rosemary, crushed
	Salt and pepper to taste

To complete the recipe:

4	ounces thinly sliced prosciutto
	Pinch of red pepper flakes, or to taste, optional
	Freshly grated Parmesan cheese for garnish

◗ Cook the rotini according to package instructions.

◗ Meanwhile, heat the oil in a medium skillet over medium-high heat. Add the squash, zucchini, and onion. Cook, stirring occasionally, for 3 minutes or until crisp-tender.

◗ While the rotini and vegetables are cooking, whisk together the vinaigrette ingredients in a small bowl. Use kitchen shears to cut the prosciutto into ½-inch pieces.

◗ When the rotini is done, drain well, and return to the pasta pan. Add the squash mixture, vinaigrette, and prosciutto. Stir gently to combine. Season with red pepper flakes (if using).

◗ Garnish the servings with Parmesan cheese.

TIP

Rosemary, thyme, oregano, savory, sage, marjoram, and bay leaf are considered to be the "robust herbs," with tough leaves that resist cold weather and heat, both from the sun and cooking. They are strong in aroma and hearty in flavor; add them early in the cooking process so their flavors will mellow and blend in with the other ingredients. Add tender fresh herbs, such as basil, cilantro, dill, and parsley, toward the end of the cooking time, or sprinkle them on top of the completed dish.

BEEF AND BROCCOLI LO MEIN

Makes **4** servings

No need to order out for Chinese. This dish, with its distinctive aroma provided by the oyster sauce, will entice your family to the table long before the deliveryman could be at your door.

For the noodles and vegetables:

8	ounces Chinese lo mein noodles
1	tablespoon canola oil
1	(16-ounce) bag broccoli coleslaw
1	cup coarsely chopped onion
1	cup sliced cremini mushrooms

For the sauce:

3	tablespoons soy sauce
3	tablespoons oyster sauce
1	tablespoon white rice vinegar
2	teaspoons minced fresh ginger
1	teaspoon dark (Asian) sesame oil

To complete the recipe:

8	ounces beef round steak or flank steak, cut into ¼-inch strips
2	teaspoons minced garlic

◗ Cook the noodles according to package instructions.

◗ Meanwhile, heat the oil in a large sauté pan over medium-high heat. Add the coleslaw, onion, and mushrooms. Cook, stirring occasionally, for 5 minutes.

◗ While the vegetables are cooking, stir together the sauce ingredients in a small bowl.

◗ Add the beef and garlic to the sauté pan; continue to cook, stirring occasionally, for 3 minutes or until the steak is the desired doneness. Add the sauce and stir until evenly combined. Remove the pan from the heat.

◗ When the noodles are done, drain well. Return them to the pasta pan, add the beef mixture, and toss.

⟶ TIP ⟵

Oyster sauce is a dark brown sauce made from oysters, brine, and soy sauce that have been cooked until thick and concentrated. A vegetarian substitute made from mushrooms and soybeans is available in many Asian markets.

FETTUCCINE CARBONARA

Makes **4** servings

A traditional and popular Italian pasta sauce, carbonara derives its name from the Italian word for charcoal. Some say it was first made as a satisfying dish for Italian charcoal producers who remained in the woods for weeks at a time and had access only to long-keeping foods. Others say it was originally prepared over charcoal grills, and it may be so-named because the specks of bacon and pepper in the pasta look like bits of charcoal. The "city" version is said to have originated at a restaurant called Carbonara in the heart of Rome.

12	ounces fettuccine
12	ounces pancetta, cut into ½-inch pieces
2	pasteurized eggs
½	cup reduced-sodium chicken broth
⅓	cup heavy cream
1	cup freshly grated Parmesan cheese
1	teaspoon minced garlic
	Salt and pepper to taste
	Finely chopped fresh flat-leaf parsley for garnish

❍ Cook the fettuccine according to package instructions.

❍ Meanwhile, heat a large sauté pan over medium-high heat. Add the pancetta; cook, stirring occasionally, for 7 minutes or until golden brown and crispy. Remove the pan from the heat.

❍ While the fettuccine and pancetta are cooking, whisk the eggs in a medium bowl. Whisk in the remaining ingredients, except the salt, pepper, and garnish.

❍ When the fettuccine is done, drain well. Return the fettuccine to the pot; add the broth mixture and the pancetta with any fat remaining in the pan. Toss to combine over medium heat for 1 minute to slightly thicken the sauce. Season with salt and pepper.

❍ Garnish the servings with parsley.

TIP

For this and other recipes where eggs are not thoroughly cooked, it's wise to use eggs that have undergone pasteurization to eliminate potential bacteria, including salmonella. You'll find pasteurized eggs along with the refrigerated eggs in most supermarkets. Or you can use pasteurized liquid eggs, which come packaged in a carton. One-quarter cup equals 1 egg.

RICE NOODLES WITH CHINESE BARBECUED PORK

Makes **4** servings

Nathan Fong prepared this dish for me after he guided me on a memorable shopping trip through Vancouver's Chinatown. The recipe is a snap to make using the flavorful barbecued pork that's already prepared and available in most Asian markets.

For the noodles:

8   ounces flat rice noodles

For the sauce:

¼   cup oyster sauce

¼   cup soy sauce

2   tablespoons white rice vinegar

2   teaspoons dark (Asian) sesame oil

1   teaspoon chili paste with garlic, or to taste

To complete the recipe:

2   tablespoons canola oil

1   cup onion in ¼-inch strips

4   green onions, diagonally cut into 1-inch pieces

1   tablespoon finely chopped fresh ginger

2   teaspoons minced garlic

8   ounces Chinese barbecued pork, cut into matchstick strips

1   (8-ounce) package fresh bean sprouts (4 cups)

◗ Cook the noodles according to package instructions.

◗ Meanwhile, stir together the sauce ingredients in a small bowl.

◗ Heat the oil in a large sauté pan over high heat. Add the onion, green onions, and ginger; cook, stirring occasionally, for 3 minutes or until the onion is crisp-tender. Stir in the garlic. Remove from the heat.

◗ When the noodles are done, drain well. Transfer the noodles to the sauté pan. Add the sauce, pork, and bean sprouts. Stir gently over medium heat just until heated through.

BEEF NOODLE BOWLS

Makes **4** servings

This is comfort, pure and simple. I particularly relish it in the winter when beef with noodles provides familiar, heartwarming sustenance. Serve the dish in deep bowls, the way Asians do, along with chopsticks if you're deft, to recreate Chinese street food of the type I often enjoy as I roam down streets in Asia.

8   ounces linguine

1   tablespoon canola oil

16   ounces beef sirloin steak, cut into ⅛-inch strips

½   cup thinly sliced onion

1   tablespoon minced garlic

1   tablespoon finely chopped fresh ginger

2   (14-ounce) cans reduced-sodium beef broth

¾   cup teriyaki sauce

3   cups broccoli florets

2   carrots, diagonally cut into ¼-inch slices

◗ Cook the linguine according to package instructions.

◐ Meanwhile, heat the oil in a large sauté pan over medium-high heat. Add the beef, onion, garlic, and ginger; cook, stirring occasionally, for 4 minutes or until the beef is lightly browned on both sides and the garlic and ginger are tender.

◐ Stir in the beef broth, teriyaki sauce, broccoli, and carrots. When the liquid comes to a boil, reduce the heat to low. Cover and cook for 2 minutes or until the broccoli and carrots are tender and the meat is thoroughly cooked.

◐ When the linguine is done, drain well. Stir it into the beef mixture. Serve in deep bowls.

BEEF, ASPARAGUS, AND CARROT STIR-FRY

Makes **4** servings

Crisp-tender asparagus and carrots contribute both color and crunch to this aromatic stir-fry, emboldened by ginger, garlic, and red pepper flakes. I like to balance these assertive elements by serving the mixture atop thin, slithery, Chinese wheat-flour noodles.

For the meat:

2   tablespoons canola oil, divided
16 ounces boneless beef top sirloin steak, cut into ⅛-inch slices

For the sauce:

½   cup dry sherry
2   teaspoons cornstarch
½   cup reduced-sodium beef broth
¼   cup soy sauce
1   teaspoon dark (Asian) sesame oil
¼   teaspoon red pepper flakes

To complete the recipe:

16 ounces asparagus, diagonally cut into 1-inch pieces
2   carrots, cut into ⅛-inch slices
¼   cup thinly sliced onion
2   tablespoons finely chopped fresh ginger
2   teaspoons minced garlic
    Coarsely chopped raw cashews for garnish

◐ Heat 1 tablespoon oil in a sauté pan over high heat. Add the beef; cook, stirring frequently, for 3 minutes or until thoroughly cooked. Transfer to a bowl and cover to keep warm.

◐ While the beef cooks, prepare the sauce. Stir together the sherry and cornstarch in a medium bowl until smooth. Stir in the remaining sauce ingredients.

◐ Heat the remaining 1 tablespoon oil in the same pan over high heat. Add the asparagus, carrots, onion, ginger, and garlic. Cook, stirring frequently, for 5 minutes or until crisp-tender.

◐ Add the sauce and beef to the sauté pan. Cook over medium-high heat, stirring constantly, for 2 minutes or until the sauce is thickened and glossy and the meat is heated through.

◐ Garnish the servings with cashews.

Beef and Broccoli Stir-Fry

BEEF AND BROCCOLI STIR-FRY

Makes **4** servings

To speed up preparation, you can stop at the salad bar to buy just the right amount of precut broccoli florets, which gets dinner on the table in minutes. I serve this colorful stir-fry over basmati rice that can cook as you prepare this dish.

For the meat:

1	tablespoon soy sauce
1	tablespoon dark (Asian) sesame oil
2	teaspoons finely chopped fresh ginger
1	teaspoon cornstarch
1	teaspoon minced garlic
8	ounces boneless beef sirloin, cut into ⅛-inch slices

For the sauce:

¾	cup reduced-sodium beef broth
2	tablespoons Chinese oyster sauce
1	tablespoon soy sauce
¼	teaspoon red pepper flakes, or to taste
2	teaspoons cornstarch

To complete the recipe:

2	tablespoons canola oil, divided
2	cups small broccoli florets
1	cup thinly sliced onion
½	red bell pepper, cut into ¼-inch strips

◗ For the meat, stir together all the ingredients, except the beef, in a medium bowl. Add the beef and stir until the mixture is evenly combined.

◗ Stir together the sauce ingredients in a small bowl.

◗ Heat 1 tablespoon oil in a large sauté pan over medium-high heat. Add the beef mixture. Cook, stirring constantly, for 3 minutes or until just cooked. Use a slotted spoon to transfer the beef to a bowl and cover to keep warm.

◗ Heat the remaining 1 tablespoon oil in the pan. Add the broccoli, onion, and bell pepper; cook, stirring constantly, for 3 minutes or until the broccoli is crisp-tender.

◗ Add the beef and sauce. Stir gently for 1 minute or until the sauce thickens.

---- TIP ----

Stir-fries are my favorite destinations for leftover odds and ends of vegetables, so keep in mind that you can substitute what you have on hand or whatever vegetables look good in the market. If you use vegetables of varying consistencies in a stir-fry, begin cooking the firmest first, and add the tender vegetables last. This ensures they all will have a pleasing consistency.

PORK COCONUT CURRY

Makes **4** servings

Curry paste is a blend of more than 10 seasonings and spices. Dried red chilies are used to make red curry paste, and fresh green chilies are used in green curry paste; they offer different, but equally addictive flavors. Here, coconut milk (choose the "lite" version) adds a smoothness and richness that balances the savory spice blend. Serve with rice.

1	tablespoon canola oil
16	ounces (½-inch-thick) boneless pork chops, cut into ¼-inch strips
½	red bell pepper, cut into ¼-inch strips
½	cup thinly sliced onion
2	teaspoons green curry paste
1	(14-ounce) can "lite" coconut milk, divided
1	cup frozen baby peas
1	tablespoon Asian fish sauce
1	tablespoon fresh lime juice
1	teaspoon sugar
⅓	cup coarsely chopped fresh Thai basil or sweet basil
	Salt to taste
	Basil leaves for garnish

◗   Heat the oil in a large sauté pan over high heat. Add the pork, bell pepper, and onion; cook for 5 minutes or until the pork is nearly cooked but still slightly pink in the center. Transfer to a plate and cover to keep warm.

◗   Spread the curry paste on the bottom of the pan and cook for 15 seconds. Add about half of the coconut milk. Stir constantly for 1 minute or until it comes to a boil.

◗   Stir in the remaining coconut milk, peas, fish sauce, lime juice, and sugar. When the liquid comes to a boil, stir in the pork mixture. Cook for 2 minutes or until the pork is thoroughly cooked. Stir in the basil and salt.

◗   Serve in bowls and garnish with basil leaves.

SAUSAGE JAMBALAYA

Makes **4** servings

Jambalaya is a revered creation on many a Louisiana table, where rustic Cajun dishes reign. Spicy, smoky andouille sausage, having the French roots that also thrive in Cajun country, is the meat of choice. Serve this jazzy dish with corn muffins or cornbread, which you can buy ready-made at the bakery, for a *lagniappe*, the Cajun word for an unexpected bonus or surprise.

12	ounces smoked andouille sausage or other smoked sausage, cut into ¼-inch slices
½	green bell pepper, coarsely chopped
½	cup finely chopped onion
2	teaspoons minced garlic
1	(15-ounce) can diced tomatoes
1	cup reduced-sodium chicken broth
1½	cups cooked rice
2	teaspoons finely chopped fresh thyme or ¾ teaspoon dried thyme
½	teaspoon salt, or to taste
¼	teaspoon pepper, or to taste
⅛	teaspoon cayenne pepper, or to taste

◗   Cook the sausage, bell pepper, onion, and garlic in a large sauté pan over medium-high heat. Stir occasionally for 3 minutes or until the sausage is lightly browned but not thoroughly cooked.

○ Stir in the remaining ingredients. Cook uncovered, stirring occasionally, for 7 minutes or until the liquid is just about absorbed.

BEEF, BELL PEPPER, AND CORN STIR-FRY

Makes **4** servings

Flank steak is a great cut to choose for this recipe because there isn't any waste—no fat to trim away. To save time when you're ready to cook, ask the butcher to cut the thin strips for you. This stir-fry is especially tasty served over rice, which absorbs every last bit of flavor from the aromatic, glossy oyster sauce that makes this dish so special.

For the sauce:

½	cup oyster sauce
⅓	cup water
3	tablespoons soy sauce
3	tablespoons dry sherry
¼	teaspoon red pepper flakes, or to taste

For the stir-fry:

2	tablespoons canola oil, divided
12	ounces beef flank steak, cut into ⅛-inch slices
2	tablespoons finely chopped fresh ginger
2	teaspoons minced garlic
1	red bell pepper, cut into ½-inch strips
1	medium red onion, cut into ½-inch wedges
2	cups sliced bok choy in ½-inch pieces, including the green tops
½	(15-ounce) can cut baby corn cobs, drained and rinsed (or substitute whole baby corn cobs and cut into 1-inch pieces)

○ Combine all the sauce ingredients in a small bowl; set aside.

○ Heat 1 tablespoon oil in a large sauté pan over high heat. Add the beef, ginger, and garlic. Cook, stirring frequently, for 4 minutes or until the beef is just cooked. Transfer to a bowl and cover to keep warm.

○ Heat the remaining 1 tablespoon oil in the same pan over high heat. Add the bell pepper and onion; cook, stirring frequently, for 2 minutes. Add the bok choy and corn; stir for 1 minute or until the vegetables are crisp-tender, the greens are wilted, and the corn is heated through. Stir in the beef.

○ Reduce the heat to medium-high. Add the sauce and stir constantly for 1 minute or until the sauce thickens and the beef and vegetables are heated through.

── TIP ──

Bok choy, sometimes called pak choy or pak choi, should have unwilted dark green leaves attached to firm, light green or white unblemished stalks; both the leaves and stalks are edible raw or cooked. Store bok choy in a plastic bag in the refrigerator for up to three days.

PORK CHOPS
WITH CITRUS COLESLAW

Makes **4** servings

These days, supermarkets offer more than ordinary shredded cabbage and carrots. Try a bag of shredded broccoli, cauliflower, carrots, and red cabbage coleslaw to add a rainbow of colors to the presentation.

For the coleslaw:

1	(15-ounce) can Mandarin oranges in light syrup; 3 tablespoons syrup reserved
¼	cup mayonnaise
2	tablespoons white rice vinegar
1	teaspoon sugar
½	teaspoon celery seed
¼	teaspoon salt, or to taste
⅛	teaspoon pepper, or to taste
1	(16-ounce) bag cabbage-and-carrot coleslaw or broccoli coleslaw

For the meat:

16	ounces boneless pork loin chops
	Dash of salt and pepper
1	tablespoon canola oil
⅓	cup water

◗ To make the coleslaw, stir together the 3 tablespoons Mandarin orange syrup, mayonnaise, vinegar, sugar, celery seed, salt, and pepper in a medium bowl. Add the coleslaw and oranges; gently toss.

◗ Lightly sprinkle both sides of the pork chops with salt and pepper. Heat the oil in a large skillet over medium-high heat. Add the chops and cook for 4 minutes per side or until lightly browned and thoroughly cooked. Transfer to a plate and cover to keep warm.

◗ Pour the water into the pan. Stir constantly for 1 minute over medium heat, scraping the bottom of the pan to loosen the browned bits.

◗ To serve, drizzle the pan juices over the pork chops and serve with the coleslaw on the side.

Pork Chops
with Citrus Coleslaw

FLANK STEAK WITH RED PEPPER PURÉE AND RED BEAN–CORN RELISH

Makes **4** servings

The blender does all the work for this velvety, vivid sauce. Ready it before guests arrive, and then listen to the compliments roll in when forks go into action.

For the red pepper purée:

1   (7-ounce) jar roasted red bell peppers, drained
¼   cup coarsely chopped red onion
1   jalapeño chili, coarsely chopped
1   tablespoon extra-virgin olive oil
1   tablespoon fresh lime juice
2   teaspoons minced garlic
¼   teaspoon salt, or to taste
    A few drops of Tabasco sauce
2   tablespoons finely chopped fresh cilantro

For the meat:

16   ounces beef flank steak

To complete the recipe:

4   cups Red Bean–Corn Relish (page 275)
    Sprigs of fresh cilantro for garnish

▶   Purée the red pepper purée ingredients, except the cilantro, in a blender until smooth. Stir in the cilantro. Transfer ¼ cup to a small bowl for brushing the steak.

▶   Heat a stovetop grill pan over high heat. Score the top of the steak by making ⅛-inch-deep diagonal cuts at 1-inch intervals. Coat the scored side with 2 tablespoons of the red pepper purée (reserve the remainder). Reduce the heat to medium-high and place the steak on the pan, scored-side down; cook for 6 minutes. Brush the top of the steak with 2 tablespoons red pepper purée. Turn and cook for 6 more minutes or until the desired degree of doneness.

▶   When the steak is done, transfer to a plate and let stand for 1 minute. Cut into thin slices.

▶   Serve the steak over the corn relish. Spoon the remaining red pepper purée over the steak. Garnish the servings with cilantro sprigs.

PORK CHOPS WITH APPLES AND RASPBERRIES

Makes **4** servings

Pork with applesauce is as familiar as pairing ham and eggs. This recipe calls for apple slices instead and updates the presentation with a fresh raspberry sauce. The easy-yet-elegant combination makes guest-worthy fare. Prepare rice or mashed sweet potatoes, and purchase or make a creamy salad dressing, such as Creamy Poppy Seed Dressing (page 270), to toss with crisp greens.

For the meat:

3   tablespoons all-purpose flour
1½   teaspoons ground cumin
1   teaspoon salt
½   teaspoon pepper
8   (2- to 3-ounce, ½-inch-thick) boneless pork chops
1   tablespoon unsalted butter
1   tablespoon olive oil

For the apples:

1	tablespoon olive oil
2	small Granny Smith apples, cut into ½-inch slices

For the sauce:

½	cup reduced-sodium chicken broth
2	tablespoons raspberry vinegar
2	tablespoons Dijon mustard
1	cup fresh raspberries
¼	cup coarsely chopped fresh flat-leaf parsley
	Salt and pepper to taste

◗ To prepare the meat, combine the flour, cumin, salt, and pepper in a large zip-top plastic bag. Add the pork chops, 4 at a time, and shake to lightly coat. (Discard the bag and excess flour mixture.)

◗ Melt the butter with the oil in a large sauté pan over medium-high heat. Add the pork chops; cook for 3 minutes per side or until lightly browned and thoroughly cooked. Transfer to a plate and cover to keep warm. Remove the skillet from the heat.

◗ While the pork chops are cooking, cook the apples. Heat the oil in a medium skillet over medium-high heat. Add the apples; cook, stirring occasionally, for 4 minutes or until lightly browned and just tender.

◗ To make the sauce, stir the chicken broth, vinegar, and mustard into the pork chop drippings in the skillet. Stir over medium-high heat, scraping the bottom of the pan as the broth comes to a boil. Stir in the apples, raspberries, and parsley. Season with salt and pepper.

◗ Serve the apples, raspberries, and sauce over the pork chops.

PICADILLO

Makes **4** servings

This is a popular specialty in many Spanish countries, each with its own vibrant version. In Cuba, to accent its lively flavors, picadillo is served with rice and black beans, which is a great way to make the meal complete. Offer tortilla chips as an accompaniment. Or omit the sliced almonds and sprinkle coarsely crumbled tortilla chips over the servings.

16	ounces lean ground beef
½	cup coarsely chopped onion
1	(14-ounce) can diced tomatoes
1	sweet-tart apple (such as Braeburn or Granny Smith), coarsely chopped
½	cup dark raisins
1	(4-ounce) can chopped green chilies, drained
1	teaspoon ground cinnamon
¼	teaspoon ground cumin
	Salt and pepper to taste
½	cup finely shredded Cheddar cheese
½	cup toasted sliced almonds

◗ Cook the ground beef and onion in a large sauté pan over medium-high heat; stir occasionally for 5 minutes or until the onion is tender and the meat is lightly browned. Drain off any excess fat.

◗ Stir in the tomatoes, apple, raisins, chilies, cinnamon, and cumin. When the liquid comes to a boil, reduce the heat to low and simmer for 5 minutes. Season with salt and pepper.

◗ Sprinkle with cheese and almonds.

PORK SAUSAGE FRITTATA

Makes **4** servings

Here's a fine-flavored dish to elevate sausage and eggs far above the ordinary. Enjoy the frittata for breakfast, lunch, or dinner served with your favorite steamed vegetables or a cup of fresh fruit.

6	eggs
½	cup jarred roasted red bell peppers, drained and cut into ¼-inch strips
¼	cup finely chopped fresh basil
8	ounces bulk pork sausage, regular or hot flavor
1	tomato, thinly sliced
2	green onions, thinly sliced
¼	cup sliced black olives
½	cup finely shredded Cheddar cheese
	Freshly ground pepper and sprigs of fresh basil for garnish

◗ Use a fork to lightly beat the eggs in a medium bowl. Stir in the bell peppers and basil.

◗ Heat a large nonstick skillet over medium-high heat. Add the sausage; cook, stirring to crumble, for 5 minutes or until lightly browned and thoroughly cooked.

◗ Reduce the heat to medium. Slowly pour the egg mixture into the skillet so that the sausage remains evenly distributed. Cook, undisturbed, for 1 minute or until the frittata begins to set around the edges. Using a spatula, gently lift the edges and tilt the skillet to let any uncooked egg run down under the bottom. Continue cooking for 3 minutes or until the eggs are almost set but still moist on top.

◗ Reduce the heat to low. Arrange the tomato slices on the top of the frittata. Sprinkle with the green onions, olives, and cheese. Cover and cook for 1 more minute or until the eggs are set on top, the cheese is melted, and the bottom of the frittata is lightly browned.

◗ Cut into 8 wedges and garnish with pepper and fresh basil sprigs.

Note: To thaw frozen bulk sausage, transfer the sausage from the package to a microwave-proof bowl. Microwave on DEFROST for 1 minute. Break the sausage into pieces. Microwave for 1 minute more.

TIP

As an alternative method for cooking a frittata, cook it in an ovenproof nonstick skillet. Position the oven rack about 5 inches from the heating element and preheat the broiler. Rather than covering the pan as the final cooking step, place the pan under the broiler. This will not only finish cooking the eggs but also will lightly brown the top.

PEPPER-CRUSTED SIRLOIN WITH SANGIOVESE-MUSHROOM SAUCE

Makes **4** servings

Pair the steak and its rich mushroom sauce with buttered julienned carrots and garlic mashed potatoes. This is a dinner worthy of special-occasion status, so light some candles and pour glasses of bold Cabernet, Merlot, or Syrah.

For the meat:

1	tablespoon mixed whole peppercorns (such as black, pink, and white), coarsely crushed
24	ounces (1-inch-thick) boneless beef top sirloin steak, cut into 4 pieces
½	teaspoon salt
1	tablespoon unsalted butter

For the sauce:

2	tablespoons unsalted butter
1	cup onion in ¼-inch slices
1	(8-ounce) package sliced cremini mushrooms
1	tablespoon finely chopped fresh thyme or 1 teaspoon dried thyme
¾	cup Sangiovese or other medium-bodied, high-acid red wine
1	teaspoon cornstarch
	Salt to taste
	Coarsely chopped fresh flat-leaf parsley for garnish

◐ Press the crushed peppercorns into the top and bottom of the steaks; sprinkle with salt.

◐ To cook the steaks, melt the butter in a large skillet over medium-high heat. Add the steaks; cook, turning once, for 9 to 11 minutes for medium-rare. Transfer to a plate and cover to keep warm. Set the pan aside, but do not rinse or wash.

◐ While the steaks are cooking, prepare the sauce. Melt the butter in another large skillet over medium-high heat. Add the onion, mushrooms, and thyme. Cook, stirring frequently, for 4 minutes or until the onions and mushrooms are tender. Reduce the heat to medium.

◐ Stir together the wine and cornstarch in a small bowl until smooth. Stir into the onions and mushrooms. Stir constantly for 1 minute or until slightly thickened. Pour the mushroom mixture into the steak drippings in the other skillet; stir, scraping the bottom of the pan to loosen all the browned bits of meat. Season with salt.

◐ Serve the steaks topped with the sauce and garnish with parsley.

——— TIP ———

Mushrooms keep best with good air circulation. If they are sealed in plastic wrap, remove the plastic and place the mushrooms in a paper bag before refrigerating. Do not wash before storing. Before using mushrooms, simply brush with a mushroom brush or wipe with a moist paper towel. If you rinse them, do it very quickly; because mushrooms are very absorbent, they should not be allowed to soak in water. They also should be cooked quickly; because mushrooms are 90 percent water, they easily become overcooked and mushy.

Filet Mignon
with Sherried Mushrooms

FILET MIGNON
WITH SHERRIED MUSHROOMS

Makes 4 servings

To many, filet mignon is a steak lover's dream. The cut has less fat than others, so it is important to cook filet mignon over high heat and not cook it for too long, which causes the meat to dry out. For an epicurean menu, accompany this perfect partnership of mushrooms and steak with buttered baby carrots. My wine expert friend, Kristine Igo, says pairing this luscious dish with Valpolicella Ripasso, an earthy and almost portlike red wine from northern Italy's Veneto region, makes her mouth water. So remember this menu for your next special dinner party.

Also try serving the tasty mushrooms with fish or chicken—and even scrambled eggs or polenta slices to please vegetarians. Or pile the mushrooms on toasted or grilled slices of French bread for a lovely appetizer.

For the mushrooms:

2	tablespoons unsalted butter
2	tablespoons olive oil
8	ounces sliced white mushrooms
1	teaspoon minced garlic
¾	teaspoon paprika
¼	cup dry sherry
1	teaspoon fresh lemon juice
1	tablespoon minced fresh flat-leaf parsley
⅛	teaspoon salt, or to taste
⅛	teaspoon pepper, or to taste

For the meat:

4	(6-ounce) beef filets mignons
	Dash of salt and pepper
2	teaspoons finely chopped fresh rosemary
2	tablespoons olive oil

❍ To prepare the mushrooms, melt the butter with the oil in a large sauté pan over medium heat. Add the mushrooms, garlic, and paprika; cook, stirring occasionally, for 5 minutes or until the mushrooms are tender and lightly browned. Add the sherry and lemon juice; stir gently for 2 minutes or until the liquid is slightly reduced. Remove from the heat and stir in the remaining ingredients. Cover to keep warm.

❍ To cook the meat, season the filets mignons with salt and pepper, and then sprinkle with rosemary. Heat the oil in a large skillet over high heat. Arrange the meat in the skillet and cook for 4 minutes per side (for medium-rare) or until desired doneness.

❍ To serve, spoon the warm mushrooms over the filets mignons.

TIP

There are thousands of varieties of mushrooms. The readily available cultivated white mushroom has a mild, earthy flavor; those labeled "button mushrooms" are immature and smaller. Cremini mushrooms are dark brown, slightly firmer, and have a fuller flavor than their paler relatives. Portobello mushrooms are the matured form of cremini mushrooms.

SPANISH CHORIZO FRITTATA

Makes **4** servings

I first tasted manchego cheese when I purchased this sheep's milk cheese for a midafternoon snack at Barcelona's Mercat la Boqueria. Here in the U.S., I can find it at most cheese markets. For this recipe, be sure to use Spanish-type chorizo, a highly seasoned pork sausage made from smoked pork that is already cooked. Make one large open-faced omelet that can be cut into wedges to generously serve four people. For brunch, I pair the frittata with juicy orange slices drizzled with pure maple syrup. For lunch or dinner, accompany it with some crusty peasant bread and a green salad.

6	eggs
¾	cup coarsely grated manchego cheese (3 ounces)
½	teaspoon Spanish pimentón or paprika
	Dash of salt and pepper
1	tablespoon olive oil
6	ounces Spanish chorizo sausage, cut into ½-inch cubes
¼	cup finely chopped red onion
	Freshly ground pepper for garnish

◗ Use a fork to lightly beat the eggs in a medium bowl. Stir in the cheese, pimentón, salt, and pepper.

◗ Heat the oil in a large nonstick skillet over medium-high heat. Add the chorizo and onion; cook, stirring occasionally, for 2 minutes or until the chorizo is lightly browned and the onion is tender.

◗ Reduce the heat to medium. Slowly pour the egg mixture into the skillet so that the sausage remains evenly distributed. Cook, undisturbed, for 1 minute or until the frittata begins to set around the edges. Using a spatula, gently lift the edges and tilt the skillet to let any uncooked egg run down under the bottom. Continue cooking for 3 minutes or until the eggs are almost set but still moist on top.

◗ Reduce the heat to low; cover and continue to cook for 1 minute or until the eggs are set on top and the bottom of the frittata is lightly browned.

◗ Use a spatula to transfer the frittata from the pan to a large serving platter. (It will be thin, about ¾ inch.) Sprinkle with pepper.

◗ Cut into 8 wedges and serve warm or at room temperature.

SOUTHWESTERN STEAK WITH BEAN SALSA

Makes **4** servings

Here's a dish inspired by the Wild West. It makes a quick-to-prepare and satisfying main course that the whole family will enjoy on a demanding weeknight. To add crunch, serve with spoonfuls of Vegetable Salsa (page 274) on the side.

16	ounces boneless beef top sirloin steak
1	tablespoon olive oil plus olive oil for brushing
½	green bell pepper, coarsely chopped
1¼	cups chunky tomato salsa, divided
1	(15-ounce) can great northern beans, drained and rinsed
¼	teaspoon ground cumin

Salt and pepper to taste

¼ cup finely chopped fresh cilantro

● Heat a stovetop grill pan over high heat. Lightly brush both sides of the steak with oil. Reduce the heat to medium-high; cook for 5 minutes per side or until the desired degree of doneness.

● While the steak is cooking, heat 1 tablespoon oil in a medium sauté pan over medium-high heat. Add the bell pepper; cook, stirring occasionally, for 4 minutes or until tender. Reduce the heat to medium; stir in 1 cup salsa, the beans, and cumin. Stir until thoroughly heated.

● When the steak is done, remove it from the pan and let stand for a few minutes. Cut into thin slices. Sprinkle with salt and pepper.

● To serve, spoon the bean mixture onto plates; top with the beef slices, the remaining ¼ cup salsa, and cilantro.

BACON AND GREEN ONION FRITTATA WITH SMOKY GOUDA

Makes **4** servings

The warm, smoky Gouda adds a complementary accent to the bacon. And this Dutch cheese makes a nice change from the traditional Cheddar. Serve the frittata for brunch with toasted brioche and your favorite fruit preserves.

8 strips bacon

8 eggs

¼ cup cold water

¼ teaspoon salt

¼ teaspoon pepper

2 tablespoons unsalted butter, divided

4 green onions, thinly sliced

1 cup finely shredded natural smoked Gouda or natural smoked Cheddar cheese

● Cook the bacon in a large nonstick skillet, turning as needed, for 12 minutes or until crisp. (Or place the bacon, 4 strips at a time, on a triple layer of paper towels on a microwave-safe plate, and cover with a double layer of towels. Microwave on HIGH for 2 minutes. Continue to microwave for 1-minute intervals until done.) Transfer to a paper-towel-lined plate to cool. Discard the bacon drippings. Crumble when cool.

● Lightly whisk the eggs, water, salt, and pepper in a large bowl until combined.

● Melt 1 tablespoon butter in the same skillet over medium-high heat. Add the green onions; cook, stirring constantly, for 1 minute or until softened. Transfer to a bowl.

● Melt the remaining 1 tablespoon butter in the same skillet. Slowly pour in the eggs. Cook, undisturbed, for 1 minute or until the frittata begins to set around the edges. Using a spatula, gently lift the edges and tilt the skillet to let any uncooked egg run down under the bottom. Continue cooking for 3 minutes or until the frittata is almost set but still moist on top.

● Sprinkle the top of the frittata with the cheese, bacon, and green onions. Reduce the heat to low; cover and cook for 1 minute or until the eggs are set and the cheese is melted.

● Cut the frittata into wedges to serve.

SPEEDY BEEF HASH

Makes **4** servings

Grand Café, a charming neighborhood restaurant in Minneapolis, serves the most delicious Kobe beef brisket. I savor every bite but can never finish the generous portion. Lucky me. The next day at home, I transform the tender leftovers into this delicious hash, which I serve topped with poached or sunny-side-up eggs to make the meal complete. I've multiplied my single serving recipe so you can share this speedy dish with your family as a day-after destination for beef. Mary Hunter, who owns the café, uses chunks of roasted potatoes in her hash, but the frozen shredded potatoes are a delicious and speedy alternative.

2	tablespoons olive oil
3	cups frozen hash browns (shredded potatoes)
½	cup finely chopped onion
½	green bell pepper, finely chopped
2	cups cooked beef in ½-inch cubes
1	tablespoon fresh thyme or 1 teaspoon dried thyme
½	teaspoon pepper, or to taste
	Salt to taste

◐ Heat the oil in a large skillet over medium-high heat. Add the potatoes, onion, and bell pepper. Cook, stirring occasionally, for 3 minutes or until the onion and bell pepper begin to become tender and the potatoes are thawed.

◐ Stir in the remaining ingredients and press with a spatula to flatten. Cook for 2 minutes or until the bottom begins to brown. Turn over in sections and continue to cook for 2 more minutes or until the hash is flecked with brown, crispy bits and the onion and bell pepper are tender.

ORANGE-GLAZED PORK TENDERLOIN WITH MANGO-LIME SALSA

Makes **4** servings

Cutting the pork tenderloin into thin medallions speeds up the cooking and makes an elegant presentation for this fast and festive meal bursting with fresh, bright flavors. To add substance and even more color, accompany the dish with sweet potatoes.

For the salsa:

2	cups jarred mango in ½-inch cubes
¼	cup coarsely chopped fresh cilantro
	Coarsely chopped green parts of 4 green onions
1	tablespoon olive oil
½	teaspoon lime zest
2	tablespoons fresh lime juice
½	teaspoon red pepper flakes, or to taste
	Salt to taste

For the pork:

20	ounces pork tenderloin
	Olive oil for rubbing
	Dash of salt and pepper
1	tablespoon olive oil
	Coarsely chopped white parts of 4 green onions
½	cup fresh orange juice

◐ Stir together the salsa ingredients in a medium bowl.

- Slice the pork crosswise into ¾-inch-thick medallions and press with your hand to flatten slightly. Rub the surfaces with oil to lightly coat and sprinkle with salt and pepper.

- Heat a large skillet over medium-high heat. When hot, add the pork in a single layer. Cook for 4 minutes per side or until lightly browned and thoroughly cooked. Transfer to a plate and cover to keep warm.

- Heat the oil in the same skillet over medium-high heat. Add the white parts of the green onions; cook, stirring constantly, for 30 seconds. Add the orange juice; stir, scraping the bottom of the pan as the juice comes to a boil. Continue to cook, stirring constantly, for 2 minutes or until the juice becomes syrupy.

- Return the pork to the skillet to reheat, and coat with the glaze.

- To serve, drizzle the remaining glaze over the pork medallions and top with the salsa.

SAUSAGE AND YAM SKILLET

Makes **4** servings

These aromas remind me of my Czech grandmother, who used to make rustic sausage and cabbage dishes like this for simple, weeknight dinners. It's not a meal destined for guests, but rather one that makes a wholesome family supper.

12	ounces precooked kielbasa sausage, cut into 16 (1-inch) pieces
2	yams (red sweet potatoes), peeled and cut into 1-inch cubes

1	(14-ounce) can reduced-sodium chicken broth
1	green bell pepper, cut into 1-inch pieces
½	cup thinly sliced onion
2	tablespoons minced fresh thyme or 1 teaspoon dried thyme
¼	teaspoon pepper, or to taste
	Salt to taste
3	cups coarsely shredded green cabbage

- Combine all the ingredients, except the cabbage, in a large sauté pan over medium-high heat. When the liquid comes to a boil, reduce the heat to medium. Cover and cook for 5 minutes.

- Stir in the cabbage. Cover and cook, stirring occasionally, for 5 more minutes or until the cabbage is wilted and the yams are tender.

- Spoon the sausage and vegetables into large shallow bowls and add ladles of broth.

───── TIP ─────

What is labeled a "yam" at the supermarket most likely is a red (or orange) sweet potato. These have a dark, uniformly colored brown skin, a shape that tapers on both ends, a bright orange flesh, and a sweet flavor when cooked. White sweet potatoes have a lighter, thinner skin, pale yellow flesh, and a less sweet flavor. Store sweet potatoes unwrapped in a cool, dry, dark, and well-ventilated place for up to two weeks; do not refrigerate.

Vegetarian

FOR MANY years I was a vegetarian. As time went on and I continued to travel and eat in many parts of the world, I realized that vegetarian eating was somewhat limiting. But I still love to cook vegetarian dishes at home, and I find that most of my friends eat meatless meals frequently, though not exclusively, just as I now do.

Nearly all cuisines include full-flavored, satisfying vegetarian dishes. And even the most devout carnivores I know appreciate the appeal of gourmet Grilled Cheese Sandwiches with Balsamic Dip (page 240), meaty Grilled Portobello Mushroom Sandwiches (page 238), and Huevos Rancheros (page 240) accompanied with cubes of juicy papaya for Sunday brunch, as well as many pasta dishes, especially Ravioli with Hazelnut and Sage Pesto (page 251).

My cooking class students often ask me for advice in dealing with the challenge of cooking for friends or family members on a meatless diet. If this is one of your concerns, too, you'll find solutions in this chapter. Many of the recipes can also serve as side dishes for others at the table who want meat, seafood, or chicken as their main course. For example, serve Greek Green Beans and Tomatoes with Feta (page 261) to accompany chicken breasts cooked on the grill, or add shrimp to Chilean Vegetable Stew (page 255).

Some dishes in this chapter are perfect for vegans, strict vegetarians who do not eat any animal meat or animal-derived foods, such as butter, cheese, eggs, or milk. They'll welcome a meal of the Mexican Vegetable Soup (page 233), Fresh Green Bean Salad with Spicy Peanut Sauce (page 222), Chinese Mapo Tofu with Wheat-Flour Noodles (page 246), and Garlic and Lemon Lentils (page 260). Other dishes can become

vegan by making simple changes, such as eliminating the cheese garnish on Chickpea Soup with Kale (page 229), Chilean Vegetable Stew (page 255), Mostaccioli with a Trio of Sweet Peppers (page 248), and Rigatoni with Swiss Chard (page 253), or omitting the cheese layer in the Grilled Portobello Mushroom Sandwiches (page 238).

Variety is the key to healthful vegetarian recipes. Here you'll find opportunities to try vegetables that may be new to you, such as kale and Swiss chard, or new flavors, like curry leaves or oyster mushrooms.

But healthful meatless meals can't be composed of vegetables alone. You will find dishes here that offer a variety of protein sources: from legumes, nuts, and soy to eggs, cheese, and other dairy products.. Try Japanese Miso Soup (page 234) with tofu and East Indian Noodles with Split Peas and Cashews (page 244). I've also included a variety of satisfying carbohydrates, such as rice, couscous, pasta, and polenta, which form a fine foundation for tasty meatless ingredients.

When making vegetarian dishes, always use top-quality vegetables. For some recipes, especially the soups, a good vegetable stock is essential. Making stock from scratch isn't really practical for 15-Minute cooking, but I have found that the choices are endless for making vegetable stock quickly: On the supermarket shelves, you will find many products, including vegetable stock concentrates, cubes, and powders. They vary significantly in flavors—some are salty, some herb fla-vored, others mild. Experiment to find the one you like best. (You'll find that I have not specified low-sodium vegetable stock because I think that some salt is necessary to add flavor.)

Keep in mind, too, that many of the recipes in other chapters of this book, especially soups, can be made vegetarian by substituting vegetable stock for chicken broth or by omitting fish, chicken, or meat. On the flip side, you can substitute chicken broth for vegetable stock if you are not a vegetarian and prefer a more robust flavor.

Endive and Apple Salad
with Blue Cheese Dressing

ENDIVE AND APPLE SALAD WITH BLUE CHEESE DRESSING

Makes **4** servings

Blue cheese, apples, and walnuts are a classic combination to snack on beside a warming fire. But there's no need to wait for winter to enjoy their compatible flavors. Use the trio to top spears of endive for a memorable summer salad.

For the dressing:

½	cup buttermilk
¼	cup coarsely crumbled blue cheese
3	tablespoons mayonnaise
2	tablespoons finely chopped fresh flat-leaf parsley
½	teaspoon minced garlic
	Salt and pepper to taste

For the salad:

3	Belgian endives, divided
2	red-skinned apples (such as Pink Lady or Braeburn), cut into ½-inch cubes
½	cup coarsely chopped walnuts

◗ Combine all the dressing ingredients, except the salt and pepper, in a blender; purée until smooth. Season with salt and pepper.

◗ Separate the leaves of one endive and arrange 3 leaves on each of 4 salad plates with the tips pointing outward.

◗ Coarsely chop the remaining 2 endives and put into a medium bowl. Add the apples and dressing. Stir until combined.

◗ Sprinkle the servings with walnuts.

STONE FRUIT SALAD WITH POMEGRANATE-RASPBERRY VINAIGRETTE

Makes **4** servings

All year long, I look forward to the stone fruits of summer because few pleasures can be compared to biting into a perfectly ripe peach. When making this salad, also add apricots and a plum, in whatever combination you'd like so that the total amount of chopped fruit is about 4 cups. There are several new hybrid fruits in the stone fruit category too, such as the Black Velvet Plumcot, a juicy cross between a plum and apricot.

2	peaches, peeled and cut into 1-inch chunks
2	apricots, cut into 1-inch chunks
1	plum, cut into 1-inch chunks
¼	cup Pomegranate-Raspberry Vinaigrette (page 271)
2	tablespoons dried currants
1	cup arugula leaves
	Coarsely chopped toasted walnuts for garnish

◗ Stir together the peaches, apricots, and plum. Add the vinaigrette and currants; stir again.

◗ Serve the salad on arugula leaves and garnish with walnuts.

PINEAPPLE CARPACCIO

Makes **4** servings

As a photographer who loves cooking and shooting beautiful food, my friend Nancy Bundt shared this recipe, which was served to her by a worldly Swedish couple. Nancy recommends using a fruity type of olive oil rather than the more bitter-tasting Tuscan oil. To make the presentation visually appealing, she arranges a circle of overlapping pineapple slices, with some basil leaves peeking through from beneath and others arranged on top. Irresistible!

20 (⅛-inch) fresh pineapple slices
  Extra-virgin olive oil for drizzling
  Fresh basil leaves and coarse freshly ground pepper for garnish

○ Arrange the pineapple slices on salad plates. Lightly drizzle with olive oil and sprinkle with pepper. Garnish with basil leaves.

TIP

Mixed baby greens, also called mesclun, come in a prewashed mix—usually including arugula, frisée, oak leaf lettuce, and radicchio leaves—which offers a variety of textures and flavors ranging from sweet to bitter.

MESCLUN SALAD WITH GRILLED PEARS, BLUE CHEESE, AND MAPLE-WALNUT VINAIGRETTE

Makes **4** servings

Sweet and savory flavors pair well together in this elegant salad. I love the look and texture of grilled pear slices, but to speed up the preparation, simply chop the pears and stir them with the vinaigrette before tossing the salad. Sometimes I also add dried cranberries. Serve this as a first course or for lunch accompanied by slices of nut bread.

2 pears, peeled, cored, halved, and cut into ¼-inch slices
  Olive oil for brushing
6 cups mesclun (mixed baby greens)
½ cup Maple-Walnut Vinaigrette (page 269)
1 cup Sugar-Spiced Walnuts (page 279)
½ cup finely crumbled blue cheese

○ Heat a stovetop grill over high heat. Lightly brush the pear slices with oil. Reduce the heat to medium-high; cook for 30 seconds per side or until tender and lightly browned. Transfer to a plate and set aside to cool.

○ Toss the mesclun with the vinaigrette in a large bowl. Divide the salad among 4 plates. Top each serving with pear slices, walnuts, and blue cheese.

Pineapple Carpaccio

AUTUMN APPLE SALAD WITH MAPLE-WALNUT VINAIGRETTE

Makes **4** servings

I love this flavor combination, especially in the fall. And I choose one green and one red apple for visual appeal. Sugar-Spiced Walnuts make the salad exceptional, but if you don't have them on hand, substitute plain walnuts, which you can quickly toast in a dry skillet on the stovetop to bring out their nutty flavor.

2	sweet-tart apples (such as Granny Smith and McIntosh), cut into 1-inch chunks
2	cups coarsely chopped romaine lettuce
½	cup Maple-Walnut Vinaigrette (page 269)
½	cup finely crumbled blue cheese
½	cup Sugar-Spiced Walnuts (page 279)

❍ Toss the apples and lettuce with the vinaigrette in a large bowl. Add the cheese and toss again.

❍ Divide among 4 salad plates and sprinkle the salads with walnuts.

ORANGE, OLIVE, AND ARUGULA SALAD

Makes **4** servings

Spain is famous for its oranges, especially in Andalusia, and that is the origin of this refreshing salad. When they're available, I like to use thin-skinned blood oranges, which offer juicy, sweet flavor, as well as their intense color.

For the vinaigrette:

¼	cup fresh orange juice
2	tablespoons hazelnut or walnut oil
1	tablespoon honey
	Salt to taste

For the salad:

3	large oranges, peeled and thinly sliced
12	black olives, pitted and coarsely chopped
12	large arugula leaves
	Finely chopped flat-leaf parsley for garnish

❍ Whisk together the vinaigrette ingredients in a medium bowl.

❍ Add the oranges and olives and toss.

❍ To serve, arrange the arugula leaves on salad plates; top with the orange mixture. Garnish the servings with parsley.

> ——— TIP ———
>
> Arugula, also called roquette or rocket, has long, spear-shaped leaves that resemble dandelion greens. They have a spicy, peppery, mustardy bitterness and aroma. Select dark green leaves 3 to 5 inches long; the more mature the green, the stronger the flavor. Wrap the roots in moist paper towels and place them in a plastic bag; store in the refrigerator for up to two days. Wash the sandy leaves thoroughly before using.

BABY SPINACH
AND ORANGE SALAD

Makes **4** servings

In January when they're available from Florida, I like to make this refreshing, light salad with honeybell oranges, which are the sweetest and juiciest of all. Top the servings with Sugar-Spiced Walnuts (page 279) to add their intriguing flavor and crunch.

For the orange vinaigrette:

¼	cup extra-virgin olive oil
¼	cup fresh orange juice
1	tablespoon red wine vinegar
1	tablespoon minced shallot
1	teaspoon Dijon mustard
	Salt and pepper to taste

For the salad:

6	cups baby salad spinach
2	oranges, cut into ½-inch cubes
½	cup very thin red onion slices
½	cup coarsely crumbled feta or blue cheese

▶ Whisk together the vinaigrette ingredients in a small bowl.

▶ Toss together the salad ingredients in a large bowl. Add the vinaigrette and toss again.

▶ Top the servings with cheese.

TOMATO AND
GOAT CHEESE SALAD WITH
BALSAMIC VINAIGRETTE

Makes **4** servings

This salad is an example of elegant simplicity. Its just-right blend of flavors, dramatic colors, and do-ahead capabilities make this a stellar dish for summer entertaining.

8	ounces medium pasta shells
½	cup Balsamic Vinaigrette (page 268)
1	cup grape tomatoes
3	green onions, thinly sliced diagonally
½	cup (4 ounces) chèvre cheese, coarsely crumbled
	Salt and pepper to taste
8	cups mesclun (mixed baby greens)
	Freshly ground pepper for garnish

▶ Cook the pasta shells according to package instructions.

▶ When the pasta is done, drain well. Rinse with cold water and drain again.

▶ Transfer the pasta to a large bowl. Add the vinaigrette, tomatoes, and green onions; toss until evenly combined. Add the cheese and toss gently. Season with salt and pepper.

▶ Serve the pasta salad on beds of mesclun. Garnish with pepper.

Watermelon
and Chèvre Salad

WATERMELON
AND CHÈVRE SALAD

Makes **4** servings

This dish was inspired by a memorable lunch in the
Bahamas, where I savored a watermelon salad on a
breezy veranda that overlooked the powdery sand
beach and the tranquil, turquoise-blue Atlantic.
This salad, too, is a feast for the senses, and it's the
perfect reason to bring out your best extra-virgin
olive oil and to buy top-quality chèvre cheese.
If you can find it, try chèvre made with coarsely
ground peppercorns, which adds a pleasing flavor
complement to the juicy, sweet melon. There's really
no reason to measure the ingredients, but here are
approximations. Take a look at the photo and begin
chopping your watermelon triangles.

12	randomly cut triangular chunks of watermelon (bases about 2 inches, height about 2½ inches)
½	cup (4 ounces) chèvre cheese in bite-size chunks
¼	cup extra-virgin olive oil
¼	cup shelled, salted pistachios
	Coarsely ground sea salt and coarse freshly ground pepper to taste

▶ For each serving, place 4 watermelon triangles
on a plate. Sprinkle the plate with chèvre. Drizzle
the watermelon, cheese, and plate with olive oil.
Scatter the plate with pistachios and sprinkle with
salt and pepper.

— TIP —

Sea salt is obtained by evaporating
sea water in enclosed, protected bays.
The salt is purified during this process,
leaving naturally present trace minerals,
including magnesium, zinc, calcium, iron, and
potassium. These elements offer a more
complex flavor than ordinary table salt,
so less is usually needed. Fine sea salt,
which dissolves almost instantly, can be
used just like ordinary table salt. Coarse
sea salt crystals are used to salt cooking
water. Or they can be finely ground in a salt
mill for use in recipes or at the table. (Make
sure that the salt mill has a stainless steel
or other noncorrosive mechanism.)

Specialty varieties of sea salt include *sel
gris*, gray in color and slightly moist, which
can be used to season foods while cooking,
and *fleur de sel*, used to add flavor at the
table. You'll find these in gourmet shops.

GAZPACHO BREAD SALAD WITH SHERRY VINAIGRETTE

Makes **4** servings

Here's a take-off on panzanella, a classic bread salad that frugal Italian home cooks developed as a way to transform day-old bread into a delicious yet practical meal. (In Italy, bread is unsalted, resulting in loaves that are fresh only the day they are baked.) You don't need to use stale bread, but it's important to use full-bodied bread that will absorb the dressing without falling apart.

For the vinaigrette:

¼	cup extra-virgin olive oil
3	tablespoons sherry vinegar
1	teaspoon minced garlic
½	teaspoon paprika
	Salt and pepper to taste

For the salad:

2	tomatoes, cut into ½-inch dice
1	cucumber, peeled, quartered lengthwise, seeded, and cut into ½-inch slices
½	red bell pepper, coarsely chopped
¼	cup finely chopped red onion
¼	cup pitted kalamata olives
¼	cup coarsely chopped fresh basil
2	cups sturdy bread in 1-inch cubes
4	hard-cooked eggs, coarsely chopped

◉ Whisk together the vinaigrette ingredients in a small bowl.

◉ Combine the tomatoes, cucumber, bell pepper, onion, olives, and basil in a large bowl. Add about half the vinaigrette and toss. Add the bread cubes and the remaining vinaigrette; toss again to mix thoroughly.

◉ Spoon the salad into bowls. Top the servings with the eggs and drizzle with the remaining vinaigrette.

GREEK TOMATO AND FETA SALAD WITH LEMON-OREGANO VINAIGRETTE

Makes **4** servings

This simple salad relies on top-notch ingredients, so be sure to use extra-virgin olive oil and fresh lemon juice. It's a rustic vegetarian lunch dish reminiscent of the popular taverna food served at outdoor tables throughout the Greek islands. For nonvegetarians, serve the salad as an uncomplicated accompaniment to grilled fish or chicken, such as Tomato-Soy Chicken Kabobs (page 83) or Cornmeal-Crusted Tilapia on Tomato Ragu (page 128).

For the vinaigrette:

1	teaspoon minced garlic
⅛	teaspoon salt, or to taste
⅓	cup extra-virgin olive oil
2	tablespoons fresh lemon juice
¼	teaspoon dried oregano

For the salad:

8	cups torn romaine lettuce leaves
½	cucumber, halved lengthwise and cut into ¼-inch slices
1	cup grape tomatoes
¼	cup coarsely chopped red onion
¼	cup coarsely chopped pitted kalamata olives

¼	cup coarsely chopped fresh basil leaves
1	teaspoon fresh lemon zest
¼	cup coarsely crumbled feta cheese
	Freshly ground pepper to taste

● To make the vinaigrette, stir together the garlic with the salt in a small bowl to make a paste. Add the remaining vinaigrette ingredients and whisk to combine.

● Put the lettuce in a large salad bowl. Top with the remaining salad ingredients, except the feta cheese and pepper. Just before serving, drizzle with the dressing and toss. Sprinkle with the feta cheese and pepper.

HEIRLOOM TOMATO AND BEET SALAD WITH BALSAMIC VINAIGRETTE

Makes **4** servings

One of summer's sweetest pleasures is exquisitely ripe heirloom tomatoes. These full-flavored tomatoes are grown from nonhybrid plants—and some varieties are quite ancient—thus the name "heirloom." You'll find them in specialty produce markets, farmers' markets, and in some supermarkets.

2	heirloom tomatoes, cut into ½-inch cubes
1	(15-ounce) can sliced red beets, cut into ½-inch squares
¼	cup coarsely chopped fresh basil
½	cup Balsamic Vinaigrette (page 268)
8	cups mesclun (mixed baby greens)
¼	cup coarsely crumbled blue cheese

● Stir together the tomatoes, beets, and basil in a medium bowl. Stir in the vinaigrette.

● Mound the mixture over greens on salad plates and sprinkle with the cheese.

HEARTS OF PALM SALAD

Makes **4** servings

Fresh hearts of palm are available in Florida, but lucky for the rest of us, the canned variety works just fine in this recipe. For an eye-catching presentation, serve the refreshing salad in martini glasses. For nonvegetarians, add cooked salad shrimp.

1	avocado, peeled, pitted, and cut into ½-inch cubes
¼	cup fresh lime juice
1	(15-ounce) can hearts of palm, drained and cut into ¼-inch slices
2	tomatoes, cut into ½-inch cubes
3	green onions, coarsely chopped
¼	cup coarsely chopped fresh cilantro
1	tablespoon seeded and finely chopped jalapeño chili, or to taste
1	teaspoon minced garlic
	Salt and pepper to taste
	Sprigs of fresh cilantro for garnish

● Toss the avocado with the lime juice in a medium bowl. Add the remaining ingredients, except the garnish, and stir gently to combine.

● Garnish with cilantro sprigs.

TABOULI

Makes **4** servings (4 cups)

Tabouli, a well-known classic Middle Eastern dish, will keep for up to three days in a covered container in the refrigerator. It can be assembled quickly and is great to have on hand in the summer to serve as a vegetarian salad or as a refreshing accompaniment to fish or chicken. Traditionally, the recipe is made with bulgur wheat, but using couscous speeds up the preparation time and yields delicious results.

¾	cup water
¾	cup couscous
¼	cup fresh lemon juice
2	tablespoons extra-virgin olive oil
1	tomato, cut into ½-inch cubes
1	cup seeded cucumber in ½-inch cubes
½	cup finely chopped fresh flat-leaf parsley
2	green onions, finely chopped
¼	cup finely chopped fresh mint leaves
¼	teaspoon salt, or to taste
¼	teaspoon pepper, or to taste

● Heat the water in a small saucepan over high heat until very hot but not boiling. Remove the pan from the heat. Stir in the couscous. Let stand, covered, for 5 minutes or until the liquid is completely absorbed.

● Meanwhile, stir together the lemon juice and oil in a medium bowl. Stir in the tomato, cucumber, parsley, green onions, and mint.

● Fluff the couscous with a fork and stir into the tomato mixture. Season with salt and pepper.

TIP

Couscous, sometimes called Moroccan pasta, is a tiny beadlike pasta made from semolina flour. It is available in both white and whole-wheat varieties in most supermarkets, usually in the rice aisle. Couscous keeps almost indefinitely in a tightly closed container in a dark, dry place. This quick-cooking pasta is prepared by combining equal amounts of couscous and hot liquid, such as water, chicken broth, or vegetable stock. Then let it stand until the couscous is tender and the liquid is completely absorbed. Couscous will double in volume as it absorbs the liquid. Fluff with a fork before serving.

Israeli couscous (as in Grilled Pesto Shrimp with Israeli Couscous, page 121) is larger, about the size of peppercorns, and requires longer cooking time.

FRESH GREEN BEAN SALAD WITH SPICY PEANUT SAUCE

Makes **4** servings

When summer's at its peak, this combination of green beans with a nutty sauce is the perfect reason to make a trip to the farmers' market for the freshest produce available.

6	cups green beans in 2-inch pieces (20 ounces)

½ cup coarsely chopped roasted, salted peanuts; 2 tablespoons reserved for garnish

⅓ cup finely chopped red bell pepper

¼ cup finely chopped red onion

½ cup Spicy Peanut Sauce (page 265)

Salt and pepper to taste

○ Fill a Dutch oven half full of salted water; bring to a boil over high heat. Add the green beans; cover and cook for 4 minutes or until tender. Drain well. Immerse in a large bowl of cold water for 1 minute or until the beans are at room temperature. Drain again.

○ Combine the green beans with the remaining ingredients, except the garnish, in a large bowl.

○ Garnish the servings with the remaining 2 tablespoons peanuts.

WARM BUTTER BEAN SALAD WITH BASIL-SHERRY VINAIGRETTE

Makes **4** servings

Sweet bell pepper and salty feta cheese complement the peppery arugula leaves. Served warm, this amiable winter salad is assertive enough to stand on its own, but to complete the meal, pass a loaf of crusty artisan bread.

For the vinaigrette:

¼ cup extra-virgin olive oil

3 tablespoons sherry vinegar

1 tablespoon fresh lemon juice

¼ cup finely chopped fresh basil

2 tablespoons minced shallots

¼ teaspoon salt, or to taste

¼ teaspoon pepper, or to taste

For the salad:

2 cups coarsely shredded romaine lettuce

2 cups baby arugula leaves

1 tablespoon olive oil

2 carrots, coarsely shredded

½ red bell pepper, coarsely chopped

⅓ cup coarsely chopped red onion

1 teaspoon minced garlic

1 (15-ounce) can butter beans, drained and rinsed

Freshly ground pepper and finely crumbled feta cheese for garnish

○ To make the vinaigrette, whisk together the extra-virgin olive oil, sherry, and lemon juice in a small bowl. Stir in the remaining ingredients.

○ To assemble the salad, layer the lettuce and arugula on large salad plates.

○ Heat the olive oil in a medium sauté pan over medium heat. Add the carrots, bell pepper, onion, and garlic; cook, stirring occasionally, for about 5 minutes or until the bell pepper is crisp-tender. Reduce the heat to low. Add the beans and the vinaigrette; gently stir for 1 minute or until warm.

○ Spoon the bean mixture over the arugula. Serve warm garnished with pepper and feta cheese.

MUSHROOM AND RED BEET SALAD WITH HONEY-MUSTARD DRESSING

Makes **4** servings

The flavor of sweet, earthy beets combined with pungent feta cheese and a drizzle of mustardy dressing makes this salad not only colorful but also an appealing contrast of flavors. Serve it as a first course or accompanied by warm rolls for a light lunch.

For the salad:

2	tablespoons olive oil
2	cups sliced cremini mushrooms
½	cup thinly sliced red onion
1	(8-ounce) can red beet slices, drained and cut into ½-inch strips

For the dressing:

¼	cup extra-virgin olive oil
2	tablespoons Dijon mustard
2	tablespoons honey
1	tablespoon water
	Salt and pepper to taste

To complete the recipe:

4	Boston lettuce leaves
½	cup coarsely crumbled feta cheese
	Freshly ground pepper for garnish

◗ To make the salad, heat the oil in a medium skillet over medium-high heat. Add the mushrooms and onion; cook, stirring occasionally, for 5 minutes or until tender. Transfer to a bowl and let cool.

◗ Meanwhile, whisk together the dressing ingredients in a small bowl.

◗ Stir the beets into the mushrooms.

◗ Place the lettuce leaves on salad plates and top with the beet-mushroom mixture. Drizzle with the dressing and sprinkle with the feta cheese and pepper.

ORZO SALAD WITH PARMESAN-PEPPERCORN VINAIGRETTE

Makes **4** servings

Be sure to use premium extra-virgin olive oil in this Italian-inspired salad because its flavor really stands out in the simple recipe. Served warm, the cheese melts slightly, enhancing both taste and texture. Served cold, this bold salad makes delicious gourmet picnic fare. It can be made in advance. Store in a covered container in the refrigerator for up to two days.

For the pasta:

1	cup orzo

For the vinaigrette:

¼	cup extra-virgin olive oil
2	tablespoons fresh lemon juice
1	teaspoon Dijon mustard
1	teaspoon minced garlic
¼	cup finely shredded Parmesan cheese
½	teaspoon coarsely ground pepper, or to taste

To complete the recipe:

½	cup toasted pine nuts
½	cup coarsely chopped pitted kalamata olives
¼	cup finely chopped red onion

2   tablespoons small (nonpareil) capers, drained and rinsed

Salt to taste

6   cups salad spinach

Freshly shredded Parmesan cheese for garnish

◗ Cook the orzo according to package instructions.

◗ Meanwhile, prepare the vinaigrette. Whisk together the olive oil, lemon juice, mustard, and garlic in a medium bowl. Stir in the Parmesan cheese and pepper.

◗ When the orzo is done, drain well. Add to the bowl of dressing. Stir in the pine nuts, olives, onion, capers, and salt.

◗ To serve, arrange the spinach on plates. Top with the orzo salad and garnish with Parmesan cheese.

GREEN BEAN AND EGG SALAD

Makes **4** servings

This eye-catching but uncomplicated dish is one of my favorites for a light summer lunch. The unexpected combination of ingredients and textures is sure to awaken heat-jaded palates.

16 ounces haricots verts (thin French green beans)

4   hard-cooked eggs

4   teaspoons small (nonpareil) capers, drained and rinsed

½   cup Basic Vinaigrette (page 268)

Coarse freshly ground pepper for garnish

◗ Put the green beans in a medium microwave-proof dish; add ¼ cup water. Cover and microwave on HIGH for 4 minutes or until crisp-tender. (Or, cook the beans over simmering water in a stovetop steamer.) Drain and rinse with cold water.

◗ Put the eggs in a medium bowl. Use a fork to finely crumble. Stir in the capers.

◗ To assemble, arrange the green beans on salad plates, top with the egg mixture, drizzle with the vinaigrette, and garnish with pepper.

⊢ TIP ⊣

To hard-cook eggs, place them in a single layer in a saucepan and cover with at least 1 inch of cold water. Cover and bring the water to a full rolling boil over medium-high heat. Remove the pan from the heat and let the eggs stand in the water, covered, for about 15 minutes for large eggs. (For larger or smaller eggs, adjust the time up or down by about 3 minutes for each size variation.) Drain off the hot water and immediately cover the eggs with cold water; let stand until the eggs are completely cool. This cooling process prevents a dark gray-green surface from forming around the yolk. (If it does occur, the greenish color is harmless and does not alter the nutritional value or flavor of the egg.) Quick cooling also causes the eggs to contract, making them easier to peel. Refrigerate hard-cooked eggs for up to a week.

STACKED TOMATO SALAD

Makes **4** servings

This simple, artistically composed salad makes a striking presentation, and it's especially delicious accompanied by warm cornbread. For guests, add swirls of Roasted Red Bell Pepper Sauce (page 267) to the plates.

4	medium beefsteak tomatoes, each cut into 3 slices, tops and bottoms sliced off and discarded
4	cups Red Bean–Corn Relish (page 275)

▶ For each serving, arrange a salad plate with alternate layers of 3 tomato slices and ½ cup relish.

CURRIED ORZO SALAD

Makes **4** servings

This salad, bursting with ingredients both sweet and savory that are boosted by East Indian flavors, is ideal for serving on a steamy summer night. Just add some fruit muffins and a tall pitcher of iced tea, and you're all set to sit back and enjoy.

For the pasta:

8	ounces (about 2¼ cups) orzo pasta

For the dressing:

¾	cup mango chutney
¼	cup canola oil

2	tablespoons fresh lemon juice
2	tablespoons red wine vinegar
1	tablespoon sugar
1	teaspoon minced garlic
½	teaspoon salt, or to taste
¼	teaspoon pepper, or to taste

To complete the recipe:

1	cup coarsely shredded carrot
1	cup finely chopped apple, such as Braeburn or Gala
1	cup roasted and salted whole cashews
½	cup golden raisins
⅓	cup finely chopped red onion
¼	cup finely chopped fresh mint leaves
	Fresh mint leaves for garnish

▶ Cook the orzo according to package instructions. Drain, rinse in cold water until cool, and drain again.

▶ While the orzo is cooking, whisk together the dressing ingredients in a large bowl. Add the orzo and the remaining ingredients and stir until evenly combined.

▶ Garnish the servings with mint leaves.

Stacked Tomato Salad

ASIAN COLESLAW WITH ROASTED SOY NUTS

Makes **4** servings

My friend Fran Lebahn generously shares beautiful herbs from her garden with me. She also contributed this tasty mixture, which makes a refreshing salad. Fran recommends advance preparation because the ingredients soften slightly and the flavors nicely blend when the coleslaw is refrigerated for about an hour. For nonvegetarians, omit the soy nuts and serve the coleslaw as a warm weather accompaniment to grilled fish.

For the dressing:

¼	cup fresh orange juice
2	tablespoons fresh lime juice
2	tablespoons dark (Asian) sesame oil
1	tablespoon soy sauce
1	tablespoon honey
2	teaspoons finely chopped fresh ginger
½	teaspoon Tabasco sauce, or to taste
⅛	teaspoon pepper, or to taste

For the coleslaw:

6	cups coleslaw
½	red bell pepper, cut into ¼-inch strips
½	green bell pepper, cut into ¼-inch strips
½	cup red onion in ¼-inch strips
4	green onions, thinly sliced
½	cup roasted, salted soy nuts

○ Whisk together the dressing ingredients in a medium bowl.

○ Add the coleslaw ingredients, except the soy nuts, and toss until evenly combined.

○ Top each serving with 2 tablespoons soy nuts.

CUCUMBER-DILL SALAD

Makes **4** servings

My friend Tom Nugent, known for being quite a gourmet cook, shared with me this salad recipe—which, ironically, is one of the simplest and quickest in the book. The tasty combination of lemon and dill is the catalyst sparking this summer lunch.

1	(12-ounce) carton large-curd cottage cheese
1	cucumber, cut into ¼-inch dice (about 2 cups)
1	cup halved grape tomatoes
2	tablespoons snipped fresh dill
3	tablespoons mayonnaise
2	tablespoons fresh lemon juice
¼	teaspoon Tabasco sauce
	Salt and pepper to taste

○ Pour the cottage cheese into a strainer. Drain the excess liquid while chopping the cucumber, tomatoes, and dill.

○ Stir together the mayonnaise, lemon juice, and Tabasco sauce in a medium bowl. Stir in the cottage cheese, cucumber, tomatoes, and dill. Season with salt and pepper.

Soups

CHICKPEA SOUP WITH KALE

Makes **4** servings (6 cups)

Here's a full-bodied, healthful meatless soup that will appeal to nonvegetarians, too. To speed up the preparation time, buy preshredded carrots. And be sure to cook the potato until very tender for easy puréeing, which will thicken the soup.

If available, use Italian Parmigiano-Reggiano cheese for the garnish to perfectly complement the bitterness of kale. I like to serve the soup with crusty bread and an assortment of full-flavored cheeses.

1	tablespoon olive oil
1	cup finely shredded carrots
¾	cup finely chopped onion
1	teaspoon minced garlic
½	teaspoon ground cumin
4	cups vegetable stock (prepared using stock concentrate, cubes, or powder) or chicken broth for nonvegetarians
1	(15-ounce) can garbanzo beans (chickpeas), drained and rinsed
1	russet potato (10 ounces), peeled and cut into ½-inch chunks
2	ounces kale, stems and center ribs cut out and discarded; leaves finely chopped (2 cups)
	Salt and pepper to taste
	Freshly grated Parmesan cheese for garnish

▶ Heat the oil in a Dutch oven over medium-high heat. Add the carrots, onion, and garlic; cook, stirring occasionally, for 3 minutes or until tender. Add the cumin and stir for 15 seconds.

▶ Stir in the vegetable stock, beans, and potato. Increase the heat to high. When the liquid comes to a boil, reduce the heat to medium and continue to cook, stirring occasionally, for 5 minutes or until the potatoes are very tender.

▶ Use an immersion blender to purée the soup until partially puréed but still somewhat chunky. (Or transfer 1 cup of the soup to a standing blender, purée, and then stir it back into the Dutch oven.)

▶ Add the kale; stir occasionally for 2 minutes or until tender. Season with salt and pepper.

▶ Top the servings with Parmesan cheese.

— TIP —

Kale, a loose-leafed member of the cabbage family, is at its best during fall, winter, and early spring. It doesn't tolerate heat well and can become bitter if grown in the summer months. Store in a perforated plastic bag in the refrigerator for up to three days; beyond that, the flavor becomes quite strong. Be sure to wash both sides of the leaves in a bowl of cold water, and remove and discard the tough center stalks before using.

GINGERED CARROT SOUP

Makes **4** servings (6 cups)

With such a small number of ingredients in this rich and colorful soup, each makes a very important contribution. For speed, I use preshredded carrots, and I love the way crystallized ginger enhances their natural sweetness. In winter, the soup is ready in minutes to banish chills. For summer days, make it early in the morning and serve cold.

1	tablespoon olive oil
8	cups finely shredded carrots
½	cup finely chopped onion
3	cups vegetable stock (prepared using stock concentrate, cubes, or powder) or chicken broth for nonvegetarians
¼	cup finely chopped crystallized ginger
¾	teaspoons salt, divided
⅛	teaspoon ground white pepper, or to taste
1	cup heavy cream, divided
	Coarsely chopped fresh cilantro for garnish

▶ Heat the oil in a Dutch oven over medium-high heat. Add the carrots and onion; cook, stirring constantly, for 4 minutes or until crisp-tender.

▶ Stir in the vegetable stock, ginger, ½ teaspoon salt, and white pepper. Cover and increase the heat to high. When the liquid comes to a boil, reduce the heat to medium. Cook for 4 minutes or until the carrots and onion are very tender.

▶ Meanwhile, pour ½ cup heavy cream and the remaining ¼ teaspoon salt into a small bowl. Use an electric hand mixer to beat until the cream forms soft peaks.

▶ Use an immersion blender to purée the soup until smooth. Stir in the remaining ½ cup heavy cream.

▶ To serve, ladle the soup into bowls. Top with dollops of the whipped cream and sprinkle with cilantro.

CREAM OF TOMATO BASIL SOUP

Makes **4** servings (5 cups)

Luscious! I love this soup, which is perfect for children—but also elegant. And the croutons add just the right texture and flavor contrast to the silky basil and tomato cream.

2	tablespoons unsalted butter
1	cup finely chopped onion
1	teaspoon minced garlic
1	(28-ounce) can diced tomatoes
1	cup vegetable stock (prepared using stock concentrate, cubes, or powder) or chicken broth for nonvegetarians
2	tablespoons tomato paste
½	teaspoon salt, or to taste
¼	teaspoon ground white pepper, or to taste
½	cup heavy cream
¼	cup finely chopped fresh basil leaves
8	Parmesan Cheese Croutons (page 281) for garnish

▶ Melt the butter in a medium saucepan over medium-high heat. Add the onion and garlic; cook, stirring frequently, for 3 minutes or until just tender. Stir in the tomatoes, vegetable stock, tomato paste, salt, and white pepper. Bring to a boil over high heat. Then reduce the heat to low, cover, and simmer for 5 minutes or until the vegetables are very tender.

▶ Use an immersion blender to purée the soup until smooth. Stir in the cream and basil. Stir over low heat for 1 minute or until heated through.

▶ Top each serving with 2 croutons.

Mexican Vegetable Soup

MEXICAN VEGETABLE SOUP

Makes **4** servings (6 cups)

This satisfying soup is effortless, thanks to the just-right combination of supermarket staples. If you'd like, add red pepper flakes to spike the bowl with a little jolt of heat.

1	tablespoon olive oil
2	small zucchini, halved lengthwise and cut into ¼-inch slices
¾	cup finely chopped onion
1	tablespoon minced garlic
1½	cups tomato juice
1	(15-ounce) can pinto beans, drained and rinsed
1	(14-ounce) can stewed tomatoes with Mexican seasonings
1	cup frozen corn kernels
1	tablespoon finely chopped fresh oregano or 1 teaspoon dried oregano
	Salt and pepper to taste
	Coarsely broken yellow corn tortilla chips for garnish

▶ Heat the oil in a Dutch oven over medium-high heat. Add the zucchini, onion, and garlic; cook, stirring occasionally, for 5 minutes or until tender.

▶ Increase the heat to high and stir in the tomato juice, beans, tomatoes, corn, and oregano. When the liquid comes to a boil, reduce the heat to low; cover and simmer for 5 minutes. Season with salt and pepper.

▶ Top the servings with corn chips.

TIP

• Extra-virgin olive oil is made from the first pressing of top-quality olives. The oil has a pronounced, full-bodied, fruity or peppery taste and low acidity. The color and fragrance vary depending on the variety of olives, the growing conditions, and to some degree, the manner in which the olives are harvested and handled. In general, the deeper the color, the more intense the olive flavor.

• "Olive oil" is the name for a more refined and less flavorful oil. It is not always made with top-quality olives, is more acidic, and comes from second or subsequent pressings. Sometimes virgin olive oil is blended in to provide fruitiness and aroma.

• "Light olive oil" is processed using a fine filtration system, resulting in oil that is light in both color and fragrance with little of the classic olive oil flavor. It contains exactly the same number of calories as other olive oils.

• Since some of the olive oil flavor dissipates under heat, "olive oil" is acceptable for cooking. "Extra-virgin" is the best choice in uncooked recipes, such as vinaigrettes, or if added for flavor in the final stages of cooking.

MISO SOUP

Makes **4** servings (8 cups)

A culinary mainstay in Japan, miso is made with fermented soybeans mashed into a paste the consistency of peanut butter. It has a wonderful salty depth and adds texture and flavor to a wide spectrum of dishes. Do not allow the soup to come to a boil after adding the miso; high temperatures alter the flavor of the miso and also will destroy its beneficial health-promoting enzymes. For variety, substitute or add other vegetables, such as small broccoli florets, finely chopped red bell pepper, or frozen baby peas.

6	cups vegetable stock (prepared using stock concentrate, cubes, or powder), divided
¼	cup white miso
2	teaspoons very finely chopped fresh ginger
1	teaspoon minced garlic
3	ribs bok choy, halved lengthwise, then cut into ¼-inch slices (green tops included)
4	green onions, finely chopped
½	cup baby carrots in ¼-inch slices
1	(12-ounce) package extra-firm or firm tofu (at room temperature), cut into ½-inch cubes
1	(4-ounce) package oyster mushrooms, caps thinly sliced (rubbery stems removed and discarded)
2	teaspoons dark (Asian) sesame oil
⅛	teaspoon red pepper flakes, or to taste

▶ Whisk together the vegetable stock and miso in a Dutch oven. Stir in the ginger and garlic. Bring to a simmer over high heat.

▶ Reduce the heat to medium. Stir in the bok choy, green onions, and carrots. Simmer for 4 minutes or until the vegetables are nearly tender. Stir in the tofu and mushrooms. Season with sesame oil and red pepper flakes. Cook, stirring occasionally, for 2 minutes or until the mushrooms are tender and the tofu is heated through.

— TIP —

Miso, an aged Japanese condiment made from soybeans and a grain, is easily digested, highly nutritious, and rich in B vitamins and protein. Look for it in Asian markets and in the refrigerated section of some grocery stores, where it is sold in vacuum-sealed pouches or tubs. There are many varieties, so keep in mind that the darker the color, the stronger, saltier, and more robust the flavor. Store miso in the refrigerator for up to two years; it keeps well because of its high sodium content.

FRESH PEA SOUP

Makes **4** servings (5 cups)

This soup, made with sweet green peas, is quicker to prepare, lighter, and fresher tasting than traditional pea soup made with dried split peas and seasoned with ham. I like to serve it with Parmesan Crisps (page 279) for a quick and easy, one-bowl lunch. Or when time permits, top the soup with homemade croutons.

1	tablespoon canola oil
2	ribs celery, finely chopped
½	cup finely chopped onion
1	teaspoon minced garlic
1½	cups vegetable stock (prepared using stock concentrate, cubes, or powder) or chicken broth for nonvegetarians
1	(16-ounce) bag frozen baby peas
3	carrots, cut into ⅛-inch slices
1½	cups half-and-half or milk, divided
¼	teaspoon ground white pepper
	Salt to taste
	Ground nutmeg (preferably freshly ground) and Garlic Croutons (page 280) or Parmesan Cheese Croutons (page 281) for garnish

▶ Heat the oil in a medium saucepan over medium-high heat. Add the celery, onion, and garlic; cook, stirring occasionally, for 4 minutes or until the vegetables are crisp-tender.

▶ Stir in the vegetable stock and peas. Increase the heat to high. When the liquid begins to simmer, reduce the heat to medium; cover and cook for 5 minutes or until the vegetables are tender.

▶ Meanwhile, put the carrots into a small, microwave-proof dish; add about 2 tablespoons water. Cover and microwave on HIGH for 4 minutes or until tender; drain well.

▶ Stir ½ cup half-and-half into the saucepan. Use an immersion blender to purée the soup until smooth.

▶ Stir in the remaining 1 cup half-and-half, the cooked carrots, and white pepper. Stir gently over medium heat for 2 minutes or until the soup is heated through. Season with salt.

▶ Garnish the servings with a sprinkling of nutmeg and croutons, if desired.

— TIP —

Freshly grated whole nutmeg is more aromatic and flavorful than preground nutmeg. Use a nutmeg grater or a grinder, which can be purchased in a gourmet shop. Whole nutmeg will keep its flavor for years if stored in a jar in your spice cabinet.

CHUNKY GAZPACHO

Makes **4** servings (3½ cups)

Rather than puréeing this chilled vegetable soup so popular in Spain, I leave my gazpacho thick and chunky. Plan to refrigerate it for at least two hours to allow the flavors to blend; then serve in chilled bowls on a blistering-hot day.

This soup will keep for up to five days in a covered container in the refrigerator. After storage, thin the soup with water or tomato juice to the desired consistency. Or spoon the thickened gazpacho over chilled grilled fish or chicken, or bring it to room temperature to serve over polenta or baked potatoes.

1	(15-ounce) can tomato sauce
2	tablespoons red wine vinegar
1	tablespoon extra-virgin olive oil
1	tablespoon honey
½	cucumber, seeded and coarsely chopped
1	tomato, cut into ½-inch cubes
½	green bell pepper, coarsely chopped
1	rib celery, coarsely chopped
2	tablespoons finely chopped red onion, or to taste
1	teaspoon minced garlic
¼	teaspoon Tabasco sauce, or to taste
¼	teaspoon pepper, or to taste
	Salt to taste
	Garlic Croutons (page 280) for garnish

○ Combine the tomato sauce, vinegar, oil, and honey in a medium bowl. Stir in the remaining ingredients, except the croutons. Refrigerate in a covered container for at least 2 hours, or until chilled.

○ Taste and adjust the seasoning before serving. Garnish with croutons.

— · TIP · —

Look for small, thin cucumbers, which are less likely to be bitter. To seed them, cut in half lengthwise; then starting at one end, scrape the seeds down the length of the cucumber with the tip of a spoon or melon baller. If the skin is thick or waxed, peel the cucumber before using. Long, slender European or English (hothouse) cucumbers are nearly seedless, thinner skinned, and available year-round.

Sandwiches and Tortillas

BLACK BEAN TACOS WITH MANGO-TOMATO SALSA

Makes **4** servings

Sweet and juicy mango is an unexpected, colorful, and refreshing complement to bold black beans with green chilies and chili powder.

For the salsa:

1	cup jarred mango in ½-inch cubes
1	large tomato, cut into ½-inch cubes
¼	cup finely chopped red onion
¼	cup finely chopped fresh cilantro
1	tablespoon finely chopped jalapeño chili or ¼ teaspoon red pepper flakes, or to taste
2	tablespoons fresh lime juice
⅛	teaspoon salt, or to taste

For the tacos:

1	tablespoon olive oil
½	cup coarsely chopped red onion
1	teaspoon minced garlic
½	teaspoon ground cumin
1	(15-ounce) can black beans, drained and rinsed
1	(4-ounce) can chopped green chilies, drained
2	tablespoons fresh lemon juice
1	teaspoon chili powder
	Salt and pepper to taste
4	(7-inch) flour tortillas
½	cup coarsely crumbled feta cheese

● Stir together all the salsa ingredients in a medium bowl.

● To make the tacos, heat the oil in a medium sauté pan over medium-high heat. Add the onion and garlic; cook, stirring occasionally, for 4 minutes or until tender. Add the remaining taco ingredients, except the tortillas and feta cheese; stir for 1 minute or until warm.

● While the taco filling is cooking, stack the tortillas between 2 paper towels. Microwave on HIGH for 45 seconds or until moist and warm.

● For each taco, spoon about ½ cup of the warm bean mixture down the center of a tortilla and top with 2 tablespoons feta cheese. Fold the sides of the tortilla to the center to overlap.

● To serve, place the filled tortillas, seam side down on plates. Top each with ½ cup of the salsa.

TIP

Mango in a jar is always the perfect ripeness and it's ready to use, making it a great choice for 15-Minute cooks. But, if you prefer using a fresh mango, here's some good information to know:

• The color of a mango is unimportant— it may be green, orange, yellow, or red—a ripe mango will yield to gentle pressure.

• To ripen, place the mango in a paper bag at room temperature for one or two days and check daily; black spots indicate overripe fruit. Once ripened, a mango will keep two to three days in the refrigerator. (But the flavor is at its best served at room temperature.)

• The simplest method to cut a mango is to hold the mango horizontally; cut it in two lengthwise, slightly off-center, so the knife just misses the flat pit. Holding a half in the palm of your hand, slash the flesh into a lattice, cutting down to, but not through, the peel. Holding the mango flesh upward, carefully push the center of the peel with your thumbs to turn it inside out, opening the cuts of the flesh. Then cut the mango cubes from the peel.

• One mango yields 1 to 1½ cups fruit.

GRILLED PORTOBELLO MUSHROOM SANDWICHES

Makes **4** servings

Thanks to their dense, meaty texture, portobello mushrooms are ideal for grilling. For entertaining, instead of sandwich buns, I like to use French onion rolls sliced in half and toasted under the oven broiler. Serve giant dill pickles on the side.

For the sandwich spread:

¼   cup oil-packed minced sun-dried tomatoes, drained

¼   cup chèvre cheese

2   tablespoons extra-virgin olive oil

1   tablespoon red wine vinegar

2   teaspoons minced garlic

½   teaspoon sugar

⅛   teaspoon red pepper flakes

⅛   teaspoon salt, or to taste

⅛   teaspoon pepper, or to taste

For the sandwich filling:

4   (¼-inch-thick) red onion slices

     Olive oil for brushing

4   large portobello mushroom caps (stems removed and discarded)

     Dash of salt and pepper to taste

To complete the recipe:

4   sandwich buns, halved horizontally and toasted

8   thin Provolone cheese slices

16   arugula leaves

▶   Combine all the spread ingredients in a food processor. Process until the mixture is nearly smooth.

▶   To make the sandwich filling, heat a stovetop grill pan over high heat. Lightly brush both sides of the onion slices with oil. Reduce the heat to medium-high; cook for 2 minutes per side or until tender. Transfer to a plate and cover to keep warm.

▶   Lightly brush both sides of the mushrooms with oil; cook for 3 minutes per side or until tender and lightly browned. (Or cook the onion and mushrooms on an outdoor grill.) Transfer to a plate and sprinkle lightly with salt and pepper. Cover to keep warm.

▶   To assemble each sandwich, spread about 3 tablespoons of the sun-dried tomato mixture on the cut sides of a bun. Layer the bottom half with 1 slice of cheese, 4 arugula leaves, 1 onion slice, another slice of cheese, and a mushroom cap. Close the sandwich, fasten with long sandwich picks, and slice in half.

SMOKY CHIPOTLE, MANGO, AND AVOCADO WRAPS

Makes **4** servings

This is a winner for anyone who loves a smoky, hot flavor. The chipotle spread packs quite a kick—beware! For even more zest, add a pinch of red pepper flakes to the mango sauce. Then sit back and enjoy.

For the mango sauce:

2   cups coarsely chopped jarred mango

½   cup fresh orange juice

For the chipotle spread:

1   (8-ounce) package cream cheese, softened

¼   cup finely chopped fresh chives

2 tablespoons fresh orange juice

1 tablespoon chipotle chili powder

To complete the recipe:

4 (10-inch) flour tortillas, sun-dried tomato or spinach flavor

½ cup fresh cilantro leaves

1 cup jarred mango in ½-inch strips

1 avocado, cut into ¼-inch slices

½ cup jarred roasted red bell peppers, drained and cut into ¼-inch slices

❍ Combine all the sauce ingredients in a blender; purée until smooth.

❍ Stir together all the spread ingredients in a small bowl until smooth.

❍ To assemble each wrap, spread a tortilla with a generous ¼ cup of the spread. Sprinkle with cilantro leaves. Starting about 1 inch up from the bottom of the tortilla, arrange 1 horizontal row of the mango strips, another row of the avocado slices, and another row of the red bell pepper slices, keeping the ingredients in the bottom third of the tortilla. Fold 1 inch of the sides of the tortilla over the filling, fold the bottom of the tortilla over the filling, and then firmly roll it away from you.

❍ To serve, cut diagonally in half. Serve with the mango sauce.

┌─────────────────────────────────────┐

— ▸ TIP ◂ —

Chipotle chilies are dried and smoked jalapeño chilies.
└─────────────────────────────────────┘

GOAT CHEESE AND FIG PANINI
Makes **4** servings

I like to serve these sweet sandwiches lightly dusted with powdered sugar, dressing them up for a weekend brunch. Bowls of fresh fruit tossed with fruit-flavored liqueur make an epicurean accompaniment.

½ cup (4 ounces) chèvre cheese

2 tablespoons apricot jam

½ cup finely chopped dried figs (about 8 figs)

8 slices cinnamon-raisin bread

4 tablespoons salted butter, softened

❍ Combine the cheese and jam in a small bowl. Stir in the figs.

❍ For each sandwich, spread one-fourth of the fig mixture on one slice of bread. Close the sandwich with another slice of bread. Generously spread the outside of the sandwich with butter.

❍ Toast the sandwiches in a preheated panini grill for 3 minutes or until the bread is golden brown and the cheese is melted.

❍ Or toast both sides of the sandwiches in a skillet or stovetop grill pan over medium heat. Place another heavy skillet, bottom down, on top of the sandwiches and press gently for even browning.

❍ Depending on the size of your panini grill or skillet, you may need to toast the sandwiches in two batches.

GRILLED CHEESE SANDWICHES WITH BALSAMIC DIP

Makes **4** servings

These aren't your ordinary grilled cheese sandwiches. Stuffed with aged Cheddar (I use five-year-old white Cheddar) and Gruyère cheese along with fresh basil leaves, toasted in a panini grill, and served with a sweet-tart, balsamic vinegar dip, these are a gourmet version of the classic, designed for adults.

If you'd like, prepare the balsamic dip in advance. Store it in a covered container in the refrigerator and bring to room temperature before serving.

For the dip:

1	cup balsamic vinegar
2	tablespoons packed brown sugar
1	tablespoon chilled unsalted butter, cut into small pieces

For the sandwiches:

1	cup (4 ounces) coarsely shredded aged white Cheddar cheese
1	cup (4 ounces) coarsely shredded Gruyère cheese
8	(½-inch-thick) slices artisan bread, such as Italian or sourdough
16	medium-size fresh basil leaves
¼	cup unsalted butter, melted

○ Bring the vinegar to a boil in a small saucepan over high heat. Boil, uncovered, for 4 minutes or until reduced to ½ cup. Remove from the heat, add the brown sugar, and stir until dissolved. Add the butter and stir until melted.

○ Combine the Cheddar and Gruyère cheeses in a medium bowl. Mound ½ cup of the cheese mixture on top of each of 4 bread slices, pressing the cheeses together slightly. Top each with 4 basil leaves. Cover with the remaining bread slices. Brush both sides of the sandwiches with melted butter.

○ Toast the sandwiches in a preheated panini grill for 3 minutes or until the bread is golden brown and the cheese is melted.

○ Or toast both sides of the sandwiches in a skillet or stovetop grill pan over medium heat. Place another heavy skillet, bottom down, on top of the sandwiches and press gently for even browning.

○ Depending on the size of your panini grill or skillet, you may need to toast the sandwiches in two batches.

○ Cut each sandwich into 4 strips and serve with the balsamic dip in a small bowl on the side.

HUEVOS RANCHEROS

Makes **4** servings

Pick your favorite tomato salsa (hot, medium, or mild) to combine with pinto beans or other varieties, such as black beans or garbanzos—or a combination. Serve this satisfying dish for brunch, lunch, or dinner accompanied with fruit, such as cubes of juicy papaya drizzled with fresh lime juice.

1	tablespoon olive oil
½	red bell pepper, finely chopped
1	teaspoon minced garlic
1	(15-ounce) can pinto beans, drained and rinsed
1	cup chunky tomato salsa

1 cup vegetable stock (prepared using stock concentrate, cubes, or powder) or chicken broth for nonvegetarians

2 green onions, finely chopped

2 tablespoons ketchup

1 teaspoon ancho chili powder

½ teaspoon ground cumin

Salt and pepper to taste

Olive oil for frying

4 (7-inch) flour tortillas

4 eggs

Finely chopped fresh cilantro for garnish

○ Heat the 1 tablespoon oil in a large sauté pan over medium-high heat. Add the bell pepper and garlic; cook, stirring occasionally, for 2 minutes or until nearly tender. Stir in the beans, salsa, vegetable stock, green onions, ketchup, chili powder, and cumin. Reduce the heat to low; cover and cook, stirring occasionally, for 2 minutes or until warm. Season with salt and pepper.

○ While the bean mixture is cooking, heat ¼-inch oil in a medium skillet over medium-high heat. Fry each tortilla for 1 minute per side or until lightly browned. Transfer to a paper-towel-lined plate.

○ Using a spoon, make 4 small wells in the bean mixture (all the way to the pan bottom) about 2 inches apart. Break 1 egg at a time into a small cup and then slide it into a well and sprinkle lightly with salt and pepper. Cover and cook over medium heat for 5 minutes or until the eggs are the desired degree of doneness.

○ For each serving, place 1 tortilla on a plate. Top with 1 egg and surround it with some of the bean mixture. Sprinkle with cilantro.

PORTOBELLO QUESADILLAS
Makes **4** servings

Here's an unconventional way to enjoy these earthy mushrooms. Their meaty taste makes them a better companion for strong flavors than many of their relatives.

2 tablespoons olive oil plus extra for brushing

4 portobello mushrooms, stems and black gills removed, caps cut into ½-inch strips

1 cup finely chopped onion

1½ teaspoons minced garlic

Salt and pepper to taste

1 cup finely shredded Mexican cheese blend

8 (10-inch) flour tortillas

Tomato salsa, Vegetable Salsa (page 274), or Mixed Fruit Chutney (page 278) for accompaniment

○ Heat the oil in a large skillet over medium-high heat. Add the mushrooms, onion, and garlic. Cook, stirring occasionally, for 4 minutes or until tender. Season with salt and pepper.

○ Evenly divide the mushroom mixture and spread on 2 of the tortillas. Sprinkle with cheese, and then top with the remaining 2 tortillas.

○ Wipe the skillet clean with a moist paper towel. Lightly brush the outsides of the quesadillas with oil. Cook one at a time over medium heat for 1½ minutes per side or until the tortillas are golden brown and the cheese is melted.

○ Cut each quesadilla into 4 wedges and serve warm with salsa or chutney.

Pasta and Noodles

CHINESE FIRECRACKER NOODLES

Makes **4** servings

I like my noodles fiery—although this recipe calls for 1 tablespoon chili paste with garlic, I always increase it to 2 tablespoons. For the less adventurous, stick with 1 tablespoon of the hot stuff. Serve mounds of these noodles warm, at room temperature, or chilled on beds of shredded romaine lettuce, Chinese cabbage, or salad spinach. "Thank you" to Nathan Fong for sharing one of his favorite noodle recipes.

For the noodles:

8	ounces thin Chinese wheat-flour noodles or thin Chinese egg noodles

For the spicy pickled ginger vinaigrette:

2	tablespoons soy sauce
2	tablespoons white rice vinegar
2	tablespoons dark (Asian) sesame oil
1	tablespoon Chinese chili paste with garlic, or to taste
1	tablespoon fresh lemon juice
1	tablespoon honey
1	tablespoon finely chopped pickled ginger
⅛	teaspoon salt, or to taste

To complete the salad:

2	cups finely shredded carrots
4	green onions, diagonally cut into ¼-inch slices
½	cup finely chopped peanuts, preferably dry-roasted
½	cup coarsely chopped fresh cilantro
	Black sesame seeds and sprigs of fresh cilantro for garnish

▶ Cook the noodles according to package instructions.

▶ Meanwhile, whisk together the vinaigrette ingredients in a small bowl.

▶ When the noodles are done, drain. Rinse in cold water, and then drain again.

▶ Transfer the noodles to a large bowl. Add the vinaigrette and toss. Add the remaining ingredients, except the garnishes, and toss.

▶ Garnish the servings with black sesame seeds and fresh cilantro sprigs.

TIP

Pickled ginger is a cool, sharp-tasting condiment made from young ginger that has been marinated in seasoned vinegar. It is available in jars in Asian markets and supermarkets. Pickled ginger is often used as a garnish for Asian dishes and is eaten in small bites to cleanse the palate, as when served with sushi.

LO MEIN WITH THAI COCONUT-PEANUT SAUCE

Makes **4** servings

Be sure to use pure natural peanut butter without added sugar. Then create a sauce that's anywhere from mild and creamy to ultra-zesty, depending on the amount of red pepper flakes you choose to add. On busy days, combine the noodles and sauce ahead of time; then chill until you're ready to dig in. Cilantro lovers: Increase the quantity to ½ cup.

For the noodles:

12	ounces lo mein noodles

For the sauce:

1	cup canned "lite" coconut milk
½	cup smooth peanut butter
2	teaspoons minced garlic
½	teaspoon red pepper flakes, or to taste
¼	cup fresh lime juice
⅛	teaspoon salt, or to taste

To complete the recipe:

1	cup snow peas, stems and strings removed
½	red bell pepper, finely chopped
4	green onions, finely chopped
¼	cup finely chopped fresh cilantro
½	cup finely chopped salted peanuts

▶ Cook the noodles according to package instructions. Also, bring a small saucepan of water to a boil.

▶ While the noodles are cooking, combine the coconut milk, peanut butter, garlic, and red pepper flakes in a medium saucepan over medium heat; stir for 1 minute or until the sauce is warm, creamy, and smooth. Remove from the heat; stir in the lime juice and salt.

▶ Immerse the snow peas in the boiling water for 30 seconds or until they become a darker green. Drain and plunge into very cold water to stop the cooking. Drain again.

▶ When the noodles are done, drain well. Return to the pasta pan. Add the peanut sauce and toss. Add the snow peas and the remaining ingredients; toss over medium heat just until heated through.

┤ TIP ├

Blanching is a method that partially cooks food by boiling or steaming. The food is briefly immersed in boiling water, drained, and then plunged in very cold water to stop the cooking. The process enhances the color and flavor of some vegetables and also loosens the skins of tomatoes, peaches, and nuts (such as almonds), making them easy to peel.

EAST INDIAN NOODLES WITH SPLIT PEAS AND CASHEWS

Makes **4** servings

The day my friend Raghavan Iyer shared this classic East Indian recipe with me, he taught me how to heat the mustard seeds until they pop, filling my kitchen with an enticing aroma. For lunch we feasted on this colorful dish that unites a unique blend of flavors and textures, including the intrigue of slightly crunchy split peas and raw cashews. Traditionally this is a vegetarian dish, but you can toss in cooked shrimp along with the noodles if you wish.

4	ounces thin rice noodles (sometimes called rice vermicelli or rice sticks)
1	tablespoon canola oil
1	teaspoon brown or yellow mustard seeds
1	red bell pepper, cut into ¼-inch strips
1	cup red onion in ¼-inch strips
1	cup raw cashews
¼	cup dried yellow split peas
1	(10-ounce) package frozen chopped spinach, thawed (do not drain)
⅓	cup fresh lime juice
¼	cup finely chopped fresh cilantro
2	green Thai chilies, finely chopped, include seeds, or to taste
8	whole fresh curry leaves, optional
½	teaspoon ground turmeric
½	teaspoon salt, or to taste

◐ Cook the noodles according to package instructions, stirring occasionally to separate as they soften. Drain in a colander and rinse with cold water. Use kitchen shears to randomly cut the noodles into shorter lengths, about 6 inches long, for easier eating.

◐ Heat the oil in a large sauté pan over medium heat. Add the mustard seeds; cover and heat for 30 seconds or until they stop popping. Add the bell pepper and onion; cook, stirring constantly, for 2 minutes or until crisp-tender. Add the cashews and split peas; cook, stirring constantly, for 2 minutes or until golden brown. Add the spinach with its liquid. Reduce the head to medium low, cover, and cook for 2 minutes or until wilted. Remove the pan from the heat. Stir in the lime juice, cilantro, chilies, curry leaves (if using), turmeric, and salt.

◐ Immerse the cooked noodles in a pan of cold water; swirl them with your hand to separate. Without draining in a colander, transfer handfuls of the noodles,

with whatever water that clings to them, to the sauté pan. Stir the mixture gently over medium-high heat just until heated through. Remove the curry leaves before serving, or eat around them.

TIPS

Whole mustard seeds are available in the spice section of most supermarkets. Compared with the yellow (or white) seeds, the brown (or Asian) seeds are smaller but more pungent in flavor. Store the seeds for up to a year in a dark, dry place.

Split peas, both yellow and green, are grown for drying. In the process, they are split along a natural seam, which explains their name. The peas are available in supermarkets and health food stores. They will keep indefinitely if stored in a tightly closed container in a cool, dry place. The flavors differ, so yellow and green split peas are not interchangeable in recipes.

Curry leaves come from a plant that is native to southern Asia. The leaves, which look like shiny lemon leaves, are available in Indian and Asian markets. They have a unique fragrance and a flavor that is essential to many East Indian dishes. Refrigerate fresh curry leaves in an airtight container for up to two weeks or freeze them for up to two months. Packaged dried curry leaves can be substituted but are less flavorful.

CHINESE MAPO TOFU
WITH WHEAT-FLOUR NOODLES
Makes **4** servings

According to Nathan Fong, my culinary friend from Vancouver, B.C., *mapo tofu* means "grandmother's tofu" and nearly every Chinese grandmother has her own version. Making this variation of his takes only minutes since it is prepared from ingredients in your pantry. Adjust the hotness to suit your taste.

1	tablespoon canola oil
½	cup finely chopped onion
2	teaspoons finely chopped serrano chili
2	teaspoons minced garlic
½	cup vegetable stock (prepared using stock concentrate, cubes, or powder)
2	tablespoons hoisin sauce
¼	cup soy sauce
1	tablespoon dark (Asian) sesame oil
1	teaspoon sugar
⅛	teaspoon red pepper flakes, or to taste
12	ounces silken extra-firm tofu, cut into ½-inch cubes (about 2 cups)
1	cup frozen baby peas, thawed
6	ounces thin Chinese wheat-flour noodles
¼	cup finely chopped fresh cilantro
	Finely chopped green onions for garnish

◉ Bring a large pan of water to a boil over high heat.

◉ Heat the oil in a large sauté pan over medium-high heat. Add the onion, chili, and garlic; cook, stirring occasionally, for 2 minutes or until the onion is crisp-tender.

◉ Meanwhile, combine the vegetable stock, hoisin sauce, soy sauce, sesame oil, sugar, and red pepper flakes in a small bowl.

◉ Add the broth mixture to the sauté pan. Reduce the heat to low; cook, stirring occasionally, for 2 minutes or until the onion is tender.

◉ While the broth mixture is cooking, add the noodles to the pan of boiling water and cook according to package instructions; drain well.

◉ Gently stir the tofu and peas into the sauté pan. Cover for 2 minutes or until the tofu and peas are heated through. Add the noodles and cilantro; toss gently.

◉ Serve in deep noodle bowls and garnish with green onions.

——— TIP ———

Tofu is made from soybeans through a process that resembles cheese making. The curds are pressed into blocks labeled soft, medium, firm, and extra-firm, depending on how much water is released. Soft and medium tofu can be blended to a smooth, creamy consistency and are the best choices for making dressings and sauces. Firm and extra-firm tofu have a denser consistency and hold their shape when cut into cubes. "Silken" tofu has a mild flavor and smooth texture.

ASIAN NOODLES WITH ASPARAGUS AND ORANGE-SHERRY SAUCE

Makes **4** servings

This is a dish with a delightfully split personality. My son likes the noodles served warm, while I especially enjoy the leftovers for lunch the next day at room temperature or slightly chilled.

For the sauce:

1 tablespoon cold water

1 teaspoon cornstarch

¼ cup dry sherry

¼ cup fresh orange juice

2 tablespoons soy sauce

1 tablespoon dark (Asian) sesame oil

1 tablespoon hoisin sauce

½ teaspoon chili paste with garlic, or to taste

⅛ teaspoon ground white pepper, or to taste

To complete the recipe:

1 tablespoon canola oil

2 cups asparagus diagonally cut into 2-inch-long pieces

1 red bell pepper, coarsely chopped

4 green onions, coarsely chopped

2 teaspoons minced garlic

6 ounces ramen noodles (discard flavoring packets)

Sprigs of fresh cilantro for garnish

◗ Bring a medium pot of water to a boil over high heat.

◗ Stir together the water and cornstarch in a small bowl until smooth. Stir in the remaining sauce ingredients.

◗ Heat the oil in a medium sauté pan over medium-high heat. Add the asparagus, bell pepper, green onions, and garlic; cook, stirring constantly, for 5 minutes or until the asparagus is crisp-tender. Add the sauce; stir constantly for 1 minute or until the mixture thickens to maple-syrup consistency. Remove from the heat; cover and set aside.

◗ Drop the noodles into the boiling water. Reduce the heat to medium-high and cook for 3 minutes or according to package instructions. As the noodles cook, stir occasionally with a fork to separate. Drain well.

◗ Add the noodles to the sauté pan; toss the mixture over medium heat just until heated through.

◗ Garnish the servings with cilantro sprigs.

TIP

Asian rice noodles are made with rice flour and water. They are recognized by their translucence that turns opaque-white after cooking; the shape can be flat and wide or thin and round. The term "rice stick" applies to thin rice noodles, which also may be called rice vermicelli. You can buy fresh rice noodles in some Asian markets. Dried rice noodles, sold in coiled nests packaged in cellophane, are found in the Asian section of supermarkets. It's important to store them away from moisture.

MOSTACCIOLI WITH A TRIO OF SWEET PEPPERS

Makes **4** servings

The sweetness of bell peppers is the flavor we're celebrating in this multicolored dish. Stir strips of grilled chicken breast into the topping for nonvegetarians. If you like, add a dash of red pepper flakes to invigorate the sweet flavors. I especially enjoy the contrast of tangy chèvre as it melts into the warm topping.

12	ounces (about 4 cups) mostaccioli
2	tablespoons olive oil, divided
1	red bell pepper, cut into ¼-inch strips
1	yellow bell pepper, cut into ¼-inch strips
1	green bell pepper, cut into ¼-inch strips
1	cup red onion in ¼-inch strips
¼	cup pine nuts
1	tablespoon minced garlic
¼	teaspoon salt, or to taste
¼	teaspoon pepper, or to taste
½	cup fresh basil chiffonade (see tip, page 144)
	Freshly ground pepper and large dollops of chèvre cheese or shredded Parmesan cheese for garnish

◗ Cook the mostaccioli according to package instructions.

◗ Meanwhile, heat 1 tablespoon oil in a large sauté pan over medium-high heat. Add the bell peppers and onion; cook, stirring occasionally, for 8 minutes or until tender. Add the pine nuts, garlic, salt, and pepper; stir for 30 seconds. Remove from the heat and cover to keep warm.

◗ When the mostaccioli is done, drain well; return to the pasta pan. Add the remaining 1 tablespoon oil and toss. Add the basil and toss again.

◗ To serve, spoon the mostaccioli into pasta bowls; top with the bell pepper mixture. Garnish with pepper and cheese.

PENNE WITH PEPPERY ARUGULA SAUCE

Makes **4** servings

The peppery taste of arugula is a natural with tomatoes and feta cheese. And shallots do double duty, providing the qualities of both onion and garlic. Using just the right proportion of these assertive ingredients is the key to creating a simple sauce with an aroma as irresistible as its flavor.

12	ounces penne
2	tablespoons olive oil
½	cup finely chopped shallots
1	(28-ounce) can diced tomatoes
3	cups coarsely chopped arugula leaves
½	teaspoon sugar
½	teaspoon pepper, or to taste
1	(4-ounce) package coarsely crumbled feta cheese
	Freshly ground pepper for garnish

◗ Cook the penne according to package instructions.

◗ Meanwhile, heat the oil in a large sauté pan over medium heat. Add the shallots; cook, stirring constantly, for 3 minutes or until tender but not browned.

● Increase the heat to high; stir in the tomatoes. Cook, stirring occasionally, for 4 minutes or until the liquid thickens slightly. Stir in the arugula, sugar, and pepper. Reduce the heat to low; cover and cook for 2 minutes or until the arugula is wilted. Remove from the heat and cover to keep warm.

● When the penne is done, drain well; return to the pasta pan. Add the sauce and toss. Add the feta cheese and toss again.

● Garnish the servings with pepper.

LASAGNA ROLLS

Makes **4** servings (8 rolls)

Lasagna doesn't need to be a time-consuming preparation destined for a crowd. Enjoy my quick, uncomplicated version that speedily provides just the right amount for four.

8	oven-ready lasagna noodles
1	tablespoon olive oil
4	cups lightly packed salad spinach
4	ounces sliced mushrooms, finely chopped
1	cup coarsely shredded carrots
2	teaspoons minced garlic
1	(15-ounce) carton ricotta cheese
½	cup freshly grated Parmesan cheese, divided
2	tablespoons finely chopped fresh basil or 2 teaspoons dried basil
½	teaspoon salt, or to taste
¼	teaspoon pepper, or to taste
2	cups chunky tomato pasta sauce

● Soak the oven-ready lasagna noodles in a large bowl of very hot tap water for 10 minutes.

● Meanwhile, heat the oil in a large sauté pan over medium-high heat. Add the spinach, mushrooms, carrots, and garlic. Cover and cook, stirring occasionally, for 3 minutes or until the spinach is wilted and the carrots are tender. Stir in the ricotta cheese, ¼ cup Parmesan cheese, basil, salt, and pepper. Remove from the heat.

● Drain the soaked noodles and pat dry. For each lasagna roll, place a noodle on a cutting board, spread with ⅓ cup of the ricotta cheese mixture, and gently roll.

● Place the rolls seam-side down in an 11 x 8-inch microwave-proof dish. Pour the pasta sauce over the rolls and sprinkle with the remaining ¼ cup Parmesan cheese. Microwave on HIGH for 5 minutes or until thoroughly warm.

─── TIP ───

Oven-ready lasagna noodles come in a box found on the grocer's shelf. Unlike traditional lasagna noodles that require boiling, these need only to be soaked in hot tap water for 10 minutes to become pliable and ready to use.

RADIATORE WITH YAMS AND SPINACH

Makes **4** servings

When I first ordered the pasta-potato combination in an Italian restaurant, I was pleasantly surprised at their compatibility. Here the potatoes, which can be cooked right along with the pasta, come to life with the addition of generous amounts of garlic and red pepper flakes. If you love "heat," increase the red pepper flakes to 1 teaspoon.

Radiatore is literally "little radiators," and this is a short, chunky pasta shape that resembles tiny radiators with rippled edges.

12	ounces radiatore or penne
16	ounces yam, peeled and cut into-1-inch cubes (3 cups)
2	tablespoons olive oil
1	cup yellow onion in ¼-inch strips
1	tablespoon minced garlic
2	cups reduced-sodium vegetable stock (prepared using stock concentrate, cubes, or powder) or 1 (14-ounce) can chicken broth for nonvegetarians
6	cups salad spinach in ½-inch strips
½	teaspoon red pepper flakes, or to taste
¼	teaspoon pepper, or to taste
½	cup freshly shredded Romano or Parmesan cheese
	Salt to taste
	Freshly ground pepper for garnish

▶ Cook the radiatore with the yam in a large pot of boiling water according to pasta package instructions or until the pasta and yam are tender.

▶ Meanwhile, heat the oil in a large sauté pan over medium-high heat. Add the onion and garlic; cook, stirring occasionally, for 5 minutes or until tender.

▶ Increase the heat to high; stir in the vegetable stock and spinach. Cover and cook for 2 minutes or until the spinach is wilted. Remove from the heat and stir in the red pepper flakes and pepper.

▶ When the radiatore and yam are done, drain well; return to the pasta pan. Add the spinach mixture; toss to combine over medium heat just until heated through. Add the Romano cheese and toss again. Season with salt. Garnish with pepper.

GNOCCHI WITH SALSA PROVENÇAL

Makes **4** servings

The appealing comfort-food texture of gnocchi serves as a base for the peppery Mediterranean mélange. Serve with garlic bread and a green salad tossed with Balsamic Vinaigrette (page 268).

16	ounces potato gnocchi
3½	cups Salsa Provençal (page 276)
	Coarsely crumbled feta cheese or freshly shredded Parmesan cheese for garnish

▶ Cook the gnocchi according to package instructions.

▶ When the gnocchi is done, drain well. Rinse the pasta pan and return the gnocchi to it. Add the salsa and gently toss over low heat for 30 seconds or until warm and evenly combined.

▶ Garnish the servings with feta or Parmesan cheese.

RAVIOLI WITH HAZELNUT AND SAGE PESTO

Makes **4** servings

This is a favorite of mine for when it's time to bid goodbye to summer and welcome back the tastes of autumn. My guests praise this distinctive pesto, including toasted hazelnuts and walnuts that complement the pungent, musty flavor of sage. It's best tossed with pumpkin-filled ravioli, which is available in the fall at some Italian specialty shops. For a sparkling burst of color and flavor, garnish with a sprinkling of brilliant red pomegranate seeds. And pair the dish with a round and rich white wine, such as South American Chardonnay from Chile, to add a just-right earthiness to the meal.

For the pasta:

12 ounces cheese- or pumpkin-filled ravioli or tortellini

For the pesto:

½ cup hazelnuts, preferably toasted
¼ cup coarsely chopped walnuts, preferably toasted
¼ cup walnut oil
1 tablespoon dried leaf sage
2 teaspoons minced garlic
¼ teaspoon pepper
½ cup freshly shredded Parmesan cheese

To complete the recipe:

Salt to taste

Freshly ground pepper and freshly shredded Parmesan cheese for garnish

❍ Cook the ravioli or tortellini according to package instructions.

❍ Meanwhile, combine all the pesto ingredients, except the Parmesan cheese, in a food processor. Process until the mixture is a slightly chunky purée. Add the Parmesan cheese and pulse once or twice to blend.

❍ When the pasta is done, drain well. Return to the pasta pan, add the pesto, and toss. Season with salt.

❍ Garnish the servings with pepper and Parmesan cheese.

MEDITERRANEAN MOSTACCIOLI

Makes **4** servings

The recipe multiplies well to accommodate and please large groups. Excellent warm, it's also delicious served at room temperature or chilled, so you can do all the preparations in advance and be a guest at your own party. Mound the mixture on your favorite platter as part of a buffet. Simply add a green salad tossed with Italian dressing or Basic Vinaigrette (page 268) and a basket of crusty bread, and your delectable meal is complete. Spaniards love their Garnacha, and it's a perfect wine to pair with this dish.

10	ounces mostaccioli
3	tablespoons red wine vinegar
2	tablespoons olive oil, divided
2	tablespoons small (nonpareil) capers, drained and rinsed
1	tablespoon fresh thyme leaves
½	teaspoon pepper, or to taste
4	cups peeled eggplant in ½-inch cubes (about 1 pound)
2	cups sliced mushrooms
1	small zucchini, halved lengthwise and cut into ¼-inch slices
¼	cup finely chopped shallots
4	plum tomatoes, cut into ½-inch cubes
½	cup coarsely crumbled feta cheese
	Salt to taste
	Sprigs of fresh thyme for garnish

▶ Cook the mostaccioli according to package instructions.

▶ Meanwhile, stir together the vinegar, 1 tablespoon oil, capers, thyme, and pepper in a small bowl.

▶ Also while the pasta is cooking, heat the remaining 1 tablespoon olive oil in a large sauté pan over medium-high heat. Add the eggplant, mushrooms, zucchini, and shallots; cook, stirring occasionally, for 5 minutes or until the eggplant is tender and lightly browned. Stir in the tomatoes and continue to cook, stirring occasionally, for 2 minutes or until softened. Stir in the vinegar mixture. Remove from the heat, cover, and set aside.

▶ When the mostaccioli is done, drain well. Return to the pasta pan. Add the eggplant mixture and toss. Add the feta cheese; toss again. Season with salt.

▶ Garnish the servings with sprigs of fresh thyme.

TIP

Feta cheese is a white Greek cheese with a rich, tangy flavor. Traditionally, it is made with goat's milk or sheep's milk, or a combination; today it is also often made with cow's milk. Fresh feta is crumbly with whey; when mature it becomes drier and saltier.

FARFALLE CROWNED WITH BRIE AND PEARS

Makes **4** servings

Brie cheese melts into warm pasta and marries its distinctive flavor with fresh pears to create a memorable dish that's ideal for special occasions. As for wine, try something new, a Spanish Albariño. The richness of this white wine complements the Brie, and the bite of the acidity balances the sun-dried tomatoes.

1	(12-ounce) package farfalle (bow-tie pasta)
1	(6-ounce) jar oil-packed julienned sun-dried tomatoes; oil drained and reserved
2	tablespoons balsamic vinegar
2	teaspoons minced garlic
¼	teaspoon pepper, or to taste
2	pears, cored, peeled, and cut into ½-inch cubes
4	ounces Brie cheese, rind removed and discarded, cheese coarsely chopped (about ⅔ cup)
½	cup fresh basil chiffonade (see tip, page 144)
	Salt to taste
	Chopped toasted walnuts for garnish

● Cook the farfalle according to package instructions.

● Meanwhile, stir together 2 tablespoons oil (reserved from sun-dried tomatoes), the vinegar, garlic, and pepper in a small bowl. Discard the remaining reserved oil.

● When the farfalle is done, drain well; return to the pasta pan. Add the olive oil mixture and toss. Add the sun-dried tomatoes, pears, Brie cheese, and basil; toss again. Season with salt.

● Garnish the servings with walnuts.

RIGATONI WITH SWISS CHARD

Makes **4** servings

Here's an appetizing way to use Swiss chard and reap its nutritional benefits. Leafy greens, such as Swiss chard and kale, are excellent sources of vitamin A (in the form of beta carotene) and vitamin C, as well as iron, magnesium, and potassium. Not only that—they taste terrific. I opt for rhubarb chard, which is especially colorful thanks to its bright red stem and veins.

10	ounces rigatoni
2	tablespoons olive oil
1	red bell pepper, cut into 1 x ½-inch strips
⅓	cup coarsely chopped onion
2	teaspoons minced garlic
1	cup vegetable stock (prepared using stock concentrate, cubes, or powder)
8	cups coarsely chopped Swiss chard leaves (stems removed and discarded)
2	tablespoons unsalted butter
½	teaspoon pepper, or to taste
2	tablespoons balsamic vinegar
¼	teaspoon salt, or to taste
¼	cup freshly grated Parmesan cheese
	Freshly shredded Parmesan cheese for garnish

● Cook the rigatoni according to package instructions.

● Meanwhile, heat the oil in a large sauté pan over medium-high heat. Add the bell pepper, onion, and garlic; cook, stirring occasionally, for 5 minutes or until the bell pepper is crisp-tender. Reduce the heat to medium; stir in the vegetable stock, chard, butter, and pepper; cover and cook for 5 minutes or until the chard and the bell pepper are tender. Remove the pan from the heat; stir in the balsamic vinegar and salt.

● When the rigatoni is done, drain well; return to the pasta pan. Add the chard mixture and toss. Add the grated Parmesan cheese and toss again. Garnish with Parmesan cheese.

MEDITERRANEAN PASTA SKILLET WITH CANNELLINI BEANS

Makes **4** servings

Bursting with distinctive Mediterranean flavors, this quick and pretty one-dish meal is vegetarian comfort food at its best. The secret to the filling and nutritious combination is in the creamy, buttery-tasting beans that make the dish oh-so satisfying. Your family will clamor for seconds—guaranteed.

8	ounces penne
1	tablespoon olive oil
½	cup finely chopped shallots
1	(28-ounce) can diced tomatoes
1	(19-ounce) can cannellini beans, drained and rinsed
1	tablespoon finely chopped fresh oregano
4	cups coarsely sliced salad spinach
½	teaspoon pepper, or to taste
	Salt to taste
1	(4-ounce) package crumbled feta cheese
	Freshly ground pepper for garnish

▶ Cook the penne according to package instructions.

▶ Meanwhile, heat the oil in a large sauté pan over medium heat. Add the shallots; cook, stirring constantly, for 3 minutes or until tender but not browned. Stir in the tomatoes, beans, oregano, and pepper. Increase the heat to high; cook, uncovered, for 4 minutes or until the liquid is reduced by about half.

▶ Reduce the heat to low; stir in the spinach. Cover and cook for 2 minutes or until the spinach is wilted. Remove the pan from the heat.

▶ When the penne is done, drain well. Add to the sauté pan, and stir gently over low heat just until heated through. Season with pepper and salt.

▶ Top the servings with feta cheese and garnish with pepper.

Stovetop Dishes

VEGETABLES IN CUMIN-SCENTED COCONUT SAUCE

Makes **4** servings

The wintertime root vegetables you're likely to have on hand in your kitchen take on an enticing blend of Indian flavors when draped in this luscious, aromatic sauce. The ingredient list appears long, but this recipe is surprisingly quick to prepare and delivers such tasty rewards, especially when paired with basmati rice.

2	medium red-skinned potatoes (about 12 ounces), peeled and cut into 1-inch cubes
3	carrots, cut into ½-inch slices
2	tablespoons sesame seeds
1½	teaspoons cumin seeds
1	cup "lite" coconut milk
1	serrano chili, halved
½	teaspoon salt, or to taste
1	large tomato, cut into 1-inch cubes
1	cup frozen baby peas
½	cup salted peanuts
2	tablespoons finely chopped fresh cilantro
1	tablespoon fresh lime juice

- ▶ Bring a large saucepan of salted water to a boil; add the potatoes and carrots. Reduce the heat to medium; cook for 8 minutes or until tender.

- ▶ Meanwhile, heat a small skillet over medium-high heat until very hot. Add the sesame and cumin seeds; cook, stirring constantly, for 30 seconds or until the seeds are lightly browned and fragrant. Remove from the heat.

- ▶ Pour the coconut milk into a blender container. Add the toasted seeds, chili, and salt; pulse until coarsely blended.

- ▶ When the vegetables are done, drain, and then return to the saucepan. Add the coconut milk mixture, tomato, and peas. Stir over medium heat for 1 minute or until warm. Stir in the peanuts, cilantro, and lime juice.

TIP

Available in both seed and ground forms, cumin provides an aromatic, nutty, and peppery flavor that is widely used in Mexican and Indian cooking. It is an essential ingredient in curry powder and chili powder. As with all seeds, herbs, and spices, it should be stored in a cool, dark place for no more than six months.

CHILEAN VEGETABLE STEW

Makes **4** servings

I like to serve this thick, colorful stew on rice, couscous, or polenta—or with warmed flour tortillas or cornbread.

2	tablespoons olive oil
1	cup finely chopped onion
1	Thai chili, finely chopped
2	teaspoons ground cumin
1	(28-ounce) can whole tomatoes with juice
1½	cups frozen corn kernels
1	(10-ounce) package frozen lima beans
¼	cup coarsely chopped fresh cilantro
¼	teaspoon salt, or to taste
¼	teaspoon pepper, or to taste
1	avocado, cut into wedges
2	tablespoons fresh lime juice
	Finely shredded Cheddar cheese for garnish

- ▶ Heat the oil in a Dutch oven over medium-high heat. Add the onion and the chili; cook, stirring occasionally, for 4 minutes or until tender. Stir in the cumin.

- ▶ Stir in the tomatoes; insert kitchen shears into the pan and coarsely chop. Stir in the corn and lima beans; cover and cook, stirring occasionally, for 8 minutes or until the lima beans are tender. Stir in the cilantro and season with salt and pepper.

- ▶ While the vegetables are cooking, toss the avocado wedges with the lime juice in a small bowl.

- ▶ To serve, spoon the stew into bowls. Top with avocado wedges and garnish with cheese.

CAULIFLOWER CURRY

Makes **4** servings

In the 1800s, East Indians came to Trinidad as indentured servants, and with them they brought their culinary traditions, including vibrant curries. Today, East Indians make up a significant portion of the island's population, and their delicious dishes remain popular. As a cookbook author, I continually gather recipes from many sources. I learned about this dish from my physician, Dr. Mumtaz Kazim, who comes from Trinidad. She proudly shared a favorite recipe, commonly served in her country, and it now has become a frequently requested dish in my own home, too. Dr. Kazim explained to me that other vegetables can be substituted, such as okra for the cauliflower, and cabbage is often added, too. Serve the vegetables and their aromatic sauce over rice.

1	tablespoon canola oil
1	cup onion in ¼-inch slices
1	tablespoon curry powder
1	(15-ounce) can diced tomatoes
2	cups cauliflower florets
1	cup frozen baby peas
½	cup heavy cream or plain yogurt
¼	teaspoon salt, or to taste
¼	teaspoon pepper, or to taste
	Lemon wedges

◖ Heat the oil in a large sauté pan over medium-high heat. Add the onion; cook, stirring occasionally, for 4 minutes or until tender. Add the curry powder; stir for 30 seconds.

◖ Stir in the tomatoes and cauliflower. Reduce the heat to medium; cover and simmer, stirring occasionally, for 7 minutes or until the cauliflower is tender. Add the peas; stir gently for 1 minute or until thawed.

◖ Reduce the heat to low. Add the cream; stir for 30 seconds or until warm. Season with salt and pepper.

◖ Accompany the servings with lemon wedges for squeezing over the vegetables at the table.

------ TIP ------

Curry powder, not classic to Indian home kitchens, is a mixture of many herbs and spices blended by the British to capture the flavors of the Raj. Standard curry powders are quite mild; imported brands, often called Madras, are usually hotter. Since curry powder quickly loses its pungency, purchase it in small quantities and store airtight in a dark, dry place for up to two months.

VEGETABLES IN HERBED TOMATO SAUCE ON POLENTA

Makes **4** servings

Barb Kennedy and I met decades ago in a cooking class. Today, we continue to share our ideas about cooking—and life. I thank her for this amiable meal, which has become one of my vegetarian favorites. Barb recommends using canned crushed tomatoes with added purée for sauciness.

For the polenta:

1	(16-ounce) package cooked polenta, cut into 12 (½-inch) slices
¾	cup freshly grated Parmesan cheese

For the vegetables and sauce:

3	tablespoons olive oil
1	(8-ounce) package sliced cremini mushrooms
1	medium zucchini, cut into 2 x ¼-inch strips
1	cup finely chopped onion
1½	teaspoons minced garlic
1	(14-ounce) can crushed tomatoes
2	teaspoons finely chopped fresh oregano or ½ teaspoon dried oregano
2	teaspoons finely chopped fresh thyme or ½ teaspoon dried thyme
⅛	teaspoon red pepper flakes, or to taste
2	tablespoons coarsely chopped fresh basil
¼	teaspoon salt, or to taste
¼	teaspoon pepper, or to taste
	Toasted pine nuts for garnish

▶ Preheat the oven to 350°F.

▶ Arrange the polenta on a foil-lined baking sheet. Sprinkle each slice with 1 tablespoon Parmesan cheese. Bake for 12 minutes or until the cheese is melted and the polenta is heated through.

▶ Meanwhile, heat the oil in a large sauté pan over medium-high heat. Add the mushrooms, zucchini, onion, and garlic; cook, stirring occasionally, for 5 minutes or until tender.

▶ Stir in the crushed tomatoes, oregano, thyme, and red pepper flakes. Reduce the heat to medium; cover and cook, stirring occasionally, for 5 minutes to allow the flavors to blend. Stir in the basil and season with salt and pepper.

▶ For each serving, place 3 polenta slices on a plate. Top with the tomato-vegetable sauce and garnish with pine nuts.

TIP

Making polenta, a staple of northern Italy, from scratch requires planning ahead because the cornmeal mixture needs to firm up in the refrigerator for at least an hour before being cooked. Lucky for the 15-Minute gourmet, premade, packaged polenta is delicious. It needs only to be sliced and then baked in the oven or browned in a skillet on the stovetop, and it's ready to make a fine foundation for many dishes.

Italian Garden Frittata

ITALIAN GARDEN FRITTATA

Makes **4** servings

Frittatas are to Italians what omelets are to the French. The ingredients may be the same, but the difference is in the cooking method. In a frittata, the filling is mixed right with the eggs, and the entire mixture is cooked together and left open-faced. To speed up preparation time, use prechopped vegetables from the supermarket salad bar. If you'd prefer, substitute other vegetables (up to 3 cups total). To make the servings more substantial and even more colorful, top with Roasted Red Bell Pepper Sauce (page 267).

3	tablespoons unsalted butter
1	red bell pepper, cut into matchstick strips
1	small zucchini, cut into ¼-inch slices
1	cup sliced mushrooms
¼	cup coarsely chopped onion
1	teaspoon minced garlic
⅛	teaspoon salt, or to taste
6	eggs
2	tablespoons water
½	cup freshly shredded Parmesan cheese, divided
¼	cup coarsely chopped fresh basil
	Dash of freshly ground pepper

● Melt the butter in a large nonstick skillet over medium-high heat. Add the bell pepper, zucchini, mushrooms, onion, garlic, and salt. Cook, stirring occasionally, for 5 minutes or until tender.

● Meanwhile, lightly beat the eggs and water in a medium bowl. Whisk in ¼ cup Parmesan cheese, the basil, and pepper.

● Reduce the heat to medium. Spread the vegetables evenly over the bottom of the pan. Slowly pour the egg mixture over the vegetables. Cook, undisturbed, for 1 minute or until the frittata begins to set around the edges. Using a spatula, gently lift the edges and tilt the skillet to let any uncooked egg run down under the bottom. Continue cooking for 3 minutes or until the eggs are almost set but still moist on top.

● Sprinkle the top of the frittata with the remaining ¼ cup cheese. Reduce the heat to low; cover and continue to cook for 1 minute or until the eggs are set and the cheese is melted.

● Serve the frittata directly from the skillet or use a spatula and slide it onto a serving platter. Cut into 8 wedges for serving.

TIP

It's best to store eggs with the large end up, the tapered end down, in the coldest part of your refrigerator. Since eggs can absorb odors through their porous shells, storing them in the carton offers protection from the aromas of other foods. If you store them out of the carton, write the expiration date on the eggshells. Although eggs will keep for up to one month in the refrigerator, they lose their fresh flavor after one week. To check for freshness, place an egg in a bowl of cool water. If the egg is fresh, it will sink to the bottom on its side. An older egg will stand up on one end. Very old eggs float and should be discarded.

GARLIC AND LEMON LENTILS

Makes **4** servings

My friend Cindy Jurgensen learned this recipe from a good friend whose work takes her to many faraway places. Now Cindy often takes this lentil dish to share with fellow world travelers at ethnically inspired pot lucks. The wonderful flavors are sure to please your vegetarian friends. I also enjoy it chilled the next day as a ready-to-serve salad.

For the lentils:

4	cups water
1	cup dried brown lentils

For the dressing:

½	cup coarsely chopped fresh cilantro
⅓	cup extra-virgin olive oil
¼	cup fresh lemon juice
1	teaspoon minced garlic
¾	teaspoon ground cumin
¼	teaspoon salt, or to taste
¼	teaspoon pepper, or to taste

To complete the recipe:

Sprigs of fresh cilantro for garnish

○ Pour the water and lentils into a 2-quart saucepan; bring to a boil over high heat. Reduce the heat to medium and simmer, uncovered, for 15 minutes or until the lentils are slightly tender. (A bit firm is good.)

○ Meanwhile, whisk together the dressing ingredients in a medium bowl.

○ When the lentils are done, drain them, rinse, and drain again. Add the warm lentils to the dressing and stir until combined.

○ Serve immediately while warm, or cover and refrigerate to serve later as a chilled salad. Garnish the servings with cilantro sprigs.

TIP

Lentils are tiny legume seeds that were dried as soon as they ripened. All lentils have an earthy, almost nutty flavor. The most common are brown lentils, which retain their shape after cooking. Red lentils (sometimes called Egyptian lentils) are smaller and orange in their dried form. They cook quickly, fall apart, and turn bright yellow during cooking.

Unlike other dried beans, lentils don't require soaking before cooking. Before using, put lentils in a colander and rinse to remove dust; also pick through them and discard any shriveled lentils or bits of gravel. You can add garlic, herbs, and spices to the lentil cooking water. Avoid adding salt and acidic ingredients, such as tomatoes, until the lentils are cooked. Adding these ingredients increases the cooking time necessary for the lentils to soften. Store lentils at room temperature in a tightly closed container, where they will keep for up to a year.

GREEK GREEN BEANS
AND TOMATOES WITH FETA

Makes **4** servings

This is reminiscent of a traditional appetizer that Greek tavernas serve at room temperature along with platters of olives. I fondly remember the flavors from a sunny afternoon in Santorini. Accompany these tasty beans with wedges of fresh pita bread or Crispy Pita Triangles (page 280).

2	tablespoons olive oil
½	cup thinly sliced onion
1	teaspoon minced garlic
12	ounces green beans, trimmed
1	(24-ounce) can diced tomatoes with basil, garlic, and oregano
¼	cup sliced kalamata olives
2	tablespoons minced fresh flat-leaf parsley
	Pinch of red pepper flakes, or to taste
	Pepper to taste
	Coarsely crumbled feta cheese for garnish

▶ Heat the oil in a large sauté pan over medium-high heat. Add the onion and garlic; cook, stirring occasionally, for 4 minutes or until tender.

▶ Meanwhile, put the green beans in a microwave-proof dish; add ¼ cup water. Cover and microwave on HIGH for 3 minutes or until crisp-tender. (Or cook the beans over simmering water in a stovetop steamer.)

▶ Stir the beans and tomatoes into the sauté pan. When the liquid begins to bubble, reduce the heat to low. Simmer, stirring occasionally, for 5 minutes. Stir in the remaining ingredients.

▶ Serve warm or at room temperature. Spoon into bowls and generously garnish with feta cheese.

MEXICAN CHIPOTLE RICE
WITH BEANS

Makes **4** servings

Beans and rice, the classic Mexican pairing, are jazzed up with smoky seasoning to make a satisfying family-style vegetarian meal. Or consider it a pleasing complement to a grilled chicken breast.

1	tablespoon olive oil
½	green bell pepper, finely chopped
½	cup finely chopped onion
2	teaspoons minced garlic
3	cups cooked rice
1	(15-ounce) can kidney beans or black beans, drained and rinsed
1	(14-ounce) can diced tomatoes with Mexican seasonings
2	tablespoons finely chopped chipotle chilies in adobo sauce (from a 7-ounce can), seeds removed
1	teaspoon ancho chili powder
1	teaspoon finely chopped fresh oregano or ½ teaspoon dried oregano
	Salt and pepper to taste

▶ Heat the oil in a large sauté pan over medium-high heat. Add the bell pepper, onion, and garlic; cook, stirring occasionally, for 4 minutes or until tender.

▶ Stir in the remaining ingredients. Warm, stirring occasionally, over low heat for 5 minutes.

Basics

THIS CHAPTER contains some basic components for your 15-Minute meals. You'll find them included as recipe ingredients in this book, but I hope they will also inspire your own culinary creations. Nearly all of these recipes will keep in the refrigerator for up to a week (or as noted), allowing you to be prepared for simple, impromptu cooking.

For example, you'll find Salsa Provençal (page 276) as an ingredient in Gnocchi with Salsa Provençal (page 250). It also makes a tasty accompaniment to grilled chicken. I always have homemade Basil Pesto (page 274) on hand in my freezer, not only for making Salmon Pesto Soup (page 105), but also as a way to add speedy flavor to pasta, sandwich spreads, and butter. Roasted Red Bell Pepper Sauce (page 267) tops my frittatas and turns leftover fish, chicken, meat, and roasted vegetables into a gourmet meal. It's my favorite sauce of all, not only because of its exceptional flavor, but also because of its versatility.

Dressings and vinaigrettes will give your salads—even a simple bowl of lettuce—personality. My refrigerator always contains a jar of Basic Vinaigrette (page 268) and Balsamic Vinaigrette (page 268) because I never tire of their beautiful flavors, which differentiate nearly any salad from the ordinary. Combine the vinaigrettes with leftover vegetables or beans for a marinated salad. Have an extra cooked chicken breast? Place slices over greens and add tomatoes; drizzle with Maple-Walnut Vinaigrette (page 269) and sprinkle with toasted walnuts.

The vinaigrettes can be whisked in bowls, or all the ingredients can be poured into a jar, tightly covered for storing in the refrigerator, and then shaken just before serving.

And although it's difficult to keep them on hand because they are so delicious, I love having Sugar-Spiced Walnuts (page 279) ready to sprinkle on salads or to set out as a cocktail snack for unexpected guests.

You can buy many of the items in this chapter premade, and it's fine to substitute them in your recipes. But once you've made your own balsamic vinaigrette, you'll never buy bottled dressing again. Homemade sauces and dressings do not keep as long as those that are bottled with preservatives, but it takes only a few minutes to prepare these recipes.

All dressings are subject to improvisation, so don't hesitate to adjust the ingredients to suit your taste. But there's one step that must never be omitted, and that is tasting the salad after tossing it with dressing. Getting the right balance of flavors and the just-right amount of salt and pepper is essential.

Sauces

LEMON-CAPER SAUCE

Makes ¾ cup

Fish and chicken catapult from mundane to marvelous when dressed up with this piquant, creamy sauce. Use it to turn a chilled, poached salmon fillet and vegetables into a gourmet salad (page 100). Try it on steamed vegetables, especially crisp-tender asparagus, too.

⅓	cup mayonnaise
¼	cup fresh lemon juice
1	tablespoon Dijon mustard
1	teaspoon honey
1	teaspoon minced garlic
1	tablespoon small (nonpareil) capers, drained and rinsed
1	tablespoon finely chopped shallot
1	teaspoon finely chopped fresh thyme or ½ teaspoon dried thyme
	Salt and pepper to taste

▶ Stir together all the ingredients in a small bowl.

SPICY PEANUT SAUCE

Makes ½ cup

This zesty sauce is a component in the Fresh Green Bean Salad (page 222). But often I simply make the sauce to serve solo as a dip for vegetables, such as red bell pepper, cauliflower florets, broccoli florets, and carrot and celery sticks.

¼	cup creamy natural peanut butter
¼	cup white rice vinegar
1	tablespoon dark (Asian) sesame oil
1	tablespoon soy sauce
2	teaspoons honey
1	teaspoon minced garlic
½	teaspoon red pepper flakes, or to taste

▶ Whisk together all the ingredients in a small bowl until smooth.

— TIP —

Buy natural peanut butter with the oil on top; stir in the oil before using. Many of the processed peanut butters are hydrogenated to prevent separation and have sweeteners, salt, and stabilizers added.

Chimichurri Sauce (top),
Roasted Red Bell Pepper Sauce (center),
Vegetable Salsa (bottom; page 274)

CHIMICHURRI SAUCE

Makes ½ cup

In Argentina, chimichurri is almost a national icon, and an indispensable accompaniment to grilled meats. It also works well to enliven poultry or fish. Recipes for the blend are very personal, so the seasonings may vary, but it is always rich with lots of parsley. Corn oil is traditional, but many people prefer using flavorful olive oil. Some cooks use half vinegar and half red wine. Chimichurri can be made thick to serve in a bowl at the table, or it may be more liquid and used to baste meats while grilling. Enjoy Chimichurri Sauce with Spiced Beef and Onion Pitas (page 183).

2	cups loosely packed fresh flat-leaf parsley leaves and tender stems
¼	cup coarsely chopped onion
2	tablespoons extra-virgin olive oil
¼	cup red wine vinegar
1	tablespoon fresh oregano leaves
4	garlic cloves or 2 teaspoons minced garlic
¼	teaspoon cayenne pepper, or to taste (or a pinch of red pepper flakes)
	Pinch of sugar
	Salt and pepper to taste

▶ Process all the ingredients in a food processor or blender until nearly smooth.

▶ The sauce seems quite acidic if sampled alone. To adjust the seasonings, taste by dipping in a piece of food, such as beef, chicken, or fish.

ROASTED RED BELL PEPPER SAUCE

Makes ¾ cup

This lovely, colorful sauce has long been one of my favorites. I appreciate its versatility, and the vibrant flavor always receives compliments from my guests. Add a pinch, or more, of red pepper flakes, if you'd like to add "heat." This sauce keeps in a tightly closed container in the refrigerator for up to three days. It's great served over chicken and seafood, and you'll find it among the pages of this book as a suggested sauce for the Scallops and Asparagus (page 143) and the Italian Garden Frittata (page 259). To add a decorative element to your plates, pour some of the sauce into a plastic squeeze bottle to use for making colorful stripes and swirls.

1	(7-ounce) jar roasted red bell peppers, drained and coarsely chopped (¾ cup)
1	tablespoon extra-virgin olive oil
2	teaspoons fresh lemon juice
1	teaspoon sugar
1	garlic clove or 1 teaspoon minced garlic
¼	teaspoon pepper, or to taste
⅛	teaspoon salt, or to taste
2	tablespoons minced fresh basil or 1 teaspoon dried basil, optional
	Dash of red pepper flakes, optional

▶ Process all the sauce ingredients, except the basil, in a blender or food processor until smooth. Stir in the basil and/or red pepper flakes (if using).

▶ Warm the sauce in a saucepan over medium heat or serve at room temperature.

Vinaigrettes and Dressings

BASIC VINAIGRETTE

Makes **1½** cups

A good vinaigrette is the little black dress of salad fixings. This one is a key ingredient in Tuna Salade Niçoise (page 93). As a versatile, all-purpose salad dressing, keep it on hand to add personality to all greens, steamed vegetables, bean salads, and potato salads. It can also transform chicken and fish into a salad meal.

1	cup extra-virgin olive oil
½	cup white wine vinegar
1	tablespoon Dijon mustard
1	tablespoon minced garlic
4	green onions, finely chopped
	Salt and pepper to taste

⬤ Whisk together the olive oil, vinegar, mustard, and garlic in a small bowl. Stir in the green onions. Season with salt and pepper.

⬤ Store in a tightly covered container in the refrigerator for up to 1 week.

BALSAMIC VINAIGRETTE

Makes ½ cup

This vinaigrette—my very favorite—will keep for up to a week in a tightly closed container in the refrigerator, so I always make sure to have some on hand for drizzling over garden-fresh tomatoes and greens for a simple but outstanding salad. You'll also find it in several of the recipes throughout this book, such as the Tomato and Goat Cheese Salad (page 217) and the Chopped Salad (page 21).

¼	cup extra-virgin olive oil
3	tablespoons balsamic vinegar
2	tablespoons fresh lemon juice
1	tablespoon finely chopped fresh basil or ½ teaspoon dried basil
1	teaspoon minced garlic
1	teaspoon Dijon mustard
1	teaspoon packed brown sugar
	Salt and pepper to taste

⬤ Whisk together all the ingredients in a small bowl.

TIP

Balsamic vinegar is wine vinegar made by boiling the juice of white Trebbiano grapes in copper pots until it caramelizes. The vinegar is then aged for up to one hundred years in small barrels made from various woods (oak, chestnut, mulberry, and juniper), each adding a hint of its woody flavor and color. The result is a vinegar with a heavy, mellow, almost-sweet flavor, and a dark color. Store balsamic vinegar in a cool, dark place for up to six months after opening.

Some less costly vinegars labeled "balsamic" are made from red wine that has been fortified with concentrated grape juice and caramelized sugar. They can be used in recipes but lack the flavor complexity of true *aceto balsamico tradizionale*.

HONEY-MINT VINAIGRETTE

Makes ½ cup

This simple, sweet dressing has proved so popular that it's become a household staple. It is equally as delicious drizzled over greens or a bowl of fresh fruit—or, perhaps, the two in tasty combination. Toss it with the classic: torn romaine lettuce, juicy strawberries, green grapes, and toasted slivered almonds.

¼	cup white rice vinegar
3	tablespoons honey
2	tablespoons canola oil
½	teaspoon poppy seeds
	Salt and pepper to taste
2	tablespoons finely chopped fresh mint

▶ Whisk together all the ingredients, except the mint, in a small bowl. Stir in the mint.

MAPLE-WALNUT VINAIGRETTE

Makes ½ cup

Walnut oil, which is used mainly for salads such as the Maple-Walnut Chicken Salad (page 24), has a distinctive, seductively nutty flavor and fragrance. I prefer roasted-walnut oil for its more pronounced flavor.

5	tablespoons walnut oil
3	tablespoons red wine vinegar
2	tablespoons pure maple syrup
1	tablespoon finely chopped shallot
1	teaspoon Dijon mustard
	Salt and pepper to taste

▶ Whisk together all the ingredients in a small bowl.

LEMON CAESAR DRESSING

Makes 1 cup

There's no need to buy bottled Caesar dressing when you can make this tasty fresh version in just minutes. Enjoy it in the Chicken Caesar Salad (page 26) and Caesar-Stuffed Tomatoes (page 100).

¾	cup mayonnaise
⅓	cup fresh lemon juice
2	teaspoons Dijon mustard
1	teaspoon anchovy paste
2	tablespoons finely chopped fresh flat-leaf parsley
2	tablespoons freshly grated Parmesan cheese
2	teaspoons minced garlic
½	teaspoon Worcestershire sauce
⅛	teaspoon pepper, or to taste
	A few drops of Tabasco sauce, or to taste
	Salt to taste

▶ Whisk together the mayonnaise, lemon juice, mustard, and anchovy paste in a small bowl. Stir in the remaining ingredients.

TIP

Tasted from a spoon, most vinaigrettes and salad dressings will seem strong or acidic, so it's best to taste by dipping a salad ingredient, such a leaf of lettuce, into the dressing.

CREAMY POPPY SEED DRESSING

Makes **1⅓** cups

If you've always loved bottled poppy seed dressing, definitely give this a try. In my opinion, this homemade version is a step above. This dressing is a key ingredient in the Chicken Salad with Red Grapes, Dried Cherries, and Toasted Pecans (page 17).

½	cup sugar
¼	cup finely chopped onion
¼	cup cider vinegar
½	teaspoon mustard powder
¼	teaspoon salt, or to taste
¼	teaspoon pepper, or to taste
¾	cup canola oil
1	tablespoon poppy seeds

○ Combine the sugar, onion, vinegar, mustard powder, salt, and pepper in a blender container. Blend at low speed until the sugar is dissolved. With the blender running at low speed, slowly add the oil. Continue to blend until very thick. Add the poppy seeds and pulse briefly just to combine.

○ Store in a tightly covered container in the refrigerator for up to 1 week.

GINGERED PLUM DRESSING

Makes ⅔ cup

This dressing adds extra pizzazz to the Crabmeat Martini Salad (page 91) and the Warm Chicken Stir-Fry Salad (page 20). It also spices up the classic combination of salad spinach, Mandarin orange segments, and toasted slivered almonds to serve as a side dish salad to accompany your Asian entrées.

¼	cup fresh orange juice
2	tablespoons Chinese plum sauce
2	tablespoons mayonnaise
1	tablespoon fresh lime juice
1	teaspoon Dijon mustard
1	teaspoon finely chopped fresh ginger
	Pinch of red pepper flakes, or to taste

○ Whisk together all the ingredients in a small bowl.

TIP

Chinese plum sauce is a thick sweet-and-sour sauce made from plums, apricots, chili peppers, sugar, vinegar, and spices. Look for it in the Asian section of most supermarkets. Store in the refrigerator after opening.

POMEGRANATE-RASPBERRY VINAIGRETTE

Makes ¾ cup plus 2 tablespoons

I first sampled pomegranate juice in Antalya, Turkey, long before it became a supermarket staple. It was fall, the season for the fruit, and pomegranates were piled high in the markets. One vendor squeezed the juice using a hand press as I waited. I couldn't get enough and savored every drop in my glass—and then ordered another. Now I crave this ruby red vinaigrette made with bottled pomegranate juice. It's especially luscious in the summer on my Grilled Chicken and Spinach Salad (page 18) and tossed into the Stone Fruit Salad (page 213). In the winter, I serve it over fresh pear slices on a bed of salad spinach or arugula leaves.

1	cup pomegranate juice
⅓	cup olive oil
2	tablespoons raspberry or white wine vinegar
2	tablespoons raspberry preserves
½	teaspoon Dijon mustard
¼	teaspoon salt, or to taste
¼	teaspoon pepper, or to taste

▶ Pour the pomegranate juice into a small heavy saucepan over high heat; boil for 6 minutes or until reduced to ⅓ cup.

▶ Pour the reduced juice into a small bowl. Whisk in the remaining ingredients. Allow to cool before using.

▶ Store in a tightly covered container in the refrigerator. for up to 2 weeks.

TERIYAKI VINAIGRETTE

Makes ⅔ cup

Serve this vinaigrette on salads that accompany your Asian meals, or use it to baste grilled chicken or fish. It's also a piquant ingredient in the Teriyaki Tuna with Spinach (page 144) and the Soba Noodle and Steak Salad (page 164).

¼	cup teriyaki sauce
¼	cup white rice vinegar
2	tablespoons dark (Asian) sesame oil
1	tablespoon plus 1 teaspoon hoisin sauce
2	teaspoons Chinese chili paste with garlic, or to taste
2	teaspoons minced garlic

▶ Whisk together all the ingredients in a small bowl.

> ——— TIP ———
>
> Chinese chili paste with garlic, sometimes labeled Chinese chili sauce or chili purée with garlic, is available in Asian markets and most supermarkets. Hot and spicy, it is made from chilies, rice vinegar, garlic, and salt, and is used in Szechuan cooking and as a condiment. After opening, store the tightly closed container in the refrigerator for up to six months.

Pestos, Spreads, and Salsas

GUACAMOLE

Makes about ¾ cup

Say *adios* to tasteless guacamole in plastic tubs. Here's the real thing. For mixing, I like to use a fork, leaving the guacamole with an appealing, slightly lumpy texture. For a smoother consistency, purée the ingredients in a blender. Use guacamole as a chip dip, sandwich spread, or as a tasty and colorful layer in Chipotle Burgers (page 178). Guacamole also makes a delicious filling for omelets topped with taco sauce and a dollop of sour cream.

1	ripe avocado, quartered
1	tablespoon fresh lime juice
2	tablespoons finely chopped red onion
1	teaspoon minced garlic
¼	teaspoon Tabasco sauce, or to taste
⅛	teaspoon pepper, or to taste
⅛	teaspoon salt, or to taste

◐ Use a fork to mash the avocado in a small bowl. Stir in the remaining ingredients.

◐ To keep at room temperature for up to 1 hour, cover with plastic wrap, pressing it directly onto the surface. To keep for up to 3 hours, cover and refrigerate.

TIP

The two most common varieties of avocados are the Fuerte, which has a smooth green skin, and the pebbly textured, almost black, rich-flavored Hass, which I prefer. Select fruits that are unblemished and heavy for their size. Most avocados require a few days of ripening after purchasing; place them in a pierced paper bag at room temperature for a day or two to speed up the process. Avocados will yield to a gentle pressure when they are ripe and ready to use. Store ripe avocados in the refrigerator for up to five days. Once cut and exposed to the air, avocado flesh discolors rapidly; to minimize this, coat the cut surfaces with lime or lemon juice and add these juices to recipes containing avocado.

Guacamole, Crispy Pita Triangles
(page 280)

BASIL PESTO

Makes ½ cup

This fragrant paste of basil, garlic, and pine nuts is a classic and for good reason: It's divine. I always have it on hand. At the end of the growing season, I pinch the leaves from my basil plants to make the aromatic blend, which I freeze for adding to recipes all winter long. It's splendid tossed with pasta, blended with mayonnaise for a sandwich spread, mixed with butter for a French bread spread, stirred into soup, such as Salmon Pesto Soup (page 105), or used in recipes such as Pesto Chicken Salad with Red Grapes (page 23) or Salmon and Noodles with Pesto Cream Sauce (page 118).

2	cups firmly packed fresh basil leaves
¼	cup pine nuts
¼	cup extra-virgin olive oil
2	garlic cloves or 1 teaspoon minced garlic
¼	teaspoon pepper, or to taste
⅛	teaspoon salt, or to taste

○ Process all the ingredients in a food processor until the mixture is a coarse purée.

Note: The pesto will keep for up to 1 week in a covered container in the refrigerator; pour a thin film of olive oil on top of the pesto to prevent discoloration. For longer storage, spoon the mixture into a foil-lined custard cup; cover tightly with foil and freeze. Once frozen, remove the foil-wrapped packet and store in a freezer bag for up to 2 months. To use, thaw in the refrigerator overnight, or remove from the foil and thaw quickly in the microwave.

Variation: To make ⅓ cup Basil Pesto Butter, stir together ¼ cup softened unsalted butter and 2 tablespoons Basil Pesto. Season with salt to taste. This makes a delicious spread for French bread and it's luscious melted into fluffy baked potatoes.

VEGETABLE SALSA

Makes about **3** cups

Spoon this colorful salsa over grilled fish or chicken. It also adds marvelous flavor and texture to the Pork Sausage Soft Tacos (page 183). Finely chop the vegetables or make the mixture chunkier by cutting them into larger cubes. To add "heat," increase the Tabasco sauce or add some chopped chilies.

1	avocado, finely chopped
1	plum tomato, finely chopped
½	red bell pepper, finely chopped
½	cup finely chopped red onion
½	cup coarsely chopped fresh cilantro
2	tablespoons fresh lime juice
1	teaspoon minced garlic
½	teaspoon Tabasco sauce, or to taste
	Salt to taste

○ Stir together all the ingredients in a medium bowl.

FRESH CORN SALSA

Makes **3** cups

Nothing says summer like fresh sweet corn, and here's a scrumptious way to enjoy the bounty of the season. This sunny salsa makes a delicious accompaniment to many foods, including fish or chicken cooked outdoors on the grill. Or serve it with Cornmeal-Crusted Tilapia on Tomato Ragu (page 128) or Salmon Patties with Cucumber-Dill Sauce (page 147). It's also enticing on its own, just begging to be scooped up with pita chips. The salsa can be made in advance; cover and refrigerate for up to two days.

3	tablespoons extra-virgin olive oil, divided
2	cups fresh corn kernels (from about 3 large ears)
2	tablespoons fresh lime juice
¼	cup finely chopped fresh cilantro
1	teaspoon ground cumin
½	teaspoon red pepper flakes, or to taste
½	teaspoon salt, or to taste
¼	teaspoon pepper, or to taste
1	large tomato, cut into ¼-inch cubes
1	small red bell pepper, cut into ¼-inch squares
⅓	cup finely chopped red onion

● Heat 1 tablespoon oil in a medium skillet over medium-high heat. Add the corn; cook, stirring often, for 6 minutes or until it begins to brown. Transfer to a plate and set aside to cool.

● Whisk together the remaining 2 tablespoons oil, the lime juice, cilantro, cumin, red pepper flakes, salt, and pepper in a medium bowl. Stir in the remaining ingredients and the cooled corn.

RED BEAN–CORN RELISH

Makes **4** cups

Here's an appealing side dish to accompany any grilled meat. It also steps in as a starring ingredient in the vegetarian Stacked Tomato Salad (page 226). Or simply serve it with pitas or Crispy Pita Triangles (page 280) as a cocktail snack.

1	(15-ounce) can red beans, drained and rinsed
1	ripe avocado, coarsely chopped
½	cup frozen corn kernels, thawed
¼	cup coarsely chopped fresh cilantro
2	tablespoons fresh lime juice
¼	teaspoon pepper, or to taste
	Salt to taste

● Stir together all the ingredients in a small bowl.

PAPAYA-PINEAPPLE SALSA

Makes about **1½** cups

Serve this tropical salsa with grilled chicken or any fish. You'll find it paired with Honey-Mustard Chicken (page 85), Caribbean Sole with Plantains (page 150), and Indian-Spiced Salmon (page 150).

1	papaya, cut into ½-inch cubes
½	cup canned crushed pineapple
¼	cup finely chopped red onion
¼	cup coarsely chopped fresh cilantro
2	jalapeño chilies, seeded and finely chopped
	Salt and pepper to taste

● Stir together all the ingredients in a medium bowl.

SALSA PROVENÇAL

Makes **3½** cups

Provençal refers to the area of southern France called Provence, where the ingredients in this salsa are plentiful. Many of them are available in jars on supermarket shelves, so they can be stored in your pantry, ready to be tossed together on a moment's notice. Combine the savory mélange with gnocchi for out-of-the-ordinary comfort food (page 250) or serve the salsa with grilled or broiled chicken.

1	(19-ounce) can fava beans, drained and rinsed
1	(7-ounce) jar roasted red bell peppers, drained and coarsely chopped
1	(6-ounce) jar marinated quartered artichoke hearts, drained
¼	cup sliced kalamata olives (about 10 pitted olives)
¼	cup coarsely chopped fresh basil
2	tablespoons extra-virgin olive oil
2	tablespoons red wine vinegar
1	teaspoon minced garlic
¼	teaspoon pepper, or to taste
¼	teaspoon salt, or to taste
⅛	teaspoon red pepper flakes, or to taste

▶ Stir together all the ingredients in a medium bowl.

—— **TIP** ——

Roasting red bell peppers takes about 30 minutes. If you prefer making your own rather than using those from jars, here's how:

•   Position the oven rack about 5 inches from the heating element, and preheat the broiler.

•   Line a rimmed baking sheet with aluminum foil.

•   For each bell pepper, remove the stem and cut the pepper in half lengthwise; discard the seeds, membranes, and stem.

•   Place the pepper halves, skin side up, on the baking sheet; flatten each with the palm of your hand. (Place as many pepper halves as you'd like on the baking sheet, arranging them in a single layer.) Lightly brush the skins with olive oil.

•   Broil for 10 minutes or until the peppers are fork-tender and the skins are blackened, charred, and blistered.

•   While they are still hot, transfer the peppers to a heavy-duty zip-top plastic bag and seal. Set aside to cool for 10 to 15 minutes. (The steam will loosen the skins.)

•   Remove the peppers from the bag; peel and discard the skins.

•   The roasted bell peppers will keep for up to two days in a covered container in the refrigerator. Drain well before using.

TAPENADE

Makes **2** cups

If you like olives, you'll love this spread. My friend Stephanie Browner, who shared her version of this classic, spoons the flavorful mixture on baked potatoes and grilled fish. She spreads it on crostini and crackers, often adds a dash to her homemade vinaigrette, and includes it as a tasty layer in tomato and mozzarella sandwiches. For me, it's a key ingredient for adding a special zest to the Italian Pepperoni Panini (page 176). Another discovery: I recently warmed leftover penne, which I tossed with tapenade and sliced cherry tomatoes for a tasty and quick lunch. With so many uses, you'll want to have a jar of tapenade in the refrigerator, where it will keep for two weeks or longer. And stir in a pinch of red pepper flakes to add a little "heat" if you wish. For the best color and flavor, stir in the fresh parsley just before serving.

2½	cups (12 ounces) mixed pitted olives (such as kalamata, black oil-cured, and green)
1	ounce (3 to 4) anchovy fillets, drained
2	garlic cloves
1	teaspoon small (nonpareil) capers, drained and rinsed
1	tablespoon extra-virgin olive oil
2	teaspoons fresh lemon juice
2	tablespoons finely chopped fresh flat-leaf parsley

► Combine the olives, anchovies, garlic, and capers in a food processor. Pulse until finely chopped. Add the olive oil and process again. (The mixture can be left slightly chunky or puréed until smooth.) Stir in the lemon juice and parsley.

⸻ · TIP · ⸻

Capers are the unopened flower buds of a shrub native to the Mediterranean and parts of Asia. After drying in the sun, the buds are pickled in vinegar brine. Capers come in several sizes. The largest have the strongest flavor. The smallest, called "nonpareil," are more subtle in taste, the most tender, and the most expensive. Capers should be rinsed before using to remove excess salt. Once the jar is opened, store capers in the refrigerator for up to three months.

HUMMUS

Makes 1¼ cups

For a snack, serve hummus as a dip for fresh vegetables or Crispy Pita Triangles (page 280). But my favorite way to enjoy hummus is to spread a layer along the ribs of fresh romaine leaves, top with a mound of Tabouli (page 222), and serve as a salad or roll as lettuce wraps. The flavors blend nicely when hummus is made in advance, so plan ahead a day or two and serve chilled.

1	tablespoon olive oil
¼	cup finely chopped red onion
1	teaspoon minced garlic
¼	cup minced fresh flat-leaf parsley
1	tablespoon minced fresh basil or ½ teaspoon dried basil
1	teaspoon minced fresh oregano or ½ teaspoon dried oregano
¼	teaspoon ground coriander
¼	teaspoon ground cumin
1	(15-ounce) can garbanzo beans, drained and rinsed
3	tablespoons fresh lemon juice
	Salt and pepper to taste

▶ Heat the oil in a small skillet over medium-high heat. Add the onion and garlic; cook, stirring occasionally, for 3 minutes or tender. Remove from the heat; stir in the parsley, basil, oregano, coriander, and cumin.

▶ Combine the garbanzo beans and lemon juice in a food processor; purée until smooth.

▶ Add the bean mixture to the skillet and stir until evenly combined. Transfer to a bowl and allow to cool before serving.

MIXED FRUIT CHUTNEY

Makes 2 cups

Fruity chutney makes an excellent accompaniment to Portobello Quesadillas (page 241) and curried entrées. It is also a key ingredient in several recipes in this book. Vary the recipe by substituting currants for raisins or peaches for pears, or by stirring in ¼ cup chopped walnuts, pecans, or slivered almonds. This chutney will keep in a tightly closed container in the refrigerator for up to two weeks. But I'm betting it will disappear much faster.

8	dried apricots, coarsely chopped
1	apple, peeled and cut into ½-inch cubes
¼	cup dark raisins
1	tablespoon lemon zest
¼	cup fresh lemon juice
2	tablespoons water
2	tablespoons white rice vinegar
2	tablespoons packed brown sugar
½	teaspoon ground cinnamon
	Dash of pepper, or to taste
2	pears, peeled and cut into ½-inch chunks

▶ Combine all the ingredients, except the pears, in a medium saucepan. Cover and cook over medium-high heat, stirring occasionally, until the liquid comes to a boil. Reduce the heat to medium and continue to cook, covered, stirring occasionally, for 5 minutes.

▶ Add the pears; cover and cook, stirring occasionally, for 5 more minutes or until all of the fruits are tender.

▶ Serve warm or refrigerate.

SUGAR-SPICED WALNUTS

Makes 1½ cups

Crunchy, sweet, and peppery, these make delicious snacks, as well as much-appreciated gifts from your kitchen. Usually, I double the recipe to have a supply on hand ready to add magic to salads, such as the Mesclun Salad with Grilled Pears and Blue Cheese (page 214), Autumn Apple Salad (page 216), and my Baby Spinach and Orange Salad (page 217).

¼	cup sugar
½	teaspoon pepper
¼	teaspoon salt
¼	teaspoon ground ginger
¼	teaspoon allspice
1½	cups walnut halves

◐ Combine the sugar, pepper, salt, ginger, and allspice in a small bowl.

◐ Heat a small nonstick skillet over medium-high heat until hot. Add the walnuts; cook, stirring occasionally, for 2 minutes or until fragrant and lightly browned. Add the sugar mixture. Reduce the heat to medium; stir constantly for 2 minutes or until the nuts are well-coated with sugar. (It's best if the sugar does not dissolve completely, leaving some grainy texture on the nuts.)

◐ Transfer the nuts to a plate; cool. Store at room temperature in a tightly closed container.

PARMESAN CRISPS

Makes **12**

These appetizing little crisps will keep for up to two days when stored at room temperature between layers of wax paper in an airtight container, so have some on hand for a ready-to-serve soup or salad accompaniment. For the best flavor, use freshly shredded authentic Italian Parmigiano-Reggiano.

¾	cup finely shredded Parmigiano-Reggiano cheese (3 ounces)
1	tablespoon all-purpose flour
¼	teaspoon pepper
1	teaspoon finely chopped fresh rosemary or thyme, if desired

◐ Preheat the oven to 375°F.

◐ Line a large baking sheet with baking parchment or a nonstick pan liner.

◐ Stir together the cheese, flour, and pepper in a medium bowl. For herb-flavored cheese crisps, also add rosemary or thyme.

◐ Arrange tablespoons of the cheese mixture 4 inches apart on the baking sheet, stirring cheese in the bowl between tablespoons to keep the flour evenly distributed. Flatten the mounds slightly to form 3-inch rounds.

◐ Bake in the middle of the oven for 8 minutes, or until the cheese is melted and the crisps are golden.

◐ Cool completely on the baking sheet and then remove carefully with a metal spatula.

CRISPY PITA TRIANGLES

Makes **24**

In place of store-bought crackers, jazz up plain-Jane pitas for a savory accompaniment to soups and salads, such as the Gazpacho Salad with Grilled Chicken (page 29)—or simply serve them as a tasty snack. Add a bowl of Hummus (page 278) or Red Bean Corn–Relish (page 275).

2	(6-inch) pita bread rounds, sliced in half horizontally
1	tablespoon olive oil
½	teaspoon dried oregano
½	cup freshly grated Parmesan cheese

▶ Position the oven rack about 5 inches from the heating element and preheat the broiler.

▶ Use a pastry brush to spread the rough sides of each pita half with oil. Place on a baking sheet, oiled sides up. Sprinkle with the oregano and Parmesan cheese. Use kitchen shears to cut each pita half into 6 wedges.

▶ Broil for 2 minutes or until the pitas are lightly browned and the cheese is melted. Watch closely. (The pitas will become crisper as they cool.)

GARLIC CROUTONS

Makes **2** cups

Make these once, and there's no turning back. Homemade croutons, especially those made using whole-wheat bread, are far superior to the packaged varieties. They'll add flavor and crunch to your soups, such as Chunky Gazpacho (page 236), and salads, such as Chicken Caesar Salad (page 26).

You'll notice that I call for dried herbs in this recipe, which are necessary instead of fresh herbs that may burn in the pan. Those bits that don't adhere to the croutons will darken, so be sure to transfer the crispy croutons to a plate using a slotted spoon.

3	tablespoons olive oil
1	teaspoon minced garlic
½	teaspoon dried basil
½	teaspoon dried oregano
2	cups ½-inch bread cubes (about 3 slices bread)

▶ Heat the oil in a large skillet over medium heat. Add the garlic, basil, and oregano. Stir for a few seconds to soften the herbs.

▶ Increase the heat to high. Add the bread cubes; stir constantly for 4 minutes or until the croutons are lightly browned and crisp. Transfer the croutons to a plate and let cool. (They will become crisper as they cool.)

▶ The croutons can be made a day in advance. Store in a tin at room temperature. They become soggy in a plastic container. To crisp again, heat the croutons on a baking sheet for about 5 minutes at 350°F.

PARMESAN CHEESE CROUTONS

Makes **4** servings

With their enticing golden brown edge and savory topping of melted cheese, these super-sized croutons look great atop the Cream of Tomato Basil Soup (page 230) or Tomato-Fennel Soup (page 40). These are best freshly made, and the recipe can easily be doubled, tripled, or quadrupled.

8	(½-inch) slices of baguette (about ¼ of a 20-inch baguette)
½	garlic clove
1	tablespoon extra-virgin olive oil
2	tablespoons freshly grated Parmesan cheese

❍   Position the oven rack about 5 inches from the heating element and preheat the broiler.

❍   Rub the cut surface of the garlic cloves over one side of each baguette slice. Brush that side with olive oil.

❍   Place the baguette slices, olive oil sides up, on a baking sheet. Broil for 45 seconds or until golden brown. Turn the slices over; lightly sprinkle with the Parmesan cheese. Broil for 30 seconds, or until the cheese is melted and the edges of the bread are golden brown.

Desserts

EVEN WHEN I prepare a delicious 15-Minute main course, the meal never seems complete without dessert. Sometimes the finale can be as simple as a sliced, perfectly ripe summer peach. But I do like to prepare tempting dessert concoctions, not only when I have guests, but also to surprise my family. With 15-Minute dessert recipes, it's easy to enjoy delectable sweets, even at the end of a busy day.

You'll find many chocolate desserts here because they're my favorites—and usually winners around any table. Who can resist Chocolate-Glazed Strawberries (page 294) or Mocha Shakes (page 293)?

The basic sauces, including two of my favorites, are easy to keep on hand in the refrigerator. Hot Fudge Sauce with Toasted Hazelnuts (page 304) and Raspberry Sauce (page 304) are so delicious that they can turn a bowl of ice cream into a gourmet dessert.

Some of these creations, such as Pears with Parmigiano-Reggiano (page 291), Balsamic-Glazed Strawberries with Ice Cream (page 285), and Affogato (page 288), are sophisticated, making perfect endings to elegant meals for guests.

Other recipes, like Vanilla Rice Pudding (page 302), Chocolate Panna Cotta (page 300), and Mexican Hot Chocolate (page 302), are soul-soothing, homey desserts that your family will love. The fact that some of these desserts, such as Grilled Pineapple (page 294) and Summer Berries with Orange Cream (page 299), are good for you is a yummy bonus.

PEACH MELBA

Makes **4** servings

It's hard to beat a juicy summer peach. Pair it with raspberries and you have an incomparable combination. I serve this dessert often for my family and warm-weather guests.

2	peaches, peeled and cut into ½-inch wedges.
4	large scoops premium vanilla ice cream
¾	cup Raspberry Sauce (page 304)
	Sprigs of fresh mint for garnish

❍ For each serving, arrange the slices from half a peach in a dessert bowl. Top with 1 scoop of ice cream and drizzle with about 3 tablespoons of the sauce. Garnish with a mint sprig.

BALSAMIC-GLAZED STRAWBERRIES WITH ICE CREAM

Makes **4** servings

My appreciation for balsamic vinegar is always enhanced when I visit Italy, where the vinegar is aged for up to 100 years, resulting in a thick, syrupy sweet richness. Here, cooking the vinegar with sugar gives it some of the qualities of those pricey imported aged balsamics, which are traditionally drizzled over fresh berries. Sometimes I put a thin layer of crumbled amaretti cookies in the dessert bowls before adding the scoops of ice cream.

2	tablespoons balsamic vinegar
2	tablespoons packed brown sugar
2	cups sliced strawberries
1½	cups premium vanilla ice cream

❍ Combine the vinegar and brown sugar in a small saucepan over medium heat. Cook, stirring constantly, for 4 minutes or until slightly thickened.

❍ Remove from the heat and let cool for 5 minutes. Stir in the strawberries.

❍ Serve the strawberries warm over scoops of ice cream.

LIMONCELLO ICE CREAM

Makes **4** servings (2½ cups)

Limoncello, a lemon-flavored liqueur, is all the rage among stylish young Italians. Fortunately, it is also available in most liquor stores in the United States. What could be simpler than to serve this cool, refreshing final course to an Italian meal?

3	cups premium vanilla ice cream
½	cup limoncello
	Long, thin strips of lemon zest for garnish

❍ Blend the ice cream with the limoncello in a blender until smooth. Serve immediately in small liqueur glasses for sipping. Top with lemon zest strips.

❍ Or if you prefer, immediately transfer the mixture to a covered container and freeze until firm. Store in the freezer for up to 1 week. Use a small ice cream scoop and serve in dessert bowls. Garnish the servings with lemon zest strips.

Spicy Pineapple Salsa with
Cinnamon-Sugar Tortilla Triangles

SPICY PINEAPPLE SALSA WITH CINNAMON-SUGAR TORTILLA TRIANGLES

Makes **4** servings

This dish always offers an element of surprise. The sweet-with-a-little-kick-of-heat salsa can be served solo, but I especially savor it over rich vanilla ice cream with the tortilla triangles tucked into the side of the bowl.

1	(20-ounce) can unsweetened pineapple tidbits
4	fresh mint leaves, coarsely chopped
1	tablespoon finely chopped red chilies, or more to taste
	Canola oil for frying
2	(6-inch) corn tortillas, each cut into 6 triangles
1	teaspoon sugar
⅛	teaspoon ground cinnamon
	Sprigs of fresh mint for garnish

○ Combine the pineapple (and juice), mint, and chilies in a small saucepan. Simmer, uncovered, for 5 minutes. Set aside to cool.

○ Pour the oil into a medium sauté pan to a depth of about ¼ inch. Heat the oil over medium heat until a drop of water sizzles. Add the tortilla triangles and cook for 3 minutes or until golden brown on both sides. Using tongs, transfer the triangles to a paper-towel-lined plate.

○ Stir together the sugar and cinnamon in a small bowl. Sprinkle over the tortilla triangles.

○ Serve the salsa in dessert bowls and accompany with the tortilla triangles. Garnish with mint sprigs.

BANANAS FOSTER

Makes **4** servings

Among my childhood culinary memories, one of the fondest is my awe over show-off desserts prepared tableside in fancy restaurants. This was—and still is—exciting. Although it's theatrical to flambé the bananas, for simplicity you can omit that step and still serve an impressive dessert.

⅓	cup unsalted butter
⅓	cup packed brown sugar
½	teaspoon ground cinnamon
¼	teaspoon ground nutmeg
¼	cup dark rum
2	tablespoons banana liqueur
3	firm but ripe bananas, peeled and halved crosswise and lengthwise
2	cups premium vanilla ice cream
	Toasted pecans for garnish

○ Combine the butter, brown sugar, cinnamon, nutmeg, rum, and banana liqueur in a large skillet over medium-high heat. Cook, stirring constantly, until the butter is melted. Reduce the heat to low and cook, stirring frequently, for 3 more minutes or until the mixture is thickened and syrupy.

○ Stir in the bananas; cook, gently stirring once or twice, for 2 minutes or until tender.

○ Serve immediately, while warm, over ice cream, and garnish with pecans.

AFFOGATO

Makes **4** servings

Affogato is a typically indulgent Italian way to enjoy ice cream that is literally "drowned" (or *affogato*) in espresso. It's one of the simplest desserts imaginable, and it's also one I relish. I freshly brew the coffee using my espresso machine, but if necessary, you can use instant espresso powder or strongly brewed coffee. Vanilla ice cream is traditional; in my opinion, chocolate is even better. You also can vary the dessert by serving more ice cream and omitting the whipped cream topping.

At a market-side café in Nice, I adored Café Ligeois, the French version, which was crowned with whipped cream and also drizzled with sweet caramel.

¼	cup whipping cream
2	teaspoons sugar
2	cups premium vanilla or chocolate ice cream
1	cup (or more) freshly brewed hot espresso
	Sweetened cocoa powder for garnish

○ Use a whisk or beaters at medium speed to whip the cream in a small bowl. Gradually add the sugar and continue beating until the sugar is dissolved and the cream holds soft peaks.

○ Scoop the ice cream into 4 dessert bowls. Bring the espresso to the table in a small pot or as 4 individual espresso shots.

○ Pour the hot espresso over the ice cream, add dollops of whipped cream, and sprinkle lightly with cocoa powder.

Here are three other ideas to make after-dinner coffee delicious and memorable.

Café Shakerato: To prepare 2 servings, pour ½ cup hot espresso and 4 teaspoons sugar into a blender. Add 1 cup ice broken into smaller pieces and blend for 15 seconds. Pour into martini glasses and garnish with thin strips of lemon zest. Serve immediately while cold and foamy.

Espresso Shake: To prepare 2 servings, scoop about ⅔ cup premium vanilla ice cream into a cocktail shaker (or a jar with a tight-fitting lid). Add ½ cup hot espresso. Close and shake until the ice cream has melted. Pour into martini glasses and drizzle with chocolate syrup.

Chocolate Spoons: For a simple meal finale, early in the day dip teaspoons into melted semisweet chocolate. Place on a wax paper–lined or parchment-lined baking sheet and refrigerate. Serve for stirring coffee or espresso.

Affogato

FROZEN CHOCOLATE TRUFFLES

Makes **4** servings

Making these truffles for a deluxe decadent snack or
for an elegant dessert takes just minutes, but be sure
to allow about half an hour of waiting time for the ice
cream balls to freeze between steps. My friend Fran
Lebahn, who developed the recipe for her chocolate
cooking classes, suggests using several varieties of ice
cream for the three truffles that make a serving. (You
may want to make extras in case three aren't enough.)
Arrange them on pretty dessert plates to create an
impressive ending for any meal.

1	pint of your favorite premium ice cream (such as chocolate, vanilla, strawberry, or coffee), or a variety
2	ounces semisweet chocolate
2	tablespoons sweetened cocoa powder

⊙   Line a 9-inch pie plate (or other small rimmed
pan) with wax paper.

⊙   Using a small (about 1½-inch) ice cream scoop,
drop 12 balls of ice cream onto the pie plate. Cover
lightly with plastic wrap and freeze for ½ hour or until
firm.

⊙   When you're ready to assemble the truffles, put
the chocolate in a microwave-safe bowl and microwave
on MEDIUM for about 1½ minutes or until liquid.
Stir the chocolate to melt any remaining chunks and
set to cool slightly.

⊙   Spread the cocoa powder on a large plate. Roll
the ice cream balls in the powder, pressing gently, and
return them to the pie plate.

⊙   Drizzle the melted chocolate over the ice cream
balls. Return the plate to the freezer for at least ½ hour
before serving.

⊙   To store for up to 2 days, cover with plastic wrap.

CURRIED PEACHES

Makes **4** servings

There's something extra-enticing about the combination
of "fire and ice." This easy-to-prepare contrast of hot
and cold makes a memorable dinner party finale.

1	tablespoon canola oil
1	tablespoon finely chopped crystallized ginger
1	teaspoon curry powder
¼	cup pineapple or fresh orange juice
1	teaspoon honey
16	ounces peaches, peeled and cut into ½-inch wedges
2	cups premium vanilla ice cream
	Coarsely chopped toasted pecans for garnish

⊙   Heat the oil in a medium saucepan over medium
heat. Add the ginger and curry powder; stir constantly
for 30 seconds.

⊙   Stir in the pineapple juice and honey. When the
honey is melted, stir in the peaches. Cover and cook,
stirring occasionally, for 2 minutes or until the peaches
are tender.

⊙   To serve, spoon the ice cream into 4 dessert bowls.
Top with the warm peach sauce and garnish with pecans.

PEARS WITH PARMIGIANO-REGGIANO

Makes **4** servings

When this sophisticated dessert is on the menu, make certain that the pears are juicy and ripe. It's also particularly important to use top-quality cheese. Italy's Parmigiano-Reggiano cheese has an incomparable, complex flavor and a granular texture that melts in your mouth. I like to coarsely grind mixed peppercorns to offer color to the simple presentation, and the walnuts add a just-right crunch

¼	cup honey
2	ripe pears, cut into ¼-inch wedges
16	thinly shaved slices of Parmigiano-Reggiano cheese
	Freshly ground mixed peppercorns
¼	cup (or more) Sugar-Spiced Walnuts (page 279), optional

❍ Pour the honey into a microwave-proof measuring cup. Heat in the microwave on HIGH for 20 seconds or until warm and runny.

❍ For each dessert, arrange the slices from half a pear on a plate. Drizzle with 1 tablespoon warm honey. Top with 3 cheese slices and sprinkle the dish with pepper. Add walnuts, if desired.

PEAR CRUMBLE

Makes **4** servings

I like to use a combination of red- and green-skinned pears for this recipe. Select those that are firm and slightly under-ripe, which makes for easier slicing and also results in a pleasing texture after cooking. Serve the warm pears with their gingersnap topping in dessert bowls with small scoops of rich vanilla ice cream.

4	gingersnap cookies
2	pears, halved lengthwise and cut into ⅜-inch slices
¼	cup dried apricots in ¼-inch pieces (about 6 apricots)
2	tablespoons packed brown sugar
1	teaspoon pure vanilla extract

❍ Put the cookies in a plastic bag or between sheets of wax paper. Use a rolling pin or can to break them into large crumbs.

❍ Stir together the pears, apricots, brown sugar, and vanilla in a large bowl. Transfer to a 1½-quart microwave-proof casserole dish.

❍ Microwave on HIGH for 1 to 1½ minutes or until the pears are tender. (They will continue to soften after being removed from the microwave.) Spoon the warm pears into small dessert bowls and sprinkle with the crumbled cookies.

Candied Brie with
Apple Wedges

MOCHA SHAKES

Makes **4** servings

Here's a gourmet shake for adults. It offers guilty pleasure as a midday snack, but better still, serve the lush, creamy blend in martini glasses for a fashionable dessert.

8	cups premium vanilla ice cream
½	cup Mocha Sauce (page 305)
½	cup coffee-flavored liqueur

> Purée all the ingredients in a blender until smooth. Serve immediately.

CANDIED BRIE WITH APPLE WEDGES

Makes **4** servings

By adding creamy Brie cheese to the all-time childhood favorite, this treat becomes candied apples for grown-ups, as elegant as it is finger-licking good. If you want to serve this treat for a substantial snack, bake a larger round of Brie (6-inch, 13 ounces), double the sauce, and slice more apples.

1	(4-inch, 8-ounce) round of Brie cheese
2	tablespoons salted butter
3	tablespoons packed brown sugar
3	tablespoons dark corn syrup
¼	cup finely chopped pecans
2	large tart apples (such as Granny Smith), each cut into 6 wedges

> Preheat the oven to 350°F.

> Place the Brie cheese on a baking sheet. Bake for 13 minutes, or until softened and warm.

> Meanwhile, to make the sauce, combine the butter, brown sugar, and corn syrup in a small saucepan. Cook over low heat, stirring constantly until the butter is melted and the mixture comes to a full boil. Remove from the heat and stir in the pecans.

> Dip the apple wedges in acidulated water (see tip).

> Place the warm cheese in a small serving bowl or on a small plate. Spoon the sauce over the warm cheese and surround with the apple wedges.

> Provide plates for your guests, as well as small knives for spreading the cheese on the apples.

TIP

To prevent the exposed cut surfaces of apples and pears from browning, toss them with lemon juice or hold them in acidulated water, which you can make by adding a small amount of an acid, such as lemon, lime, or orange juice to tap water.

CHOCOLATE-GLAZED STRAWBERRIES

Makes **16**

Brilliantly cloaked in glossy dark chocolate, these berries make an impressive entrance. The same chocolate-glazing technique can be used for other fruits, such as orange segments, or for dried fruit or nuts. Prepare early the day they are to be served; just cover and refrigerate.

16	large strawberries, with hulls and stems attached
6	ounces semisweet chocolate
	Sprigs of fresh mint for garnish

○ Heat water until simmering in the bottom pan of a double boiler over high heat. Wash the berries and dry thoroughly. Line a baking sheet with baking parchment or wax paper.

○ Put the chocolate in the top pan of the double boiler and place it over the simmering water.

○ Reduce the heat to medium; stir occasionally as the chocolate melts. Remove the pan from the heat.

○ Using a small rubber spatula or spoon, work over the pan as you spread each berry, about half way up the sides, with chocolate. As the berries are completed, place them on the prepared baking sheet.

○ Refrigerate for 10 minutes or until the chocolate is set. Transfer the berries, in a single layer, to a covered container and refrigerate.

○ Arrange the chilled strawberries on a plate garnished with mint.

TIP

Chocolate should be stored, tightly wrapped, in a cool, dry place, where it will keep for years. Because chocolate scorches easily, it should be melted slowly over low heat, such as in a double boiler or a microwave at 50 percent power.

GRILLED PINEAPPLE

Makes **4** servings

My friend Nancy Bundt shared this idea with me, and it is simply delicious. Nancy likes to drizzle the warm pineapple rings with fresh lime juice. I recently received rave reviews for serving the grilled fruit in pools of Raspberry Sauce (page 304).

8	(½-inch) fresh pineapple rings
	Canola oil for brushing
2	tablespoons packed brown sugar

○ Heat a stovetop grill pan over high heat. When a drop of water sizzles, lightly brush both sides of the pineapple rings with oil and place on the pan. Grill for 2 minutes per side or until lightly browned.

○ For each serving, transfer 2 pineapple rings to a dessert plate and, while the pineapple is very warm, sprinkle with about ½ tablespoon brown sugar. Serve warm.

Chocolate-Glazed Strawberries

GINGERED BLUEBERRY-RICOTTA DESSERT

Makes **4** servings

In the summer, blueberries are harvested in the northern U.S., particularly in Michigan and Maine. In the winter, they come from South America. Lucky for us that we can enjoy the great flavor of fresh blueberries—and benefit from their antioxidants—all year round.

10	chocolate wafer cookies
1	banana, cut into ¼-inch cubes
3	teaspoons orange juice, divided
1	cup ricotta cheese
2	tablespoons sugar
1	tablespoon finely chopped crystallized ginger
3	tablespoons blueberry preserves
1	cup fresh blueberries
	Orange zest for garnish

◗ Put the cookies into a large zip-top plastic bag. Use a rolling pin to crush them into fine crumbs.

◗ Stir together the banana and 2 teaspoons orange juice in a small bowl.

◗ Stir together the ricotta cheese, sugar, and ginger in a medium bowl. Stir in the banana mixture.

◗ In another small bowl, combine the preserves and the remaining 1 teaspoon orange juice. Add the blueberries and stir to coat.

◗ To assemble, layer in each of 4 small dessert bowls, 2 tablespoons cookie crumbs, ⅓ cup ricotta-banana mixture, and ¼ cup blueberries.

◗ Serve immediately, or cover with plastic wrap and refrigerate for about 1 hour to allow the dessert to chill and the flavors to blend. Garnish with orange zest.

— TIP —

Crystallized, or candied, ginger has been cooked in sugar syrup and coated with coarse sugar. This sweet ginger is generally used as a confection or added to desserts. Store it in your spice cabinet in a jar with a tight-fitting lid.

PEACHES IN RED WINE

Makes **4** servings

Use a red wine with a fruity flavor and aroma, such as Dolcetto, for this dessert, which is elegant and light after a substantial Italian meal. Accompany with crisp, little amaretti macaroon cookies.

½	cup fruity Italian red wine
1	teaspoon granulated sugar
2	large ripe peaches, peeled and thickly sliced
½	cup ricotta cheese
1	tablespoon powdered sugar
½	teaspoon pure vanilla extract
	Sprigs of fresh mint for garnish

○ Combine the red wine and sugar in a medium bowl; stir until the sugar is dissolved. Add the peaches and stir gently.

○ Stir together the ricotta cheese, powdered sugar, and vanilla in a small bowl.

○ To serve, spoon the peaches and wine into dessert bowls. Add dollops of the ricotta mixture and garnish with mint sprigs.

ZABAGLIONE

Makes **4** servings

This foamy custard is a traditional Italian dessert that's best eaten right after preparing, but it doesn't take long to make this sensual delight while your guests wait. The secret is not to let the mixture get too hot, but to let it get hot enough to thicken and cook the egg yolks. I like to have fresh berries ready in advance to sprinkle over small servings of the rich, warm custard. For extra dazzle, use pretty stemmed glasses and accompany the sweet indulgence with a tray of Italian sponge fingers or little biscotti for dipping.

3	egg yolks, at room temperature
¼	cup sugar
¼	cup sweet Marsala wine

○ Half fill a small saucepan with water and bring to a simmer (not a boil) over medium heat.

○ Pour the egg yolks and sugar into a heatproof bowl that will fit into the saucepan. (A copper bowl is traditional for making this dessert, but not essential.) Or you can use a double boiler. Beat the egg mixture with a hand-held electric mixer or whisk until pale and creamy.

○ Place the bowl or top of the double boiler into the saucepan and gradually pour in the Marsala wine. Continue to beat with the mixer or a whisk for 4 minutes or until it reaches a temperature of 140°F and begins to thicken. (It's important not to overheat or the eggs may curdle.) Continue beating for 3 more minutes to ensure that the eggs are cooked. The mixture will become light and frothy, it will approximately triple in volume, and the mixture will make a trail when dropped from the beaters.

○ Serve immediately in small dessert bowls.

--- TIP ---

The best Marsala wine is imported from Sicily. It has a rich, smoky flavor that can range from sweet to dry. Like port, sherry, and other dessert wines, Marsala is a "fortified" wine, which means brandy or another spirit has been added, increasing the alcohol content and enhancing the flavor.

Summer Berries with
Orange Cream

SUMMER BERRIES WITH ORANGE CREAM

Makes **4** servings

It's hard to improve on a bowl of fresh, juicy summer berries, though a dollop of liqueur-scented crème fraîche does gild the lily with elegance and sophistication.

6	cups mixed berries, such as raspberries, strawberries, blueberries, and blackberries
3	tablespoons sugar, divided, or to taste
¾	cup (6 ounces) crème fraîche
2	tablespoons orange-flavored liqueur, such as Cointreau
2	teaspoons pure vanilla extract
	Orange zest and sprigs of fresh mint for garnish

◐ Stir the berries with 1 tablespoon sugar in a medium bowl. Taste and adjust the sweetness.

◐ Whisk together the crème fraîche, the remaining 2 tablespoons sugar, the liqueur, and vanilla in a small bowl.

◐ Spoon the berries into individual dessert bowls and top with the crème fraîche mixture. Garnish with a sprinkling of orange zest and mint sprigs.

WARM APPLES WITH VANILLA CREAM SAUCE

Makes **4** servings

I usually prepare this dessert just before serving because I love the aroma in my kitchen as the apples cook. But I have found that it also can be made early in the day, refrigerated in a covered container, and reheated in the microwave for about 2 minutes on HIGH.

The warm apples are wonderful served over premium vanilla ice cream, along with gingersnaps, or spooned over slices of gingerbread cake. Or top the warm apples with vanilla yogurt and add a sprinkling of granola or toasted chopped pecans.

6	tablespoons unsalted butter
⅓	cup sugar
2	crisp, semisweet apples (such as Braeburn or Granny Smith), peeled, cored, and cut into ½-inch cubes
½	cup dried cranberries
½	cup half-and-half
1	teaspoon pure vanilla extract
	Ground nutmeg (preferably freshly grated) for garnish

◐ Melt the butter in a large skillet over medium heat. Add the sugar; stir for 1 minute or until it begins to melt.

◐ Add the apples; cook, stirring occasionally, for 10 minutes or until the apples are tender and the butter is lightly browned.

◐ Meanwhile, put the cranberries in a small microwave-proof custard cup with 2 tablespoons water. Cover with waxed paper and microwave on HIGH for 1½ minutes or until the cranberries are softened. Drain any water remaining.

◐ Stir the half-and-half, vanilla, and softened cranberries into the apples. Reduce the heat to medium-low; cover and simmer for 2 minutes or until the sauce thickens.

◐ Serve warm in small dessert bowls. Garnish with nutmeg.

TIRAMISU PRONTO

Makes **4** servings

Tiramisu is a popular dessert in many Italian restaurants, but it always seemed like too much trouble to prepare at home—that is, until I developed this speedy version. So quick, so easy, and so delicious.

1	(8-ounce) carton whipped cream cheese
¼	cup heavy cream or milk
3	tablespoons sugar, divided
½	cup coffee-flavored liqueur, such as Kahlúa
8	(⅜-inch-thick) slices pound cake
¼	teaspoon sweetened cocoa powder for garnish

○ Whisk together the cream cheese, cream, and 2 tablespoons sugar in a small bowl.

○ In a separate small bowl, combine the liqueur and the remaining 1 tablespoon sugar. Stir until the sugar is dissolved.

○ For each serving, place 1 slice of cake in each of four 1 ¼-cup ramekins. Drizzle 1 tablespoon of the liqueur mixture over the cake. Spread with 1 heaping tablespoon of the cream cheese mixture. Repeat layers.

○ Cover with plastic wrap and refrigerate for at least 1 hour or for up to 8 hours. Sprinkle with the cocoa powder sifted through a fine mesh strainer just before serving.

CHOCOLATE PANNA COTTA

Makes **4** servings

Panna cotta is Italian for "cooked cream," and this eggless custard is thickened with gelatin and flavored with chocolate. It takes less than 10 minutes to prepare, but be sure to allow at least 3 hours for the dessert to chill and set. I like to serve this rich panna cotta in pretty little dessert bowls topped with fresh raspberries and chocolate curls or dollops of crème fraîche.

1	tablespoon cold water
1	teaspoon plain gelatin
1½	cups heavy cream
1	tablespoon packed brown sugar
3	ounces semisweet chocolate, coarsely chopped

○ Pour the water into a small bowl and sprinkle with the gelatin. Let stand for 3 minutes or until softened.

○ Stir together the cream and brown sugar in a small saucepan over medium-high heat. When the liquid begins to form bubbles around the edges, stir in the gelatin mixture. Reduce the heat to low and continue stirring for 30 seconds or until the gelatin is dissolved. Add the chocolate and whisk for 1 minute or until the chocolate is melted and the mixture is smooth.

○ Divide the mixture among 4 small dessert bowls. Let cool for a few minutes, and then cover with plastic wrap. Refrigerate for at least 3 hours or up to 8 hours.

MEXICAN HOT CHOCOLATE

Makes **4** servings

I have fond memories of sipping hot chocolate at the central market in Acapulco, where I watched it became frothy as the vendor skillfully poured it from one cup to another. She also used a *molinillo*, a chocolate whisk made of turned wood that is held between the palms and rotated back and forth to whip the beverage with style. Hot chocolate in Mexico is flavored with aromatic spices, and children drink it with breakfast. At home, I serve the rich-tasting beverage for a snack or dessert to take the chill off a winter night.

¼	cup unsweetened cocoa powder
¼	cup sugar
½	teaspoon ground cinnamon
¼	teaspoon ground nutmeg
4	cups whole milk
1	teaspoon pure vanilla extract
4	cinnamon sticks

◐ Combine the cocoa, sugar, cinnamon, nutmeg, and milk in a medium saucepan over medium heat. Stir occasionally until the cocoa and sugar are dissolved. In about 5 minutes or when the liquid begins to bubble around the edges of the pan, remove from the heat and stir in the vanilla.

◐ Beat with a portable electric mixer at medium speed until frothy.

◐ Pour the hot chocolate into mugs and insert a cinnamon stick into each serving.

Variation: Rather than using a portable electric mixer to froth the cocoa, heat 3 cups milk in the pan and froth 1 cup of the milk using a cappuccino machine. Stir the frothed milk into the milk in the pan, or mound the frothed milk atop the servings and sprinkle lightly with nutmeg or sweetened cocoa powder.

VANILLA RICE PUDDING

Makes **4** servings

No one ever grows tired of rice pudding, the classic comfort food from childhood days. Dress it up for grown-ups by substituting almond extract for the vanilla extract. I like to serve this wholesome dessert topped with slices of juicy fresh peaches.

1½	cups cooked white rice (cook until soft rather than firm, cool before using)
1¼	cups half-and-half
3	tablespoons packed brown sugar
1	tablespoon salted butter
½	teaspoon pure vanilla extract
	Pinch of salt

◐ Combine the rice, half-and-half, and brown sugar in a medium nonstick saucepan; bring just to a boil over medium-high heat. Reduce the heat to low; cover and cook, stirring frequently, for 10 minutes or until the cream is partially absorbed into the rice but the mixture is still very creamy.

◐ Remove from the heat. Stir in the butter, vanilla, and a scant pinch of salt.

◐ Transfer to small dessert bowls and serve warm. Or when the pudding is cool, cover the dishes with plastic wrap, and refrigerate to serve later the same day.

Dessert Sauces

BLUEBERRY-ORANGE SAUCE

Makes **1** cup

I love this quick and easy, fruity sauce spooned over lemon–poppy seed cake that I purchase ready-made at my favorite bakery.

¼	cup grape jelly
1	cup fresh blueberries
2	tablespoons orange-flavored liqueur, such as Grand Marnier or Cointreau
	Orange zest for garnish

▶ Heat the jelly in a small saucepan over medium heat, stirring constantly for about 1 minute or until it liquefies. Reduce the heat to low and add the blueberries and liqueur. Continue to stir for about 30 seconds.

▶ Serve the sauce warm and garnish with orange zest.

TIP

To remove citrus zest, use a zester, which has a short, flat blade with a beveled end and five small holes. When drawn firmly over the skin of a citrus fruit, the tool removes thin strips of the colored zest. (Do not strip off the white pith beneath; it has a bitter flavor.) Or use a vegetable peeler to remove strips of the zest. Then use a sharp knife to thinly slice the strips.

AMARETTO HOT FUDGE SAUCE

Makes ¾ cup

This warm, sensuous, smooth sauce turns ordinary vanilla ice cream into gourmet hot fudge sundaes—or banana splits—for adults. It adds panache to pound cake, poached pears, or crêpes, too. For variety, substitute another nut-flavored liqueur, such as Frangelico, or a fruit-flavored liqueur, such as Cointreau.

4	ounces semisweet chocolate, coarsely chopped
½	cup heavy cream or half-and-half
2	tablespoons almond-flavored liqueur (Amaretto)

▶ Heat water until simmering in the bottom pan of a double boiler over high heat.

▶ Combine the chocolate, cream, and liqueur in the top pan of the double boiler and place it over the simmering water. Reduce the heat to medium; stir constantly for 5 minutes or until the chocolate is melted and the sauce is smooth.

▶ This sauce will keep for up to 1 week in a covered container in the refrigerator. It thickens as it chills; before serving, reheat to its creamy consistency in a double boiler or in the microwave oven on LOW.

HOT FUDGE SAUCE WITH TOASTED HAZELNUTS

Makes **4** cups

My friend Judy Tills—food stylist, recipe tester, and exceptional cook—shared the secrets for her truly decadent fudge sauce. Judy makes countless batches at Christmastime to have on hand for hostess gifts. As a chocolate aficionado, for me it was love at first bite. That's why it's a little dangerous to have this sauce around—there is always the temptation to eat spoonfuls directly from the jar. Judy warms the sauce slightly before serving it over premium ice cream. She recommends using high-quality chocolate, such as Scharffenberger or Valrhona.

1	cup hazelnuts
½	cup unsalted butter
6	ounces unsweetened chocolate, coarsely chopped
1	(12-ounce) can evaporated milk
3	cups powdered sugar
1½	teaspoons pure vanilla extract
⅛	teaspoon salt

◖ Preheat the oven to 350°F. Spread the nuts on a small, rimmed baking sheet or in a shallow baking pan. Bake for 10 minutes or until deep brown and the skins begin to flake. Transfer the nuts to a thin kitchen towel and fold it over the warm nuts. Rub vigorously to remove the skins. Then coarsely chop the nuts.

◖ While the nuts are toasting, melt the butter and chocolate in a medium saucepan over low heat, stirring frequently. Stir in the evaporated milk and powdered sugar. Bring to a boil over medium-high heat, stirring occasionally. Reduce the heat to low and simmer,

stirring constantly, for 1 minute or until the sauce is thick and glossy.

◖ Remove from the heat. Stir in the vanilla, salt, and toasted hazelnuts.

◖ Serve the sauce immediately while warm. Or let the sauce cool and transfer it to a covered container. It will keep in the refrigerator for up to 1 year.

◖ To reheat, transfer the sauce to a microwave-proof container and heat on HIGH in the microwave until softened and warm.

RASPBERRY SAUCE

Makes **1** cup

This is one of my all-time favorite sauces, and I make it all year round. In summer, it stars atop Peach Melba (page 285), and in winter, it's excellent on fresh or poached pears. And any time at all, it turns a ho-hum dish of vanilla ice cream into a glorious dessert.

1	(12-ounce) bag frozen unsweetened raspberries, thawed
¼	cup sugar
⅓	cup water

◖ Pour the raspberries into a fine-mesh sieve over a bowl. Stir with a wooden spoon, pressing on the solids and allowing the liquid to drain into the bowl. Discard the solids.

◖ Combine the sugar and water in a small saucepan; stir over low heat until the sugar dissolves. Stir in the liquid from the raspberries.

○ Store the sauce in a covered container in the refrigerator for up to 1 week. (It will thicken somewhat as it cools; it can be thinned by gently heating or by adding water.)

MOCHA SAUCE

Makes **1⅔** cups

This incredibly simple sauce is a lovely surprise that will impress even your most discriminating guests. Serve immediately after preparing or make it in advance and store in a tightly closed container in the refrigerator for up to two weeks. The sauce thickens as it cools, so thin the amount you need in the microwave on LOW heat and serve warm over ice cream, cake, or poached pears. Or blend it with ice cream to make Mocha Shakes (page 293).

10	ounces semisweet chocolate, coarsely chopped
1	cup freshly brewed strong coffee
2	tablespoons coffee-flavored liqueur, such as Kahlúa

○ Heat water until simmering in the bottom pan of a double boiler over high heat. Put the chocolate in the top pan of the double boiler and place over the simmering water.

○ Reduce the heat to medium; stir occasionally as the chocolate melts. Add the coffee and stir for 2 minutes until the sauce is smooth and slightly thickened.

○ Remove the top pan of the double boiler and let cool for 5 minutes. Stir in the liqueur.

—— TIP ——

A double boiler is a double pot, with one pot sitting partway inside the other. The lower pot is used to hold simmering water, which gently heats the mixture in the top pot. Adjust the level of the water so it does not touch the bottom of the top pot. Use a double boiler to cook heat-sensitive foods, such as custards, delicate sauces, and chocolate. If you don't have a double boiler, use a stainless-steel bowl set over a saucepan of simmering water.

BLUEBERRY-GINGER SAUCE

Makes **1½** cups

Drizzle the warm sauce over angel food cake at dinner or pancakes in the morning. And the luscious sauce is also scrumptious served chilled over lemon sorbet or vanilla ice cream.

⅓	cup water
¼	cup sugar
1	teaspoon finely chopped fresh ginger
2	cups blueberries

○ Stir together the water, sugar, and ginger in a small saucepan over high heat. Bring to a boil. Add the berries and stir constantly for 2 minutes or until they begin to burst.

Index